Cooking with the 60-Minute Gourmet

◇ ◇ ◇

1

Cooking with the 60-Minute Gourmet

❖ ❖ ❖

300 Rediscovered Recipes

from Pierre Franey's Classic

New York Times *Column*

PIERRE FRANEY and BRYAN MILLER

Foreword by Jacques Pépin
Introduction by Claudia Franey Jensen

TIMES BOOKS

RANDOM HOUSE

Copyright © 1999 by The New York Times Company

Illustrations copyright © 1999 by Paul Hoffman

All rights reserved under International and Pan-American Copyright Conventions. Published in the United States by Times Books, a division of Random House, Inc., New York, and simultaneously in Canada by Random House of Canada Limited, Toronto.

All of the recipes that appear in this work were originally published in *The New York Times*.

Library of Congress Cataloging-in-Publication Data
Franey, Pierre.
    Cooking with the 60-minute gourmet : 300 rediscovered recipes
  from Pierre Franey's classic *New York Times* column / by Pierre
  Franey and Bryan Miller : foreword by Jacques Pépin;
  introduction by Claudia Franey Jensen. —1st ed.
        p.   cm.
    Includes index.
    ISBN 0-8129-3094-0
    1. Quick and easy cookery.   I. Miller, Bryan.   II. Title.
  III. Title: Cooking with the sixty minute gourmet.
  TX833.5.F66 1999
  641.5'55—dc21   98-49621
                                                               CIP

Random House website address: www.atrandom.com

Printed in the United States of America on acid-free paper

9 8 7 6 5 4 3 2

First Edition

Art direction by Naomi Osnos

Designed by Helene Wald Berinsky

SPECIAL SALES
Times Books are available at special discounts for bulk purchases for sales promotions or premiums. Special editions, including personalized covers, excerpts of existing books, and corporate imprints, can be created in large quantities for special needs. For more information, write to Special Markets, Times Books, 201 East 50th Street, New York, New York 10022, or call 800-800-3246.

For Diane, Joseph, and Ryan Kaspareck

◈ ◈

For Lucia Schaldenko and Raphaelle Franey

Contents

Chapter 2: Salads

CONTENTS

Chapter 5:   Beef, Pork, and Veal

Chapter 6: Lamb

Chapter 7:   Seafood

Chapter 8: Pasta

Chapter 9: Vegetables

Chapter 10: Desserts   277

Foreword

I fell under the formidable shadow of Pierre Franey within days of my arrival in the United States in September 1959. As soon as I unpacked my bags in New York City, I walked over to Le Pavillon, then one of America's most influential restaurants, to meet Chef Franey. Thus began my working career here and, more importantly, a warm, lifelong friendship with Pierre. I worked under him at the Pavillon and then moved with him to the Howard Johnson Company, where we continued to work closely together for ten years.

Pierre was too young to be a father figure to me, but he certainly was an "older brother" and a dear friend. He opened his heart to me and brought me into his family. The first couple of years that I spent in the United States, I would enjoy many weekends at his house in East Hampton, Long Island. I was young, unattached, and barely able to express myself in English. Pierre, his wife, Betty, and their daughters, Claudia and Diane, became my "family." Through Pierre, I also met Craig Claiborne, who was to become Pierre's partner and collaborator in cooking and writing about food. I became part of that close, convivial team, a circumstance that would forever influence my career.

Pierre's greatest qualities were his simplicity and cordiality. He was a superb chef, though he would transcend that position to become much more as a columnist for *The New York Times*, cookbook author, television personality, and mentor to many young chefs. Yet, he never lost his focus; first and foremost, he was a chef—and not just any type of chef. Between the "pencil chef" often found in big hotels, who work with secretaries, food costs, and food orders, and the "skillet chef," who works at the stove sweating, cooking, mixing, and chopping, there is no question that Pierre remained a skillet chef. Although he was able to organize and run a large kitchen, his heart was at the stove, where he loved to get his hands into the food. This outlook, this vision, never changed for him; it was his temperament, and I always felt close to this point of view.

Pierre was always interested in new projects: writing recipes, producing cookbooks, consulting for restaurants. He would become visibly excited about anything associated with food. Always willing to learn and explore, this Burgundian French chef enjoyed all kinds of ethnic fare and dabbled in cooking everything from Asian to Mexican to Russian food. He loved sharing these discoveries with friends and family.

The dozens of meals we cooked together (including my wedding feast), on glorious summer days in East Hampton with the gang—Pierre, Craig Claiborne, Henry, Jean Vergnes, Roger Fessaguet, Ed Giobbi, and many others—will always remain in my mind as essential in my learning about food and understanding the culture and bonds between food, cooking, and friendship. Pierre liked life, food, wine, and friends, and more than anything else, he enjoyed the cooking camaraderie with his many friends—chefs and amateur cooks alike.

As a major French chef trained in a classical manner, Pierre was deeply interested, as I was, in his work at Howard Johnson's. It was a new experience for us to work with large production and be able to create recipes for thousands of people all over the United States. Pierre was happy to work on classic American fare, like New England clam chowder, clam croquettes, Salisbury steak, short ribs, and chicken pot pie. We developed and kept improving these dishes, and Pierre was proud of them. He always got a kick out of serving that food, often reheated from the frozen state (which was new at the time), to other French chefs without telling them that these dishes were mass-produced and frozen. We did good work under his guidance.

Pierre was my role model. He was also one of the first French chefs to support the young American chefs who were starting out a quarter of a century ago. He would remain supportive and helpful to young chefs until the end of his days. This open-mindedness and the eclecticism of his recipes are certainly evident in the entire "60-Minute Gourmet" series. From Spanish tortillas and Cajun-style chicken fingers to award-winning New England clam chowder, whole red snapper with lime butter, a classic roasted lemon-garlic chicken, or a linguine with fresh mussels, the variety as well as the originality in these books echoes the essential Pierre.

More than anything, taste is the primary ingredient in Pierre's cooking. For him, presentation was always secondary to taste. I miss my old friend and mentor and our frequent conversations about flavors and the marvelous alchemy of cooking. Happily, there is consolation, because we can still enjoy the many books, columns, and television programs he served up to us over the years. In this posthumous book of Pierre's, he leaves us his legacy of taste. There is fun, joy, and spirit in these dishes. They reflect Pierre's *joie de vivre*, which he offers us as a last gift. As we cook along with him, Pierre is forever with us.

—Jacques Pépin

Preface

How do I pay tribute to a man who for more than fifteen years was my culinary mentor, a restaurant-reviewing companion, a travel mate, a confidant, and the kind of father figure everyone should be lucky enough to have? Trying to distill all of my impressions of Pierre on one page is nearly impossible—like reducing a cow to a bouillon cube.

Pierre achieved great fame in his long career, as a chef, food columnist, author, teacher, and a television personality. But my most vivid memories are of the times we spent together creating recipes for articles and books at his home in East Hampton, on Long Island. Usually, I would rise about 6:30 A.M. and head down to the kitchen to find that Pierre had already pedaled to town on his bike to fetch the newspaper, made coffee, set out some of his homemade bread, and scribbled down a half-dozen recipe ideas. To the background chatter of the *Today* show— he tuned in every morning but never looked at it—we planned our day.

Then we would head out to the local supermarket. Pierre always bought ingredients at local stores so readers wouldn't be exasperated by trying to locate Peruvian blue onion or Mexican jicama. He seemed to know everybody at the supermarket: the butcher, the produce man, the checkout girls, the manager. Inevitably, a wide-eyed shopper would roll her cart over to him and exclaim, "Oh, Pierre, you have changed my life!" All of this badinage made for a long expedition at the market, but Pierre loved talking about food with everybody. Finally, loaded with groceries, we drove back to the house and organized our provender. As we started chopping and slicing, a palpable transformation overcame Pierre. He became more animated, and jocular, as if physical contact with food had some intoxicating effect on his spirits.

At these times I noticed another sure sign of Pierre's culinary glee. He whistled. No particular tune, just a random, oscillating pitch, like a little kid loping home from school. This was the essential Pierre, standing at the stove in his khaki shorts, juggling pots and pans, and creating wonderful meals. By day's end, we had cooked enough food to feed the Montauk fishing fleet. Sometimes friends dropped by, and the chef thoroughly enjoyed watching everyone swoon over his cooking. Pierre is responsible for 90 percent of my culinary knowledge. Two of his cooking axioms ring in my ears to this day: "Always taste the food before you serve it!" and "Don't burn the garlic!" The latter became his mantra of sorts, both in print and later on television. One day, we were walking down Fifth Avenue when a taxi slowed down alongside us. The driver rolled down his window and shouted, "Hey, Pierre, don't burn the garlic!"

When I was the restaurant critic for *The New York Times*, I often invited Pierre out to dinner. It was daunting to see him taste a dish and then break it down into components like a chemist. "Too much sage," he would say. Or "This veal stock is too reduced." Similarly, when we were cooking at his house, he could sense immediately if a dish were swerving off the road, and he knew exactly how to make a midcourse correction so it came out perfectly. Through him, I learned that, while one may be born with a good palate, there is no substitute for years of cooking and tasting.

Pierre remained young at heart, both professionally and personally, by always keeping an open mind to new ideas and new challenges. One of his most daring ventures was appearing on his own television series. At first, he took to the medium like a fish to tennis. Pierre was no actor— he was just Pierre. He could not put on a different face for the camera. In the beginning, he was visibly uncomfortable under the spotlights and tended to shout at the camera, as if that would make up for his thick French accent. But in a short time, he began to relax and chat as if he were cooking with me at home. His honesty and passion shone through his technical shortcomings, and the shows became a big hit.

For all of the encomiums he received during his professional life, Pierre always retained humility and a sense of humor. I will always remember my friend not for what he did, but for who he was: a man content with his life, and someone who spread happiness and love via food to all around him. I am certain that, wherever Pierre is now, he is whistling down at us.

—Bryan Miller

Introduction

It was with great sadness that my family said a final good-bye to my father in October 1996. We are a close family, and Papa's absence is still very profoundly felt by my mother, sister, brother, our spouses, and our children. But we take great comfort in our wonderful memories of him and knowing that he really lived a full life. And, of course, many of these memories take place in his kitchen and revolve around all the delicious meals he cooked for us.

Papa was a man whose passion for food never took a day off. He woke every morning thinking about what he would be eating and cooking that day. When I was a child and he was executive chef of Le Pavillon in New York City, he always cooked the family meal on Sunday, his one day off. For him, it was not work, but a way of unwinding and relaxing. Cooking came naturally to him. He cooked to live; he lived to cook.

One of the real pleasures that my father enjoyed was writing his column, "The 60-Minute Gourmet." It was syndicated in hundreds of newspapers around the country and ran for many years. Besides having his own byline for the very first time, he loved the opportunity to tell people how to make a delicious meal in under an hour. He took classic French recipes that would have scared anyone away with their long lists of ingredients and complicated instructions and he simplified them. He reassured all of us that we didn't need to spend torturous hours preparing a fine dinner. We could give an elegant dinner party and have the time to sit down with our guests. Or we could come home from work tired and still be able to cook a quick and satisfying meal. He showed us that preparing a meal, whether for guests or for ourselves, is both a pleasure itself and a source of pleasure for others—"le plaisir de la table."

My mother, Betty, recalls how the column inspired my father to create and adapt recipes. Although born and raised in France and schooled in a strict, classic French cuisine, Papa was very curious about, and receptive to, foods of other cultures. He traveled extensively throughout the United States and loved meeting with young American chefs and seeing what they were creating in their own kitchens. He would return home and test out these ideas, adding his own twist. With carte blanche to cook whatever he wanted (or sometimes what my mother was in the mood for), he would take off each morning in his yellow VW beetle with Luc, his black Lab (the best-fed dog in America), in the backseat, and go food shopping. Together they would visit the farmers' market, the fish shop, the butcher, and the local supermarket in East Hampton. His creative juices would start flowing once he saw what was available—what was in season, what looked fresh. He would then head home and create a new "60-Minute Gourmet" recipe, which would appear in the newspaper a few weeks later.

How he demystified the mysteries of the kitchen for all of us! Last year, while in San Diego, I had the pleasure of having lunch at a restaurant with a young woman who had been a great fan of my father's. She was holding a copy of what she referred to as her "bible"—the first volume of *The 60-Minute Gourmet*, published in 1979. The cover was battered, sauce-stained pages were falling out, and penciled notes were written in the margins. It was stuffed with aging newspaper clippings of past "60-Minute" recipes that had appeared in her local paper. She recounted how grateful she was to my father for showing her the way in the kitchen, and she begged that we publish a book with more of the "60-Minute Gourmet" recipes.

So that is what we are doing today. My family and I hope that this collection of "60-Minute" recipes will make cooking a pleasurable experience and will help to show off your culinary talents to your family and friends. And it gives us great comfort knowing that "The 60-Minute Gourmet" lives on in our hearts and in our kitchens. *Bon appétit.*

—Claudia Franey Jensen

Things You Should Know

Before charging ahead to make any of the recipes in this book, you should know a few things about the ingredients we choose to use.

- Milk is always whole. You can substitute low-fat or skim milk, but it gives soups and sauces a thinner, less creamy consistency.

- Use unsalted butter so that you can control the amount of salt in a dish. We don't recommend substituting margarine, which has just as many calories per tablespoon (100) as butter and inferior flavor.

- Unless otherwise noted, all eggs are large.

- All dry ingredient measurements are level. Brown sugar is measured and firmly packed.

- All salt is common table salt and pepper is freshly ground. We seldom specify measured amounts of salt and pepper because every cook has a different palate. Sample the recipe several times during preparation to taste for seasoning and add salt and pepper to taste when we instruct you to do so.

And keep the following general tips in mind:

- Read through each recipe at least once to make sure that you have all the necessary ingredients and utensils, understand all the steps, and have enough preparation time.

- Be sure to use the proper-size pan when a measurement is given.

- Preheat ovens, broilers, and grills at least 15 minutes before cooking begins. Place all food on the middle rack of the oven unless the recipe says otherwise.

- Most of the recipes in this book are written to serve four. You can reduce by half or double many of them to satisfy two or eight diners.

THINGS YOU SHOULD KNOW

Stocking Your Pantry

Cooks are like Boy Scouts—they must always be prepared. Having a well-stocked pantry makes cooking infinitely easier. If you have spices, canned and frozen goods, condiments, cheese, and fruits on hand, all you need to do is shop for the main ingredients. And when you are in a jam, you can always toss something together without shopping at all. Following is an inventory of pantry items that you should have on hand.

DRY GOODS

COFFEE (regular and decaffeinated).

COLD AND HOT CEREALS.

BREADS—all breads can be frozen for 6 to 8 months.

DRY BEANS AND GRAINS—store in airtight containers. White beans (navy), lentils, red beans, couscous, rice, etc.

HERBAL AND REGULAR TEAS—store in an airtight canister in a cool place.

MACARONI AND PASTA—these are essential, and lifesavers when you need to create a quick meal from the pantry.

DRY HERBS, SPICES, AND SEASONINGS

DRIED HERBS—these are indispensable. Use them when you can't get fresh herbs. Among those you should have are basil, bay leaves, dill, marjoram, oregano, rosemary, sage, tarragon, thyme, and parsley. Keep them sealed in a cool place.

It is best to buy dried herbs in
small quantities because they
lose their potency over time.
Also, to get the most flavor from
dried herbs, crush them between
your fingers before adding them
to food.

SALT AND PEPPER—table salt, black peppercorns, whole or ground white pepper, and red pepper flakes.

SPICES

Allspice, chili powder, cinnamon, cloves, ground cumin, curry powder, ginger, dry mustard, nutmeg, and paprika.

BOTTLED AND CANNED GOODS

ASSORTED OILS (vegetable, olive, peanut).

TOMATO PASTE—this comes in handy for flavoring and thickening stews, soups, and sauces. To save leftover tomato paste, open both ends of the can, remove the cylinder of paste and enclose tightly in plastic wrap, then refrigerate.

WINES—have on hand a dry red and a dry white for deglazing and flavoring dishes. Fortified wines like Madeira and port come in handy, too—not to mention being nice to sip after dinner once in a while.

ANCHOVIES—for salads, pizzas, some pasta sauces. Buy anchovies packed in olive oil.

ARTICHOKE HEARTS MARINATED IN OLIVE OIL—toss in salads, pasta sauces, vegetable plates, and sauces.

BEANS—kidney, garbanzo, and baked beans can be used in soups, salads, vegetable dishes, and casseroles.

CANNED BROTHS—always have plenty of chicken and beef broth for making quick pan sauces.

CANNED CLAMS AND CLAM JUICE—you can make a quick pasta with clam sauce. The clam juice can pinch-hit for fish stock.

CANNED TUNA FISH—stock up on this for sandwiches and salads.

CAPERS—for flavoring sauces, casseroles, and salads.

HOT SAUCE—there are times when you want to stoke up a sauce or soup. Tabasco is the most famous hot sauce, but there are scores out there to try.

OLIVES—green, black, and pimiento-stuffed for salads, sandwiches, pasta dishes, and more.

TOMATOES (canned)—these are indispensable when ripe summer tomatoes are not available.

CONDIMENTS

DIJON-STYLE MUSTARD—see how many times this is called for in this book. It is the basis of vinaigrette, dips, some sauces, and as a condiment with meats of all kinds.

KETCHUP—for hamburgers and as an ingredient in barbecue sauces.

MAYONNAISE—this is used all the time, for sandwiches, salad dressings, cold meats, cold sauces, and more.

SUNDRY RELISHES—relishes made with tomatoes, corn, onion, and the like are good for sandwiches and roasted meats.

HORSERADISH (in jar)—use when you don't have time to grate it fresh. Goes in salad dressings, with all kinds of meats, and sauces.

PASTA SAUCES (in jars)—when you are really desperate, these come in handy. You may want to jazz them up with garlic, sautéed onions, olives, salsas, herbs, or cheese.

SOY SAUCE—adds a salty edge to marinades and Asian-style dishes.

SUN-DRIED TOMATOES—a luxury, but they come in handy for enhancing sauces of all kinds, dressings, and salads.

BAKING GOODS

ALL-PURPOSE FLOUR (5-pound bag)—not only is this necessary for baking, you also use flour for dredging meat and fish to give it a crispy crust. It keeps for months if you take it out of the bag and store in an airtight container.

BAKING POWDER—an all-purpose leavening agent for cakes, cookies, and quick breads. Baking powder loses its punch over time. To test it: Mix 1 teaspoon baking powder with ⅓ cup water. If it fizzes, it's okay.

BAKING SODA—another leavening agent, used in batters that contain acid like vinegar or buttermilk. An open box in the refrigerator absorbs odors.

GRANULATED SUGAR (5-pound bag)—used every day. Best stored in a sealed container to keep out ants.

CONFECTIONERS' SUGAR—for sprinkling over desserts and for making quick frostings.

BROWN SUGAR—used in baking, for making barbecue sauce, and for glazing meats like ham.

CORNMEAL—a bag of yellow cornmeal comes in handy for making quick muffins, crunchy toppings for stews and casseroles.

HONEY—used for all kinds of glazes, syrups, and dressings, and for sweetening tea.

VANILLA EXTRACT—for flavoring whipped cream and many desserts.

VANILLA BEAN—more intense than vanilla extract, it also is used in many desserts.

REFRIGERATED AND FROZEN STAPLES

EGGS—you always need eggs, for breakfast, omelets, frittatas (page 21), sauces, and much more. Eggs can be stored 4 weeks beyond the expiration date.

MILK—another absolute necessity. Always check the expiration date—milk lasts only about a week beyond it.

PASTAS—it's always a good idea to have good-quality prepared ravioli on hand so that you can serve it with a quick sauce. Do not defrost before cooking. Drop it right into boiling water.

CHEESES—you don't want too many cheeses lying around, so store only those that you will use up within a few weeks to a month. Parmesan or Romano comes in handy as an all-around garnish.

Goat cheese makes a nice appetizer with fresh herbs sprinkled on top, or rolled in crushed black pepper. Cover cheese in plastic wrap and refrigerate. Take it out at least 1 hour before serving.

PIE CRUSTS (frozen)—in a pinch, these are great to have. They keep in the freezer up to 8 months. Fill with a quiche mixture, fresh fruits and custards, pie fillings, and much more.

Cooking with the 60-Minute Gourmet

◇ ◇ ◇

Appetizers

◇ ◇ ◇

Tapenade

Seviche of Squid

Chicken Livers with Garlic and Rosemary

Shrimp in Beer Batter with Sweet-and-Sour Sauce

Sweet-and-Sour Sauce

Provençal Eggplant Loaf

Individual Gruyère Soufflés

Céleri Rémoulade

Cornmeal-Fried Oysters with Mustard Sauce

Chicken Fingers with Garlic Butter

Salmon Marinated with Ginger and Fennel

Gravlax

Steamed Mussels Provençal

Gazpacho Mousse

Lemony Chickpea-and-Tuna Spread

Baked Clams with Garlic Butter

Frittata with Red Peppers and Potatoes

Cold Lobster with Spicy Mustard Sauce

Sweet Corn and Pepper Fritters

Mussels with Mexican Vinaigrette

Mexican Vinaigrette Sauce

Guacamole

Oven-Roasted Tomatoes

Skewered Shrimp and Zucchini

Anchovy Butter

Shrimp and Squid with Vinaigrette Sauce

Tapenade

◇ ◇

Tapenade, a rich and saline spread made with anchovies, olives, and capers, is one of my favorite appetizers from the South of France. In this version, I add some tuna, so it could actually double as a light lunch. Spread it on toast triangles and serve it with an apéritif.

Yield: About 2 to 2½ cups, depending on whether or not you use figs.

1 cup imported pitted black olives, preferably oil-cured (see note below)

¼ cup (about ⅛ pound) fillets of anchovies, drained (packed in oil best)

¾ cup tuna in oil, well drained

⅔ cup drained capers

1 tablespoon English mustard (prepared by blending 1 tablespoon powdered dry mustard with 1 tablespoon water—let stand 20 minutes before using)

½ cup dried figs, stems removed (optional)

½ cup olive oil

Juice ½ lemon

1. Combine the olives, anchovies, tuna, capers, mustard, and figs in the container of a food processor or blender.

2. Start processing while gradually adding the oil. Add the lemon juice. The tapenade should be coarse textured.

NOTE: For tapenade, it is almost essential to use imported black olives. California black olives lack sufficient flavor. One 6½-ounce jar of oil-cured olives, when pitted, will yield about 1 cup.

Rinse the squid and pat dry. Put the squid, one at a time, on a flat surface. Grab the squid's head and innards as far inside the body as you can and pull out gently. Set aside. If you do not get the pen—the firm, thin bonelike structure that runs the length of the squid—reach back in and pull it out. Then, using a sharp knife, cut off the removed tentacles at a point just above the eye. Squeeze out the small, round, marblelike beak. Discard the beak and innards. Although the skin is edible, you may wish to remove it. You can use coarse salt to rub and pull it away. Rinse the squid.

COOKING SQUID

❖

You have to be careful when cooking squid. Because of its firm, chewy texture, it needs to be cooked either very quickly (as in this recipe) or very slowly (as in braising). If you fall somewhere in between, the squid will be leathery. Count on about 8 ounces of cleaned squid per person. Squid is ideally suited for deep-frying, too.

Seviche of Squid

❖ ❖

Once you learn to clean a squid, you can experiment with all kinds of international recipes. The zesty appetizer here, a recipe of Mexican inspiration, calls for fresh squid.

Yield: 6 to 8 servings.

2 pounds squid, cleaned (see sidebar)
Salt to taste
½ pound tomatoes, cored and cut into ½-inch cubes (about 2 cups)
1 cup coarsely chopped onions
1 tablespoon finely minced garlic
1 tablespoon finely chopped fresh or canned serrano chiles
1 tablespoon finely chopped fresh coriander
1 tablespoon finely chopped parsley
¼ cup freshly squeezed lime juice
½ cup olive oil
Freshly ground pepper to taste

1. Cut the squid bodies into rings, each about ½ inch wide. Cut the tentacles into bite-sized pieces. There should be about 3 cups. Set aside. Bring enough water to a boil to cover the squid when added. Add salt.

2. Add the squid. When the liquid returns to a boil, turn down heat to simmer for about 1 minute. Drain immediately. Let cool.

3. Place the squid into a mixing bowl and add the remaining ingredients. Toss well to blend. Serve chilled or at room temperature.

Chicken Livers with Garlic and Rosemary

◇ ◇

I love chicken livers, and I use them in all sorts of spreads, stuffings, and terrines. Here is a quick and easy recipe that makes a tasty appetizer.

Yield: 4 servings.

1¼ pounds chicken livers
Salt and freshly ground pepper to taste
¾ cup flour
4 tablespoons vegetable oil
2 tablespoons butter
2 tablespoons olive oil
1 tablespoon finely chopped garlic
¾ cup skinless, seedless diced tomatoes
2 tablespoons chopped fresh rosemary or 1 tablespoon dried
2 tablespoons finely chopped parsley

1. Place the livers, one at a time, on a flat surface. Cut away and discard any tough connecting membranes. Cut the livers into quarters.

2. Place them in a bowl and sprinkle with salt and pepper.

3. Add the flour to the livers and stir to coat well.

4. Remove the livers to a baking sheet, separating them.

5. Heat the vegetable oil in a large nonstick skillet. When it is quite hot, add half of the livers, one at a time, and cook over high heat, turning the livers as they brown. One batch of livers takes 4 to 5 minutes to cook. When the livers are cooked, transfer them with a slotted spoon to a colander. Keep warm. Add the remaining livers and cook them in the same manner.

6. Wipe out the skillet and heat the butter and olive oil over high setting. Add the garlic, cook briefly, but do not brown. Add the tomatoes, rosemary, and drained livers. Cook, shaking the skillet and stirring, until the mixture is piping hot. Sprinkle with parsley and serve immediately.

NOTE: You can freeze the chicken livers that come inside roasting chickens. When you have enough, make this garlicky appetizer. Serve with a stout red wine.

(Continued on next page)

◆

The first time I visited Belgium, many years ago, I was intrigued by the number of dishes that were made with beer-leavened batters. The technique makes great sense, since the effervescence of beer keeps a batter light. Beer batters are ideal for fried seafood, poultry, and shrimp. The batters must be well seasoned so flavors integrate with the food.

The shrimp batter here is made with flour, salt, pepper, nutmeg, and ground coriander. Note that oil is spread on top of the batter as it sits in a bowl to prevent gas from escaping. Egg whites are then folded in for extra lightness. Cook each shrimp about 50 seconds in 350-degree oil and drain well before serving.

NOTE: We added half olive oil and half butter to the hot pan to prevent the butter from burning. Always do this when you are cooking on a high setting.

Shrimp in Beer Batter with Sweet-and-Sour Sauce

◆ ◆

The sweet-and-sour sauce that accompanies this shrimp can be made in large batches and kept refrigerated in a jar. Start with a good bitter orange marmalade, which can be found in most supermarkets. To this, add some peach jam and grated fresh ginger. The heat comes from freshly grated horseradish and dry English mustard. You may adjust the proportions according to taste. The sauce needs to stand only 15 minutes or so before using.

Yield: 4 servings.

24 large shrimp (about 2 pounds)
1 cup flour
Salt and freshly ground white pepper to taste
¼ teaspoon freshly grated nutmeg
1 tablespoon ground coriander
½ cup beer
1 teaspoon vegetable or corn oil, plus enough oil for deep frying
2 egg whites
Sweet-and-sour sauce (see page 9)

1. Peel and devein the shrimp.

2. Put the flour in a mixing bowl, and add salt, pepper, nutmeg, and coriander. Gradually add the beer, stirring with a wire whisk until smooth. Brush the top of the batter with 1 teaspoon oil. This prevents gas from escaping. Cover with plastic wrap and let stand in a warm place for 30 minutes.

3. Whisk egg whites until they are in soft peaks and fold them into the batter with a rubber spatula.

4. Heat the oil in a deep fryer to 350 degrees as determined by a deep-fat thermometer. Using a pair of chopsticks or a two-pronged fork, dip the shrimp, one at a time, into the batter. Drop the shrimp into the oil without crowding them. Cook each shrimp about 30 seconds, or until golden brown on one side. Turn the shrimp and cook an additional 20 seconds, or until golden brown all over. Drain on paper towels. Serve hot with the sweet-and-sour sauce.

NOTE: To devein shrimp, take a sharp paring knife and make a shallow incision, about ⅛ inch deep, along the back. You will see the thin black vein. Remove with the tip of your knife and your hand.

Sweet-and-Sour Sauce
◇ ◇

Yield: About 1¼ cups.

½ cup bitter orange marmalade
½ cup peach jam
2 teaspoons grated fresh ginger
1 tablespoon freshly grated horseradish
1 teaspoon dry English mustard
1 teaspoon cider vinegar
3 tablespoons freshly squeezed orange juice
Salt and freshly ground pepper to taste

1. Combine all ingredients in a bowl and let stand for 15 minutes.

Provençal Eggplant Loaf
◇ ◇

This is an unusual appetizer made of eggplant slices blended with chopped egg and anchovies, plus olive oil and vinegar. It can be made the day ahead so the flavors meld.

Yield: 8 or more appetizer servings.

1 eggplant (about 1 pound)
3 hard-cooked eggs
Salt to taste
Freshly ground pepper to taste
½ cup drained small capers
2 tablespoons finely minced garlic
1 2-ounce can anchovies, drained and finely chopped
1 cup finely chopped parsley
1 cup olive oil, approximately
2 tablespoons red wine vinegar, approximately

1. Preheat a charcoal grill or a kitchen broiler.

2. Cut off the ends of the eggplant. Cut the eggplant widthwise into slices about ¼ inch thick. There should be about 18 slices.

3. Remove the yolks from the eggs and put them through a fine sieve. Finely chop the whites. Combine the two. Put in a mixing bowl.

4. Place the eggplant slices, a few at a time, over the charcoal or under the broiler and cook, turning once, until charred and soft.

5. Remove the slices and sprinkle with salt and pepper.

6. Add the capers, garlic, anchovies, and parsley to the eggs and toss to blend well.

7. Line a 6-cup loaf pan lengthwise with one layer of eggplant slices. Sprinkle with 1 tablespoon oil and ½ teaspoon vinegar. Cover with ¼ cup of the egg mixture. Add another layer of eggplant slices and sprinkle as before with the same amount of oil and vinegar. Add another layer of the egg mixture and cover with a layer of eggplant slices. Sprinkle with the same amount of oil and vinegar.

8. Continue making layers until all the eggplant slices and the egg mixture are used, ending with the egg mixture. Sprinkle the final layer with 1 tablespoon of vinegar and 10 tablespoons of olive oil. Press down with your fingers. Cover tightly with clear plastic wrap and let stand 24 hours in the refrigerator. When ready, the dish may be cut into crosswise slices.

Individual Gruyère Soufflés

◇ ◇

Whenever I give cooking demonstrations, people invariably ask about how to make a proper soufflé that doesn't collapse before it gets to the table. If well made—and that requires getting the proportions correct and maintaining even heat in the oven—a soufflé should stay puffed for 5 to 10 minutes. Whether sweet or savory, soufflés should be crisp and golden on the outside, moist but not overly runny inside. I like to make cheese soufflés for lunch or a light dinner.

Yield: 4 servings.

6 large eggs
4 tablespoons butter
3 tablespoons flour
2 cups milk
Salt and freshly ground white pepper to taste
⅛ teaspoon freshly grated nutmeg
Pinch of cayenne pepper
2 tablespoons cornstarch
3 tablespoons water
⅓ pound Gruyère or Swiss cheese, cut into small cubes
3 tablespoons grated Gruyère cheese

1. Preheat the oven to 425 degrees.
2. Place four ½-cup soufflé dishes into the refrigerator to chill.
3. Separate the eggs, placing the yolks in one bowl and the whites in a larger bowl. Beat the yolks.
4. With 1 tablespoon of the butter, grease the bottom and sides of each soufflé dish, paying special attention to the sides. Return to the refrigerator.
5. Melt the remaining butter in a saucepan and add the flour, stirring with a wire whisk. Blend well, but do not brown the flour. Add the milk, stirring rapidly with the whisk. Add the salt and pepper, nutmeg, and cayenne. Bring to a boil and reduce to a simmer. Stir for 30 seconds.
6. Blend the cornstarch and water and add to the simmering milk mixture. Stir and cook for about 2 minutes. Add the yolks, stirring vigorously. Cook, stirring, for about 1 minute. *(Continued on next page)*

7. Spoon and scrape the mixture into a large mixing bowl. Add the cubed Gruyère, and blend well with a wire whisk. Set aside.

8. Beat the egg whites in a mixing bowl, preferably copper, with a flexible balloon-shaped wire whisk or a hand beater. They should be stiff and thick. Add half of the whites to the soufflé mixture and mix thoroughly. Add the remaining whites, folding them in quickly but gently with a rubber spatula.

9. Spoon and scrape even amounts of the mixture into each soufflé dish. The mixture should fit inside the dish to about ¼ inch from the top. With your thumb, create a shallow channel around the periphery of the dish to allow for expansion. Sprinkle the top with the grated Gruyère.

10. Place the dish on a baking sheet on the bottom rack of the oven and bake for 12 to 15 minutes. Serve immediately.

NOTE: The recipe here calls for Gruyère alone, which results in a faintly sharp flavor. You could add some Cheddar and Parmesan if you like. Or use goat cheese, which is a popular soufflé cheese. Goat cheese can be delectably mild or tart, depending on the age of the cheese.

Soufflés are particularly good served with grilled vegetables, a green salad, or cold meats.

Céleri Rémoulade

◇ ◇

Celery knob, also called celeriac, is a large, brownish, edible root. It is often sliced and cooked in boiling water, but it also makes a good, earthy raw salad.

Yield: 8 to 10 servings.

3 or 4 bulbs celery knob (enough to make 3 to 4 cups when
   shredded)
1 egg yolk
1 tablespoon white wine vinegar
2 tablespoons Dijon mustard
¼ teaspoon cayenne pepper
1¼ cups vegetable oil or olive oil
1 tablespoon lemon juice
Salt and pepper to taste

1. Peel the celery and drop into cold water. Trim off all the dark spots and slice the celery as thinly as possible, using a mandoline, a food processor, or even a sharp knife.

2. Stack the slices and cut them into fine julienne strips. There should be about 3 to 4 cups.

3. In a large mixing bowl, combine the egg yolk, vinegar, mustard, and cayenne. Start beating with a wire whisk or an electric beater, gradually adding the oil. Continue beating until all the oil is used and the mayonnaise is thick. Add the lemon juice and salt and pepper to taste. If too thick, add a little water.

4. Place the julienne strips in the mayonnaise mixture and blend well. Check for seasoning and chill. Serve cold as an appetizer or first course. This is particularly good when served with garlic sausage or any cold meat or seafood.

◇

I have been an oyster lover since I first tasted this exotic treat in Paris when I was about fourteen years old. I have since learned to serve them in dozens of ways. There are five major types of oysters on the market, and many more subspecies. Each has its own characteristics—salty, briny, sweet, firm, soft, and so on. Here is a brief rundown on oyster types.

EASTERN OYSTERS. *These grow along the East and Gulf coasts and have a clear, briny flavor. In general, cold-water oysters are better than those from southern waters. Southern oysters also go by the names Wellfleet and Apalachicola.*

PACIFIC OYSTERS. *Mostly grown on the West Coast, these are not terribly briny but have a distinctive flavor that you either like or detest. Also known as Quilcene and Hama-Hama.*

EUROPEAN FLATS. *Native to Western Europe and the West Coast and Maine, these have an oceanic and slightly metallic flavor. Also called Snow Creek flats and Holmes Harbor flats.*

OLYMPIAS. *No larger than a half-dollar, these prized oysters are sweet and fairly briny. They are best eaten on the half shell.*

Cornmeal-Fried Oysters with Mustard Sauce

◇ ◇

In this recipe, the spicy mustard, crunchy batter, and briny oysters make for terrific nibbling. Just be sure not to overcook the oysters.

Yield: 4 servings.

16 large oysters
1 cup oyster liquor or a blend of oyster liquor and clam broth
¼ cup finely chopped shallots
¼ cup white wine vinegar
2 teaspoons finely minced garlic
1 cup dry white wine
¾ cup heavy cream
⅓ cup Dijon-style mustard
6 tablespoons cold butter
1 cup cornmeal, preferably stone-ground (available in health-food stores)
Salt to taste
Freshly ground pepper to taste
1½ teaspoons paprika
½ teaspoon chili powder
1 cup vegetable oil
Green leaf lettuce or radicchio

1. The oysters may be shucked at home or by the fish dealer, reserving the liquor. If there is less than a cup of liquor, add enough bottled clam broth to make a cup.

2. Combine the oyster liquor, shallots, vinegar, garlic, and wine in a saucepan. Bring to a boil and cook 45 minutes or more, until the liquid is reduced to about ⅓ cup. Add the cream. Bring to a simmer and cook about 20 minutes, until reduced to 1 cup.

3. Stir in the mustard and bring back to a simmer. Add the butter in small pieces, stirring rapidly with a wire whisk. Line a bowl with a sieve, preferably of the sort known in French kitchens as a chinois. Strain the sauce, pressing with the back of a spoon to extract as much flavor as possible from the solids. There should be about 1 cup of strained sauce. Set the saucepan in a bowl of simmering water to keep it hot.

4. Blend the cornmeal, salt, pepper, paprika, and chili powder in a shallow dish. Dredge each oyster in the mixture and shake off the excess.

5. Heat the oil in a skillet over medium-high flame and add the oysters without crowding. Cook for 1 to 2 minutes per side, depending on the size of the oysters. Do not overcook—they should be light brown. As they are cooked, transfer the oysters to paper towels to drain.

6. Line serving plates with lettuce. Spoon the sauce to one side of the plate and arrange 4 cooked oysters on the lettuce.

KUMAMOTOS. *Originating in southern Japan, Kumamoto oysters were transplanted to the American Northwest in the 1940s to supplant the declining Olympias. Generally eaten on the half shell, they are prized for their large meat and addictive salinity and sweetness.*

Chicken Fingers with Garlic Butter
◇ ◇

Over the years, I have probably devised more chicken breast recipes than anything else. And the demand never ends. Chicken breast is one of the most appealing foods in the supermarket because it is ready to cook, versatile, low in fat and high in protein. But if one falls into a rut by simply broiling or baking chicken breasts, dinner can be mighty boring.

This recipe for chicken fingers with garlic butter is simple yet tasty. And you can vary the seasonings in countless ways.

Yield: 4 servings.

4 skinless, boneless chicken breast halves
Salt and freshly ground pepper to taste
1 tablespoon chopped fresh oregano or 2 teaspoons dried
2 tablespoons flour
2 tablespoons butter
2 tablespoons olive oil
4 ripe plum tomatoes, skinned, seeded, and diced small
1 tablespoon chopped garlic
4 tablespoons chopped fresh coriander or basil
2 tablespoons fresh lime juice

1. Using a sharp knife, cut the breast halves in half crosswise, then lengthwise into strips ½ inch wide.

(Continued on next page)

Dark-fleshed fish, like salmon, tuna, and bluefish, can stand up to robust sauces better than mild-tasting fish. I love to smoke bluefish and serve them with a light fresh herb sauce. Dill has a natural affinity with rich fish, especially salmon. Here is a quick recipe for salmon gravlax, the Scandinavian dill-cured fish, a terrific appetizer, especially served with a mustard dill sauce.

Cut the tough stems from 2 bunches of fresh dill. Get a 4-pound salmon fillet. Cut the fillet widthwise into two equal-sized pieces. Pull out the small white bones with tweezers.

Combine in a bowl some salt, sugar, and black pepper. Rub this all over the fish. Spread a third of the dill over the bottom of a flat dish. Put one of the fillets, skin side down, over the dill. Cover the fish with another layer of dill. Place the other piece of salmon, skin side up, on top of the dill. Cover with remaining dill. Weight the salmon down with a heavy plate and place in the refrigerator for 48 hours, turning every 12 hours. When serving, slice thinly on the bias. Serve with mustard dill sauce.

2. Thoroughly blend salt, pepper, oregano, and flour in a flat dish. Add the chicken pieces in one layer. Stir to season, keeping each strip separate.

3. Heat the butter and oil over high heat in a skillet large enough to hold the chicken pieces in one layer. Add the chicken, cook and stir until lightly browned, about 3 minutes. Add the tomatoes and garlic and cook, stirring, for 3 minutes more. Add the coriander and lime juice and continue cooking. Blend well and serve immediately.

TIP: To get the most juice out of a lime or lemon, roll it on a countertop while pressing down. Another method is to pop it in the microwave for 30 seconds, just to warm it.

Salmon Marinated with Ginger and Fennel
❖ ❖

This invigorating appetizer pairs the rich, buttery taste of fresh salmon with the zesty flavors of ginger and fennel.

Yield: 8 to 10 servings.

2 pounds skinless salmon fillets (have your fish market remove the
   skin)
½ cup fresh lime juice
1 cup thinly sliced fennel bulb
2 tablespoons white wine vinegar
2 tablespoons olive oil
1 tablespoon grated fresh ginger
¼ teaspoon hot red pepper flakes
Salt and freshly ground pepper to taste
Lettuce for garnish

1. Slice the salmon crosswise into strips about ¼ inch wide. Place the strips in a large mixing bowl. Add the lime juice, fennel, vinegar, oil, ginger, red pepper flakes, and salt and pepper. Stir gently and cover with plastic wrap. Refrigerate for 4 to 5 hours. Taste for seasoning (you may need more salt).

2. Line small serving plates with lettuce and place a portion of salmon over the lettuce.

Steamed Mussels Provençal

◇ ◇

In the South of France, where mussels are a staple, this is a very popular appetizer. Once you get the hang of it, you may substitute herbs and spices of your choice.

Yield: 4 servings.

5 pounds fresh mussels
3 tablespoons olive oil
1 tablespoon finely chopped garlic
½ cup finely chopped fennel
½ cup finely chopped onions
1 sweet red pepper, cored, seeds removed, and finely chopped
1 cup crushed canned tomatoes
½ teaspoon saffron threads (optional)
1 teaspoon ground turmeric
⅛ teaspoon red pepper flakes, or to taste
½ cup dry white wine
4 sprigs fresh thyme or 2 teaspoons dried
1 bay leaf
Salt and pepper to taste
4 tablespoons chopped fresh basil or parsley

1. Scrub the mussels, remove beards and barnacles, and wash in cold water, agitating with the hand; repeat until the water remains clear. Drain well.

2. Heat oil in a large saucepan or pot. Add garlic, fennel, onions, and sweet red pepper, and cook briefly over medium-high heat until wilted. Do not burn the garlic. Stir often.

3. Add tomatoes, saffron, turmeric, pepper flakes, wine, thyme, bay leaf, salt and pepper. Bring to a boil and simmer 2 minutes.

4. Add mussels and basil. Cover tightly, and cook over high heat until all mussels are opened, 5 to 6 minutes. Serve immediately with French bread or a crusty Italian loaf.

MUSTARD DILL SAUCE

◇

Mustard can be flavored in all sorts of ways. Just pick your favorite herb and follow these directions.

In a bowl, combine ½ cup Dijon-style mustard, 2 teaspoons mustard powder, and 5 tablespoons sugar. With a wire whisk, stir in ¼ cup white wine vinegar, ⅓ cup vegetable oil, and ⅓ cup olive oil. Whisk well. Add dill and salt to taste. Stir.

YIELD: 1½ CUPS.

*The easiest way to peel a tomato
is to cut a small X in the bottom
then drop it into boiling water.
Ripe tomatoes should stay in the
water for 20 to 30 seconds.
Remove with a slotted spoon and
let cool. Then use a sharp paring
knife to lift off the skin.*

*To remove seeds from
tomatoes, slice them in half
widthwise (that is, holding the
tomato with its stem end up).
Squeeze each half gently, cut
side down, over a sieve (with a
bowl underneath to catch any
juices that fall). Use your finger
to flick out the seeds.*

Gazpacho Mousse

◇ ◇

I love the Spanish soup gazpacho. In fact, I love all kinds of fresh vegetable purées when my garden is in full bloom. This is a delicious twist on gazpacho. The soup is seasoned, then bound with a little gelatin. It makes a great seasonal starter.

Yield: 4 servings.

½ cup fine fresh bread crumbs
1 teaspoon finely minced garlic
2 tablespoons virgin olive oil
¾ cup peeled, seeded, and finely diced tomatoes
¾ cup peeled, seeded, and finely diced cucumber
2 tablespoons red wine vinegar
2 tablespoons finely chopped scallion
4 tablespoons cored, seeded, and finely diced sweet red pepper
½ cup tomato juice
1 teaspoon sugar
2 tablespoons chopped fresh basil, loosely packed
1 envelope granular gelatin
3 egg whites (about ⅓ cup)

1. Put the bread crumbs, garlic, and oil into the container of a food processor or electric blender. Blend thoroughly.

2. Add ½ cup of diced tomatoes, ½ cup diced cucumber, the vinegar, chopped scallion, diced red pepper, the tomato juice, sugar, and half the basil. Blend as smoothly as possible. Scrape the liquid into a mixing bowl and add the remaining tomatoes, cucumber, and basil. Blend well.

3. Pour about ¼ cup of the sauce into a pan and add the gelatin. Cook, stirring, over very low heat until the gelatin dissolves. Combine the rest of the gazpacho with the gelatin mixture and blend well. Let cool but do not allow the mixture to set.

4. Beat the egg whites until they stand in soft peaks. Scrape them into the gazpacho mixture and blend well with a whisk.

5. Lightly oil the inside of 4 individual half-cup soufflé dishes, ramekins, or other molds. Spoon or ladle equal portions of the gazpacho mixture into each mold. Cover with plastic wrap and refrigerate overnight. To serve, run a knife around the inside of each mold. Set the molds briefly in a basin of warm water. Wipe off the bottom of the molds, and invert each on a plate.

Lemony Chickpea-and-Tuna Spread

◇ ◇

When I first bought a food processor in the mid-1970s, it seemed like a gift from heaven for cooks. Suddenly, a whole world of quick purées, spreads, terrines, and soups opened up to the home cook. With a food processor or blender, this zesty spread can be made in 10 minutes. Serve over pita bread or garlic toast.

Yield: 4 to 6 servings.

1 15-ounce can of chickpeas, drained
⅓ cup sesame paste (tahini), stirred well
1 clove garlic, peeled
2 scallions, chopped
¼ cup water
½ teaspoon sesame oil
1 teaspoon cumin powder
¼ cup chopped fresh coriander (optional)
⅓ cup canned water-packed tuna, drained
2 tablespoons fresh lemon juice
Tabasco to taste
Salt and freshly ground black pepper to taste

1. Combine all ingredients in the bowl of a food processor. Purée to a coarse texture. Cover and keep cool until ready to serve.

*Both clams and oysters should
be well iced in the store and their
shells firmly shut. The way to
tell if an open clam or oyster is
alive is to pinch the shell shut—
if it remains shut, it is alive; if it
remains open, it has moved on to
shellfish heaven.*

*It goes without saying that
all shellfish should be consumed
as soon as possible. If you need
to refrigerate for a short time, put
the clams or oysters in plastic
bags with a little hole on top to
allow some air inside.*

Baked Clams with Garlic Butter

◇ ◇

In summertime, I love to go clamming on Gardiners Bay in East
Hampton. There is nothing like a briny fresh clam with a squeeze
of lemon juice. This recipe for baked clams with garlic butter
could not be easier. Serve it with country bread.

Yield: 4 servings.

24 cherrystone clams
6 tablespoons soft butter
Salt and a generous grinding of black pepper
1 tablespoon finely minced garlic
1 tablespoon finely chopped shallots
4 tablespoons chopped fresh chervil or parsley
4 tablespoons freshly grated Gruyère or Parmesan cheese
   (optional)

1. Preheat the broiler to high.

2. Open the clams, discarding the top shell, and loosen the clams on
the bottom half of the shell.

3. Blend together in a bowl the butter, salt, pepper, garlic, shallots,
and chervil. Do not add too much salt because the clams are salty.

4. Spoon an equal amount of the herb butter on top of each clam
and smooth it slightly. Arrange the clams on a baking dish and sprinkle
cheese over each clam.

5. Place the clams under the broiler 5 to 6 inches from the heat.
Broil about 3 to 4 minutes until hot and golden brown. Do not overcook.

Frittata with Red Peppers and Potatoes

◇ ◇

The frittata here calls for red potatoes, sweet peppers, white onions, basil, and Gruyère cheese. It cooks in 2 minutes, so don't leave the stove. It is done when a spatula or knife can be run around the edges easily. A cast-iron pan is excellent for making frittatas because it cooks gently.

Yield: 4 servings.

4 small red waxy potatoes (about ½ pound)
2 tablespoons vegetable oil
1½ cups sweet red pepper, cut into ½-inch cubes
1½ cups green pepper, cut into ½-inch cubes
½ cup thinly sliced white onions
8 eggs
2 tablespoons finely chopped fresh basil or parsley
Salt and freshly ground pepper to taste
¼ pound cheese, preferably Gruyère or Swiss, cut into small cubes
2 tablespoons olive oil

1. Wash the potatoes and cut them, unpeeled, into thin slices.

2. Heat the oil in a large nonstick skillet or cast-iron pan and add the potatoes. Cook over medium heat, shaking and tossing, about 5 minutes. Add the peppers and the onions. Cook, shaking the skillet and stirring, about 5 minutes.

3. In a bowl, beat the eggs with the basil; add salt and pepper, and beat in the cheese.

4. Over high heat, add the olive oil and the egg mixture to the potatoes and cook, stirring gently but firmly with a plastic spatula, about 1 minute. Cover tightly and reduce to medium heat. Cook about 2 minutes, or until it sets. Run a spatula or knife around the outside of the frittata. Invert a large round plate over the skillet and invert the skillet and plate quickly, letting the frittata fall into the plate. It should be golden brown on top. Serve immediately.

OMELETS AND FRITTATAS

◇

Omelets play a major role in my history as a cook. When I was just a teenager, the first test for employment in a kitchen was making an omelet. The boss, usually the chef, watched your every move. The omelet had to come out light, fluffy, and perfectly smooth. One day, after I had been employed by a prestigious restaurant in Paris, the chef watched me make an omelet for a customer and shouted, "That is a grandmother omelet!," referring to the wrinkles on the surface. He then whacked me on the backside with his cane. I became so furious that I flung the omelet in his face.

Certain that I was fired, I gathered my belongings and headed out the door. The chef came after me. When I turned around to face him, he said, "What I did was wrong. And you acted like a real man. Come back to the kitchen."

Making the perfect omelet— smooth and golden outside, moist, well seasoned, and perfectly folded—is a technique that all home cooks would do well to master.

(continued on next page)

Italians have their own version of an omelet, called the frittata, and the strategy for making a superior one is similar. The fundamental difference between the two is that an omelet is made with eggs and seasonings, then filled with sundry ingredients, whereas the frittata mixture incorporates the ingredients and the result is thicker and slightly drier. Moreover, the omelet is cooked in an open pan, while the frittata pan is usually covered.

The ingredients that can go into a frittata are endless. Like omelets, they can be served at any time of the day—as an appetizer, at breakfast, as a lunch entrée or a light supper. Some can even be served cold. They can be filled with diced ham, chopped sweet peppers, cheese and herbs, any cold meats with herbs, sundry vegetables, or just plain with plenty of seasonings.

◇

Cold Lobster with Spicy Mustard Sauce
◇ ◇

When buying lobster, make sure that the creature is in clean water and shows signs of life. The more active the lobster, the fresher it is. Lobsters die rather quickly in captivity so you have to make sure. Also, touch the claw shell. It should be thick and hard. Softness indicates it has recently shed its shell—and the meat inside may be very small.

I frequently look for contrast when composing dishes: salty and sour, acid and richness, hot and sweet. The sweet flavor of lobster meat goes particularly well with this spicy mustard sauce.

Yield: 4 servings.

Salt for cooking water, to taste
4 live lobsters (about 1½ pounds each)
1 egg white
2 teaspoons Dijon-style mustard
2 tablespoons red wine vinegar
Freshly ground pepper to taste
¼ teaspoon chopped, cored, and seeded jalapeño pepper
1 clove garlic, peeled
1 large sweet red pepper, cored, seeded, and cut into large pieces
½ cup olive or vegetable oil
12 fresh basil leaves

1. Pour about 2 inches of water or seawater in the bottom of a large steamer. Add salt, unless seawater is used. Bring the water to a boil.

2. Place the lobsters on a steamer rack and cover the pot. Cook over high heat for 10 to 12 minutes. Remove the lobsters from the steamer and let cool.

3. Split the lobsters in half lengthwise and crack the claws. Remove and discard the small sac near the eyes and the intestine through the middle of the tail.

4. Combine all the remaining ingredients and salt to taste in a blender or a food processor. Use the pulse lever three or four times to blend everything to a fine texture. Serve the sauce with the lobsters.

Sweet Corn and Pepper Fritters

◇ ◇

In France, fresh corn is a rarity, so for those of us who have moved to the United States it is a fabulous treat. These fritters are a great way to use fresh corn in season. You can garnish them in numerous ways: a fresh tomato sauce, sour cream and chives, herbed yogurt sauce and more.

Yield: 12 fritters.

1¼ cups whole-kernel corn, preferably fresh, although frozen may
    be used
1 cup finely chopped sweet pepper, preferably red, although green
    may be used
1 cup finely chopped scallions
1 teaspoon finely minced hot green pepper, such as jalapeño
    (optional)
1 teaspoon ground cumin
1¼ cups flour
2 teaspoons baking powder
Salt to taste if desired
Freshly ground pepper to taste
1 cup milk
4 tablespoons corn, peanut, or vegetable oil, approximately

1. Put the corn in a mixing bowl and add the chopped sweet pepper, scallions, and hot pepper. Sprinkle with cumin, flour, baking powder, salt, and pepper and stir to blend. Add the milk and stir to blend thoroughly.

2. Heat enough oil to just cover the bottom of a skillet, preferably nonstick. Spoon about ¼ cup of the batter in the skillet for each fritter (you will probably fit two) and cook about 2 minutes or until golden brown on one side. Turn the fritters and cook about 2 minutes on the second side. Drain on paper towels and keep warm. As you finish each batch of fritters, add more oil to the pan as necessary.

Mussels with Mexican Vinaigrette
◇ ◇

In summertime, I pick fresh mussels near my home on Eastern Long Island. They are great cooked with some shallots and white wine. Sometimes, I make a slightly spicy sauce like the one here, which complements the sweet fresh mussels.

Yield: 4 servings.

24 mussels (about 1 pound)
½ cup water
Mexican vinaigrette sauce (see recipe below)
2 tablespoons finely chopped coriander
Lime wedges for garnish

1. Pull off and discard the stringy beard from the mussels. Scrub the mussels as necessary and drain them well (see page 17).
2. Put the mussels in a pot and add the water. Cover closely and bring to the boil. Cook 4 or 5 minutes or until all the mussels are open. Drain. Discard the cooking liquid.
3. Pull the mussel meat from the shells and save both the meat and half of the shells. Return one mussel to each shell and arrange them on a plate. Spoon an equal portion of the vinaigrette sauce over each. Sprinkle the mussels with coriander. Garnish the platter with lime wedges.

Mexican Vinaigrette Sauce
◇ ◇

Yield: ⅔ cup.

1 tablespoon lime juice
3 tablespoons olive oil
1½ teaspoons finely seeded and minced jalapeño peppers
1 teaspoon finely chopped fresh coriander
Salt to taste
Freshly ground black pepper to taste
¼ cup finely chopped tomatoes
2 tablespoons finely chopped red onion

1. Put the lime juice in a small mixing bowl and whisk in the oil. Add the remaining ingredients and stir to blend.

Guacamole

◇ ◇

I have always liked the seasonings in Mexican cooking, especially the combinations of citrus—lemon or lime—with hot peppers. This mildly spicy dip can be used with tortilla chips, crackers, or raw vegetables. It also makes a nice side dish to grilled meats and fish.

Yield: 4 to 6 servings.

2 firm, ripe, unblemished avocados (about 1 pound each)
¾ cup finely chopped red onion
Juice of 1 lime
1 cup peeled, seeded, cubed ripe red tomato
3 pickled serrano chiles or any small, green hot tomatoes, finely
    chopped (about 1 tablespoon)
Salt to taste if desired
Freshly ground pepper to taste

1. Peel avocados. Cut in half and remove and discard pits. Cut avocados lengthwise into thin slices. Finely dice slices. There should be about 3 cups.

2. Put 1 cup of cubed avocado, ½ cup of onion, and half of the lime juice into the container of a food processor or electric blender. Blend until finely puréed. Transfer to a bowl.

3. To the blended mixture, add remaining avocado, remaining chopped onion, tomato, and chopped chiles. Add more lime juice if desired. Add salt and pepper to taste. Stir to blend.

Oven-Roasted Tomatoes

◇ ◇

This tasty side dish could not be simpler. I make it in late summer when my garden is sagging under the weight of ripe tomatoes. If you like, put some paper-thin slices of garlic cloves into the cut side of the tomato before broiling.

Yield: 4 servings.

4 ripe red unblemished tomatoes (about 1¾ pounds total)
Salt to taste
Freshly ground pepper to taste
2 tablespoons olive oil
½ teaspoon fresh rosemary or ¼ teaspoon dried

1. Preheat broiler to high.
2. Cut away core of each tomato. Bring a pot of water to a boil. Add tomatoes and let stand about 45 seconds. Let cool and remove skin with a sharp knife.
3. Cut each tomato in half widthwise.
4. Arrange each tomato half, cut side up, in one layer in baking dish. Sprinkle with salt and pepper. Blend oil and rosemary and brush the tomatoes with the mixture. Place under the broiler for 3 to 5 minutes.

VARIATION: You can sprinkle some grated Parmesan or Romano cheese over the tomatoes before broiling.

Skewered Shrimp and Zucchini

◇ ◇

You can substitute sea scallops for shrimp in this recipe.

Yield: 4 servings.

20 large shrimp (about 1¼ pounds)
2 small zucchini (about ½ pound)
Salt to taste if desired
Freshly ground pepper to taste
1 teaspoon coarsely chopped garlic
1 tablespoon finely chopped fresh parsley, or herb of choice
3 tablespoons olive oil
1 bay leaf, broken into small pieces
3 tablespoons fresh lime juice
1 teaspoon chopped fresh thyme or ½ teaspoon dried
Anchovy butter (see page 28)

1. Prepare a gas-fired or charcoal grill, or preheat a broiler to high.

2. Shell and devein the shrimp (see page 9).

3. Trim off the ends of the zucchini and cut them into 20 ¼-inch rounds.

4. In a bowl, combine the zucchini rounds and the shrimp. Add salt, pepper, garlic, parsley, olive oil, bay leaf, lime juice, and thyme. Blend well.

5. Arrange alternate pieces of shrimp and zucchini on each of 4 skewers. (It is best when skewering the shrimp to skewer them through the thick upper part and then fold the shrimp over to skewer the small tail. That way, they will lie flat on the grill.) Brush the skewered foods with any oil remaining in the bowl.

6. If the skewered foods are to be broiled, arrange the skewers on a baking sheet and place them 4 or 5 inches from the heat source. Broil about 3 minutes on one side and turn. Broil about 3 minutes on the second side.

7. If the skewered foods are to be grilled, place them over the hot coals and let cook about 2 or 3 minutes on one side. Turn and cook about 2 or 3 minutes on the second side. Serve with anchovy butter.

◇

When I don't have time to make a sauce, I often resort to compound butters—essentially, flavored butters—several of which I keep in the refrigerator at all times. They are excellent on steaks, vegetables, seafood, and as the basis for an à la minute sauce.

Anchovy butter is just one of many flavored butters that you can make. Compound butters are a cinch to make. The classic one is called maître d' hôtel, a blend of soft butter, minced parsley, and fresh lemon juice. For garlic butter, blanch the garlic for 5 minutes and mash it into butter with minced herbs of your choice. Watercress butter is particularly tasty, or use any fresh herbs you like. Flavored butter—tarragon or chive—is particularly good on steaks.

Once you have flavored the softened butter, place it in the middle of a sheet of waxed paper. Mold it into a cylinder, roll up the waxed paper, and refrigerate. Then you can just slice off a piece whenever you need it.

Anchovy Butter

◇ ◇

Yield: About ¼ cup.

4 tablespoons butter, at room temperature
1 teaspoon anchovy paste or finely chopped anchovy
2 tablespoons finely chopped chives
1 teaspoon lemon juice

1. Put the butter in a small bowl and add other ingredients. Beat with a wire whisk until light and creamy. Keep cool.

Shrimp and Squid with Vinaigrette Sauce

◇ ◇

To my taste, exquisitely fresh ingredients need minimal enhancement. In this recipe, if you have pristine squid and shrimp, you do not want to mask their flavors with a strong sauce. A little vinaigrette is all they need.

Yield: 6 to 8 servings.

1½ pounds squid, cleaned (see page 6)
1 pound shrimp, shelled and deveined
Salt to taste
12 black peppercorns
1 bay leaf
½ teaspoon dried hot red pepper flakes
3 sprigs fresh parsley
1 tablespoon minced garlic
½ cup finely chopped parsley
1 cup diced heart of celery
1½ cups coarsely chopped red onions
¼ cup lemon juice
½ cup olive oil

1. Cut the squid bodies into rings, each about ½ inch wide. Cut the tentacles into bite-sized pieces. There should be about 2½ cups.

2. Put the squid into a saucepan and add the shrimp. Add cold water to barely cover and salt lightly. Add the peppercorns, bay leaf, half of the pepper flakes, and the parsley sprigs. Bring to a boil and continue cooking 1 minute. Remove from the heat and let cool.

3. Drain. Put the squid and shrimp in a mixing bowl and add the remaining pepper flakes, garlic, chopped parsley, celery, onions, lemon juice, and oil. Toss to blend well and check seasonings. Serve at room temperature.

Salads

◇ ◇ ◇

Arugula and Red Onion Salad

Garlic Sausages

French Potato Salad

Arugula, Mushroom, and Endive Salad

Lemon-Garlic Vinaigrette

Arugula, Endive, and Orange Salad

Warm Shrimp and Spinach Salad

Cold Crabmeat and Shrimp Salad

Tomato and Lentil Salad

Spiced Carrot Salad

Avocado and Tomato Salad

Goat Cheese and Mixed Greens Salad

Provençal Salad with Seared Tuna

Warm Fresh Tuna and Scallop Salad with
Orange-Coriander Vinaigrette

Warm Skate Salad with Chinese Cabbage

Chinese Cabbage Salad

Fennel and Avocado Salad

Green Bean and Red Pepper Salad

Arugula and Red Onion Salad

◇ ◇

I grow a lot of arugula in my garden, and use it for salads, soups, and sauces. Its peppery flavor enlivens any dish. This is a quick, invigorating salad that you can whip together in minutes.

Yield: 4 servings.

½ pound arugula leaves, approximately
1 cup chopped red onion
½ cup finely chopped parsley, preferably flat-leaf Italian parsley
1½ tablespoons red wine vinegar
Salt to taste
Freshly ground pepper to taste
¼ cup olive oil

1. Pick over the arugula leaves and discard any tough stems. Rinse and drain leaves very well. Pat dry. There should be 5 to 6 cups, loosely packed. Put the leaves in a salad bowl and add onion and parsley.

2. Put the vinegar in a bowl and add salt and pepper. Start beating while gradually adding the oil. Pour the sauce over salad and toss to blend.

Garlic Sausages
◇ ◇

Yield: 6 to 8 servings.

2 uncooked garlic sausages (sometimes called *cotechini*) (about 1
 pound each)
2 bay leaves
½ teaspoon dried thyme

1. Put the sausages in a pot and add cold water to cover.

2. Add the bay leaves and thyme and bring to a boil. Let simmer 30 minutes. Serve sliced, hot or cold, with the French Potato Salad (see recipe below).

French Potato Salad
◇ ◇

This French-style salad can be served cold or at room temperature. It is relatively low-cal because it has no mayonnaise—but it does have a dousing of white wine.

Yield: 4 to 6 servings.

2½ pounds white potatoes, halved (skin left on)
Salt and freshly ground black pepper to taste
⅓ cup dry white wine
½ cup olive oil

1. Rinse the potatoes and place them in a large pot with cold water to cover. Bring to a boil, reduce heat, and simmer for about 20 minutes, or until the potatoes are tender but not mushy.

2. Preheat oven to 200 degrees.

3. Drain the potatoes. Cut them into ¼-inch-thick pieces and put them in an ovenproof bowl or casserole. Add salt, pepper, wine, and oil. Toss gently. Cover the bowl with foil and put in the warm oven to heat them gently. Transfer to a serving dish.

Arugula, Mushroom, and Endive Salad

◇ ◇

If you can't find arugula for this salad, watercress is a good substitute.

Yield: 4 to 6 servings.

½ pound white mushrooms or mushrooms of your choice, sliced
    thin (about 3 cups)
1 bunch of arugula, trimmed, rinsed, and dried well
2 cups endive, sliced thin
Lemon-garlic vinaigrette (see recipe below)

1. Mix the mushrooms, arugula, and endive in a salad bowl and toss with the lemon-garlic vinaigrette dressing.

Lemon-Garlic Vinaigrette

◇ ◇

Yield: About ¾ cup.

1 tablespoon Dijon-style mustard
½ teaspoon finely minced garlic
2 tablespoons fresh lemon juice
2 tablespoons dry white wine
Dash of Tabasco sauce
⅓ cup olive oil
Salt to taste
Freshly ground pepper to taste

1. Put the mustard and garlic into a mixing bowl. Using a wire whisk, start beating.
2. Beat in the lemon juice, white wine, and Tabasco.
3. Gradually add the oil, beating vigorously. Add salt and pepper.

◇

The balsamic vinegar you buy in supermarkets has little to do with authentic balsamic vinegar, which comes from Modena in Italy. The real thing is usually aged for more than 25 years in a series of wooden casks to achieve a sublime sweet-woody flavor. Real balsamic vinegar is prohibitively expensive—more than $100 for a tiny bottle. The supermarket version is usually regular vinegar that has been colored and sweetened. It may or may not have been aged. In any case, it has a pleasant flavor and is a nice change of pace from regular red wine vinegar.

Arugula, Endive, and Orange Salad

◇ ◇

Generally, I don't care for fruit with salads. But this snappy, cleansing combination is particularly good before a meal. The colors are beautiful, too.

Yield: 4 servings.

1 pound arugula
2 endives
2 teaspoons Dijon-style mustard
3 tablespoons balsamic vinegar
½ cup olive oil
Salt and freshly ground pepper to taste
½ cup chopped red onion
1 medium-size orange, peeled and sectioned
2 tablespoons chopped parsley

1. Trim off and discard the stems of the arugula and the endives. Cut the endives into 2-inch pieces crosswise.

2. To make the dressing, put the mustard in a salad bowl. Add the vinegar. Start beating with a wire whisk while adding the oil. Add salt and pepper. Add the chopped onion. Blend well.

3. Add the arugula, endive, orange sections, and parsley and toss well. Serve.

Warm Shrimp and Spinach Salad

◇ ◇

I enjoy serving shrimp appetizers when entertaining because the salad can be assembled beforehand and the shrimp takes no time to cook. This quick sauté would work equally well with scallops. Remember to taste for seasonings before serving.

Yield: 4 servings.

1¼ pounds medium-size shrimp
2 sweet red peppers
¾ pound spinach, trimmed of stems, washed and well dried
4 thin slices of red onion, broken into rings
6 tablespoons olive oil
Salt and freshly ground pepper to taste
2 teaspoons finely chopped garlic
3 tablespoons balsamic vinegar or red wine vinegar
½ cup chopped fresh basil leaves or parsley

1. Peel and devein the shrimp and set aside (see page 9).
2. Cut out and discard pepper cores and seeds. Cut peppers into ½-inch pieces crosswise.
3. Arrange spinach leaves on 4 dinner plates.
4. Arrange an equal portion of the onion rings in the center of each.
5. Heat oil in a large nonstick skillet and add the red peppers. Add salt and pepper. Cook, stirring, about 2 minutes over high heat. Add garlic and cook, stirring, 1 minute more. Add vinegar, cook and stir 45 seconds. Add the shrimp and cook another 3 minutes. Add half the basil and toss. Spoon shrimp and sauce equally over onion rings. Sprinkle with remaining basil and serve immediately.

In this crab and shrimp salad I
call for cooked lump crabmeat.
Unless you have a few hours to
spare—and nimble fingers—
this is the best option. Blue crabs
take a lot of work to clean. The
yield is roughly 12 percent meat
to total weight.

When buying whole crabs
(to steam), make sure that they
are alive and moving around.
Soft-shell crabs are blue crabs
that have shed their shells and
have not yet developed hard new
ones. Store crabs immediately in
the refrigerator and eat as soon
as possible.

When buying lump
crabmeat, make sure it does not
have any off odor or
discoloration. It should be well
iced at the store.

Cold Crabmeat and Shrimp Salad

I have served this rich, luxurious salad as a starter for Sunday brunch, and as a light entrée. The radicchio leaves make for a splendid presentation.

Yield: 4 servings.

1 pound medium shrimp, deveined, with shells left intact
Salt and freshly ground pepper to taste
1 bay leaf
2 sprigs parsley
¾ pound fresh cooked crabmeat, preferably lump
1 tablespoon Dijon mustard
1 tablespoon lime juice
2 tablespoons red wine vinegar
1 teaspoon honey
4 tablespoons olive oil
½ cup finely chopped scallions
1 jalapeño pepper, cored, seeded, and finely chopped
16 large, unblemished spinach leaves, trimmed of the stems, rinsed
    well and patted dry
16 radicchio leaves, washed and dried
1 head romaine or escarole, cut into bite-sized pieces
3 sprigs chervil or coriander for garnishing

1. Place shrimp in a saucepan and add salt, pepper, bay leaf, and parsley. Add cold water to barely cover and bring to a boil. Remove from the heat and let the shrimp stand until they reach room temperature. This step can be done ahead of time.

2. Pick over the crabmeat to remove bits of cartilage and shells.

3. In a bowl, combine Dijon mustard, lime juice, vinegar, honey, olive oil, scallions, jalapeño pepper, and salt and pepper to taste. Blend well with a wire whisk. Add shrimp and crabmeat and toss lightly to blend without breaking crabmeat lumps.

4. Arrange 4 spinach leaves on each of 4 large serving plates. Arrange the radicchio alternately between the spinach leaves. Place equal portions of romaine leaves in the center of each serving.

5. Spoon equal portions of the crabmeat and shrimp salad over the center of each plate. Garnish with the chervil sprigs. Serve chilled.

Tomato and Lentil Salad

◇ ◇

Lentils are a good source of fiber and protein, aside from being delicious when tossed in a salad.

Yield: 4 *servings.*

½ pound dry lentils
1 small onion, stuck with 1 clove
1 cup finely diced carrots
2 sprigs fresh thyme or ½ teaspoon dried
1 bay leaf
Salt and freshly ground pepper to taste
3 cups water
½ cup finely chopped onion
2 teaspoons finely chopped garlic
1 tablespoon red wine vinegar
3 tablespoons olive or vegetable oil
4 ripe plum tomatoes, cored and cut into small cubes
2 tablespoons chopped parsley

1. Combine in a saucepan lentils, onion, clove, carrots, thyme, bay leaf, salt, pepper, and water. Bring to a boil and simmer for 20 minutes or until the lentils are tender. Don't overcook. Drain.

2. Remove and discard the onion, thyme sprigs, and bay leaf.

3. Transfer the lentils to a salad bowl and add the chopped onion, garlic, vinegar, oil, tomatoes, salt, and pepper. Toss well and sprinkle with parsley.

Spiced Carrot Salad

◇ ◇

Notice that in this carrot salad I poach whole garlic cloves before adding them to the salad. This gives them a much milder flavor. I often do that when I want to make a subtle sauce, like a white wine and herb sauce for chicken.

Garlic is also excellent roasted whole. Peel off the papery outside of the head of garlic and roast it until it is soft to the touch—about 40 minutes (depends on the size of the head). Squeeze out the soft garlic pulp and spread it on toast.

Yield: 6 servings.

1 pound fresh carrots (about 12)
3 large garlic cloves, peeled but left whole
Salt to taste
½ cup fresh lemon juice
⅛ teaspoon cinnamon
½ teaspoon cumin
½ teaspoon paprika
⅛ teaspoon cayenne
¼ cup olive oil
Chopped parsley for garnish

1. Trim and scrape the carrots, and place them in a pot.
2. Cover the carrots with water and add the garlic and salt. Bring to a boil and cook for 10 minutes or until tender. Drain. Then cut the carrots into ½-inch-thick rounds (there should be about 2½ cups).
3. In a bowl, combine the lemon juice, cinnamon, cumin, paprika, and cayenne. Blend well. Add the carrots. Mash the garlic with a fork and add to salad. Add half of the oil. Stir well.
4. Spoon out individual portions, and sprinkle the remaining oil over them evenly. Garnish with parsley and serve.

Avocado and Tomato Salad

◇ ◇

Pick a nice ripe avocado—soft to the touch—for this salad. If your avocado is still hard, you can hasten the ripening process by placing it in a brown paper bag and letting it stand overnight.

Yield: 4 servings.

2 ripe avocados
2 tablespoons lemon juice
4 ripe plum tomatoes
1 medium-size red onion, cut into thin slices
2 hard-cooked eggs, peeled and quartered
2 teaspoons finely chopped garlic
2 tablespoons red wine vinegar
6 tablespoons olive oil
4 tablespoons coarsely chopped fresh coriander
½ teaspoon ground cumin
Salt and freshly ground pepper to taste

1. Peel the avocados and cut them in half. Discard the pit and cut each half into 4 lengthwise slices. Cut the slices into large cubes and sprinkle with lemon juice to prevent discoloration.
2. Cut the tomatoes into 1-inch cubes.
3. Combine all the ingredients in a salad bowl. Toss well and serve.

Goat Cheese and Mixed Greens Salad

◇ ◇

Goat cheese is one of my favorite additions to a salad. Just remember that the older the cheese, the more tart the flavor. To judge the age of goat cheese, just squeeze it—if it is soft and creamy, it is young; if it is firm, it is old and sharp-tasting. If it is extremely hard, it is over the hill. A salad like this is best with a relatively young cheese. Supermarkets today sell goat cheese with fresh herbs and black pepper. Either would work well in this salad.

Yield: 4 servings.

1 tablespoon Dijon mustard
2 tablespoons red wine vinegar
1 tablespoon finely chopped garlic
2 tablespoons minced basil
5 tablespoons olive oil
Salt and freshly ground pepper to taste
3 cups green-leaf or other favorite lettuce, washed and dried
2 cups radicchio, washed and dried
¼ pound goat cheese, crumbled or cubed

1. To make the dressing, place the mustard in a salad bowl and add vinegar and garlic. Add the minced basil. Start beating with a wire whisk and add oil slowly, then salt and pepper to taste. Blend well.
2. Add the lettuce, radicchio, and cheese. Toss well and serve.

Provençal Salad with Seared Tuna

◇ ◇

My local fish market has wonderful tuna in the summer. I like to sear it and serve it with this sunny blend of herbs and greens. This tuna is cooked medium-rare—be sure not to overcook it. In this salad, you could add any other vegetables that you like.

Yield: 4 servings.

◇

The term Provençal *refers to the flavors and aromas of the South of France. Such dishes invariably contain garlic and olive oil, usually tomatoes, as well as herbs like rosemary, thyme, tarragon, and basil.*

For the fish

2 center-cut tuna steaks, 1 inch thick (about 1½ pounds)
1 tablespoon olive oil
Salt and freshly ground pepper to taste
2 sprigs fresh thyme or 1 teaspoon dried
¼ teaspoon red pepper flakes
2 teaspoons grated lemon rind

For the salad

1 yellow squash (about ¼ pound)
1 zucchini (about ¼ pound)
4 ripe plum tomatoes (about ½ pound)
4 tablespoons olive oil
1 large sweet red pepper, cored, seeded, and cut into ½-inch
  pieces
1 large green pepper, cored, seeded, and cut into ½-inch pieces
1 red onion, chopped coarsely (about ¼ pound)
¼ pound snow peas or snap peas, trimmed
Salt and freshly ground pepper to taste

1 tablespoon minced garlic
2 tablespoons red wine vinegar
1 tablespoon balsamic vinegar
4 tablespoons chopped fresh basil or coarsely chopped Italian
  parsley

(Continued on next page)

1. Put the tuna on a flat surface and cut away and discard the dark part, if there is any. Spoon the oil over the fish and sprinkle with salt, pepper, thyme, pepper flakes, and lemon rind. Coat well on both sides. Cover with plastic wrap and let stand at room temperature for 15 minutes.

2. Heat a nonstick or cast-iron skillet over high setting. Add the tuna steaks and cook 3 minutes; turn and cook 3 to 5 minutes more on the other side, or until the tuna is pinkish in the center.

3. Remove the fish, cut it into ½-inch cubes, and set aside. Keep it warm.

4. For the salad, trim the yellow squash and zucchini and cut them into ¼-inch rounds.

5. Core the tomatoes and cut them into ¾-inch cubes.

6. Heat the oil over high setting in a large nonstick skillet. Add the red and green peppers, squash, zucchini, onion, snow peas, tomatoes, salt, and pepper. Cook, stirring and tossing, about 5 to 8 minutes, or until the peppers are soft.

7. Add the garlic; stir but do not let it brown. Add the vinegars, tuna cubes, and basil. Stir and toss well. Serve hot immediately.

Warm Fresh Tuna and Scallop Salad with Orange-Coriander Vinaigrette
◇ ◇

The coriander in this salad was an experiment on my part. I wanted something to counteract the sweet orange. It worked marvelously.

Yield: 4 servings.

The vinaigrette

2 teaspoons Dijon-style mustard
2 tablespoons freshly squeezed lemon juice
⅓ cup olive oil
1 tablespoon red wine vinegar
1 tablespoon minced fresh coriander
2 tablespoons orange zest, cut into 1-inch strips
Salt and freshly ground white pepper to taste

The salad

- 1 head each of different salad greens, such as radicchio, Bibb lettuce, and arugula
- 2 heads Belgian endive
- 2 oranges, sectioned neatly and trimmed of the tough membranes between each wedge
- 1 tablespoon vegetable oil
- ¾ pound bay scallops or quartered sea scallops
- ¾ pound skinless tuna fillets, cut into ½-inch cubes
- 2 tablespoons minced shallots
- Salt and freshly ground white pepper to taste

1. To make the vinaigrette, combine the mustard and half of the lemon juice in a small bowl. Beat briskly until the mixture begins to thicken. Gradually add the olive oil, the remaining lemon juice, and the vinegar while continuing to beat. Add coriander, orange zest, and salt and pepper. Mix well.

2. To make the salad, tear the greens and endive into bite-sized pieces and mix them with the orange sections in a large bowl. Pour two-thirds of the dressing over the salad and toss well. Divide the salad into 4 portions and arrange on serving plates.

3. Coat the bottom of a nonstick pan with the vegetable oil. Over high heat, sauté the scallops for 1 minute while shaking the pan. Add the tuna and shallots. Salt and pepper well. Toss briskly and cover. Cook for another minute, or until the tuna is pink in the center, shaking the pan occasionally. Remove the pan from the heat and let the seafood cool, uncovered, for 2 to 3 minutes. Drizzle the remaining vinaigrette over the tuna and scallops and distribute them among the 4 plates.

◈

Living on Eastern Long Island, I have access to excellent fresh scallops, sea scallops, and local bay scallops. There are four hundred species of scallops in the world's oceans, although fewer than twenty are harvested commercially. The main types are bay, ocean, and calico. Bay scallops, the most expensive, generally measure no more than 3 inches across. They come from shallow bays along the East Coast, especially from Long Island to northern Massachusetts. Exquisitely sweet and tender, they command a hefty price.

Sea scallops, which generally measure 5 inches or so across, are harvested primarily in the icy waters of the North Atlantic. Sea scallops can be delicious if cooked properly (just until the center loses its wet look). Bay or sea scallops would be best for the salad here. If the sea scallops are very large, cut them in half before cooking.

Calico scallops, which are inferior in flavor and can be slightly tough, are also found along the East Coast, mostly from Florida to the Carolinas.

SALADS 45

Warm Skate Salad with Chinese Cabbage

◇ ◇

Skate has been a delicacy in France for as long as I can remember, but only recently did it become popular here—primarily in restaurants. Skate is found on the sandy ocean bottoms off the New England and mid-Atlantic coasts. The edible part of the fish, the wings, have a corrugated texture and are extremely tender. The most common preparation is skate *aux beurre noir*, or skate wings with brown butter sauce. The sweet flesh also works well in this salad.

Yield: 4 servings.

2 Golden Delicious apples (about ¾ pound)
3 ripe red plum tomatoes (about ½ pound)
4 skinless, boneless skate wings (about 1½ pounds)
4 cups cold water
2 tablespoons red wine vinegar
¼ teaspoon dried thyme
1 bay leaf
3 sprigs fresh parsley
Salt to taste if desired
6 whole peppercorns
Chinese cabbage salad (see page 47)

1. Cut the apples into quarters. Cut away and discard the skin, core, and seeds. Cut the quarters crosswise into thin slices. There should be about 2 cups. Keep cool.

2. Drop tomatoes into boiling water for 10 seconds. Remove with a slotted spoon, let cool, and peel them. Cut tomatoes from top to bottom into quarters. Set aside.

3. Arrange skate wings in one layer in a skillet or casserole and add the cold water, vinegar, thyme, bay leaf, parsley, salt, and peppercorns. Bring to a boil. Remove from heat and let stand 5 minutes.

4. Divide each skate wing into bite-sized pieces and put them in a bowl. Discard the cooking liquid and spices. Add apples, tomatoes, and Chinese cabbage salad recipe. Toss gently.

5. Arrange equal portions of Chinese cabbage salad on each of 4 large plates. Top with equal portions of warm skate salad and serve.

Chinese Cabbage Salad

◇ ◇

Yield: 4 servings.

1 large Chinese cabbage
1 cup trimmed, peeled, finely shredded carrot
2 tablespoons finely chopped parsley
2 tablespoons Dijon-style mustard
3 tablespoons finely chopped shallots
¼ cup white vinegar
1 cup olive oil
Salt to taste if desired
Freshly ground pepper to taste

1. Cut cabbage lengthwise into quarters. Place each quarter on a flat surface, and slice crosswise into very thin pieces. Slice only the tender tops. Discard less tender bottom portion. There should be 7 to 8 cups. Put cabbage in a large bowl and add carrot and parsley. Blend well.

2. Put mustard, shallots, and vinegar in a mixing bowl. Start beating with a whisk while gradually adding the oil. Add salt and pepper.

3. Add about ½ cup of the sauce to the cabbage and carrot mixture and toss to blend. Use remaining to drizzle over the hot skate salad.

Fennel and Avocado Salad

◇ ◇

Fennel, which has a faint anise flavor, is one of those vegetables people either love or hate. I fall into the former camp.

Its refreshing flavor and snappy texture make it well suited to salads. Fennel also adds a nice Provençal accent to soups and stews. When buying it, look for bulbs that are firm to the touch, with no soft spots or blemishes. The stem is generally cut off and used in soups or as a garnish.

Yield: 4 to 6 servings.

2 small bulbs fresh fennel
2 firm, ripe, unblemished avocados
½ cup lemon juice
2 small red onions (about ½ pound)
2 ripe tomatoes, cored
6 tablespoons red wine vinegar
¾ cup corn, peanut, or vegetable oil
Salt to taste if desired
Freshly ground pepper to taste
½ teaspoon hot dried red pepper flakes
4 teaspoons finely chopped fresh coriander (optional)

1. Trim off and discard fennel stems. Trim off and discard the tough outer skin. Cut the fennel bulbs into quarters. Cut the quarters crosswise into thin slices. There should be about 1½ cups. Put in a mixing bowl.

2. Peel the avocados and cut them around the middle, removing and discarding the pits. Cut the halves lengthwise into quarters. Cut the wedges crosswise into ½-inch pieces. Add these to the bowl. Add lemon juice and toss gently to blend.

3. Cut the onions in half widthwise. Cut each half crosswise into very thin slices. Break the slices into individual pieces. Add to the bowl.

4. Cut the tomatoes lengthwise in half. Cut each half into 8 crosswise pieces. Add to the bowl.

5. Add the vinegar, oil, salt, pepper, pepper flakes, and coriander. Toss and serve.

Green Bean and Red Pepper Salad

◇ ◇

Yield: 4 servings.

1 pound green beans, trimmed
1 medium-size sweet red pepper, cored and seeds removed
½ cup finely chopped red onion
2 teaspoons Dijon mustard
1 tablespoon red wine vinegar
¼ teaspoon ground cumin
Salt and freshly ground pepper to taste
⅓ cup olive or vegetable oil

1. Bring to a boil enough water to cover the beans. Add the beans and, when the water returns to a boil, cook until tender, about 8 minutes. Do not overcook. Drain well and put them in a salad bowl.

2. Preheat a broiler.

3. Place the pepper under the broiler and cook it on all sides until the entire skin is well charred. Put the peppers in a paper bag and close it. Let sit for 10 minutes. Remove the peppers, and peel off the charred skin. Cut into strips about ¼ inch wide. Add them to the beans. Add the onion.

4. Place the mustard, vinegar, cumin, salt, and pepper in a small mixing bowl. Start stirring with a wire whisk, and gradually add the oil. Blend well.

5. Add the dressing to the bean mixture. Stir and blend well.

Lobster and Wild Rice Salad
◇ ◇

I like the contrast here between the sweet, tender lobster and the nutty wild rice.

Yield: 4 to 6 servings.

3½ to 4 cups cooked wild rice (see recipe below)
2 cups cooked lobster meat, cut into bite-sized cubes
2 medium-size avocados
1 tablespoon lemon juice
½ cup coarsely chopped red onion
1 tablespoon Dijon mustard
2½ tablespoons red wine vinegar
½ cup olive oil
½ teaspoon finely minced garlic
Salt and freshly ground pepper to taste
2 tablespoons finely chopped parsley

1. Put the rice in a mixing bowl, let cool, and add the lobster.
2. Peel the avocados and slice in half. Remove the pits. Cut the avocados into cubes and sprinkle with lemon juice to prevent discoloration. Add the cubes to the mixing bowl. Sprinkle with onion.
3. Put the mustard and vinegar in a small mixing bowl and beat lightly with a wire whisk. Gradually add the oil, beating briskly with the whisk. Add the garlic, salt, pepper, and parsley. Stir. Pour over the salad and toss. Serve at room temperature.

Wild Rice
◇ ◇

Yield: About 3½ to 4 cups.

1 cup wild rice
3 cups water
Salt to taste if desired

1. Combine the wild rice, water, and salt in a heavy saucepan. Bring to a boil. Cover and cook over gentle heat for about 45 minutes. The rice should be slightly firm.
2. Spoon the rice into a mixing bowl and let cool.

Wild Rice and Almond Salad

◇ ◇

Yield: 4 to 6 servings.

3½ to 4 cups cooked wild rice (see recipe page 50)
½ cup sliced almonds
½ cup Greek or French black olives, pitted
1 cup raisins
1 cup peeled, seeded, and diced tomatoes
¼ cup red wine vinegar
½ cup olive oil
Salt to taste if desired
Freshly ground pepper to taste
3 bottled hot cherry peppers or pickled jalapeños, chopped
   (optional)
1 tablespoon finely chopped fresh coriander (optional)

1. Put the rice in a mixing bowl and let it cool.

2. Preheat oven to 375 degrees.

3. Put the sliced almonds in a small skillet and place in the oven. Bake 5 minutes or longer, shaking the skillet occasionally, until the slices are nicely browned. Let cool.

4. Add to the rice the almond slices, olives, raisins, tomatoes, vinegar, olive oil, salt, pepper, cherry peppers, and coriander. Toss to blend and serve at room temperature.

Warm Chicken Salad

◇ ◇

This low-calorie and savory salad makes a great lunch entrée. You could add any fresh herbs you like. Also, turkey breast could be substituted for chicken.

Yield: 4 servings.

2 whole skinless, boneless chicken breasts (about 1 pound total weight)
Salt to taste if desired
Freshly ground pepper to taste
1 tablespoon butter
1 tablespoon Dijon-style mustard
3 tablespoons red wine vinegar
½ cup olive oil
16 Belgian endive leaves
16 small pieces red leaf lettuce
4 cups salad greens torn or cut into bite-sized pieces
¼ cup finely chopped chives

1. Preheat oven to 400 degrees.

2. Trim chicken breasts of fat and cartilage. Cut each in half lengthwise. Sprinkle with salt and pepper.

3. Heat butter in a skillet and add chicken pieces. Cook briefly on both sides, about 1 minute. Place the skillet in the oven and bake 10–15 minutes, or until the chicken is cooked in the center.

4. Meanwhile, put mustard and 2 tablespoons of vinegar in a small mixing bowl and beat with a wire whisk. Gradually add oil, beating constantly. Add salt and pepper.

5. Put the endive and red leaf lettuce into a small bowl and add 2 tablespoons of the dressing. Stir to blend. Arrange 4 pieces endive and 4 red leaf lettuce on each of 4 plates.

6. Put remaining salad greens in mixing bowl and toss with 2 more tablespoons dressing. Spoon equal portions in center of each plate.

7. Cut chicken pieces on bias in thin slices. Arrange uniformly over salad greens.

8. Spoon remaining dressing into a small saucepan and add remaining tablespoon of vinegar. Stir over low heat, using wire whisk. Remove from heat and stir in chives. Spoon equal portions of warm dressing over the chicken and serve.

Lettuce, Endive, and Mushroom Salad

◇ ◇

Yield: 4 servings.

½ head green leaf lettuce
2 large, compact heads Belgian endive
½ pound fresh mushrooms of choice
¾ cup finely grated Gruyère or Swiss cheese
½ teaspoon finely chopped garlic
1 tablespoon Dijon mustard
½ cup sour cream
Salt to taste if desired
Freshly ground pepper to taste
2 tablespoons red wine vinegar
¼ cup olive oil

1. Trim off and discard any tough stem ends from the lettuce. Put the tender leaves in a salad bowl.

2. Cut off the bottoms of each head of endive. Cut each head lengthwise into 1-inch-thick strips and separate the leaves. There should be about 2 cups. Add to the salad bowl.

3. Rinse the mushrooms and pat dry. Cut them into thin slices. There should be about 1½ cups. Add to the salad bowl.

4. Sprinkle the greens with the cheese.

5. Blend in a separate bowl the garlic, mustard, and sour cream. Add salt and pepper. Stir in the vinegar and the oil.

6. Pour the dressing over the salad greens and toss well.

◇

I stress to cooking students that making a good vinaigrette is more than just tossing the ingredients into a bowl and whisking. You have to balance the mustard, oil, and vinegar so the flavor is tart but not overwhelmingly so. The basic vinaigrette made with oil, vinegar, mustard, salt, and pepper is just a launchpad for all kinds of other dressings, both cold and warm. Always trust your taste more than a recipe because ingredients change in intensity from one dressing to another. Here are a few quick options that would go with just about any salad in this chapter. Each makes about 1 cup.

JAPANESE STYLE. Combine in a bowl 2 tablespoons miso (fermented soybean paste, available at Oriental markets), ½ cup rice vinegar, ¼ cup olive oil, 2 scallions (chopped), 1 teaspoon sugar.

ARUGULA MAYONNAISE. Place in a bowl 3 tablespoons mayonnaise, 1 tablespoon lemon juice, ⅓ teaspoon Dijon-style mustard, ½ teaspoon salt, freshly ground black pepper to taste, and 1 cup minced arugula (or watercress). Blend well.

(continued on next page)

TOMATO-CHERVIL. *In a blender, combine 1 ripe tomato (cored and quartered), ½ cup fresh chervil (or ¼ cup basil), 2 tablespoons white wine vinegar, ½ cup olive oil, salt and freshly ground black pepper to taste, Dijon-style mustard to taste.*

CITRUS. *Whisk together in a bowl ¼ cup fresh lemon juice, salt and freshly ground black pepper, 2 tablespoons balsamic vinegar, and ½ cup olive oil.*

HERB-HORSERADISH. *Whisk together in a bowl 2 teaspoons red wine vinegar, salt and freshly ground black pepper, 2 tablespoons olive oil, 2 tablespoons cream, 1½ teaspoons grated fresh horseradish (or prepared), ½ cup chopped watercress (or herb of choice).*

SESAME. *Combine in a bowl 1 tablespoon sesame oil, 2 tablespoons olive oil, 1 tablespoon soy sauce, 1 clove garlic (minced), and freshly ground black pepper.*

YOGURT-SCALLION. *Whisk together in a bowl ½ cup unflavored yogurt, 2 shallots (minced), ⅓ cup chopped basil, 2 teaspoons Dijon mustard, salt and freshly ground pepper to taste.*

Fresh Tuna Salad with Tomatoes
◇ ◇

When I have exquisitely fresh tuna, it doesn't need much embellishment. Tomatoes are a perfect accompaniment.

Yield: 4 servings.

2 pieces tuna steak, each about 1 inch or more thick (about 1½ pounds total)
3 whole cloves
6 parsley sprigs
2 tablespoons white vinegar
4 cups water, approximately
Salt to taste if desired
8 peppercorns
¼ cup red wine vinegar
6 tablespoons olive oil
1 teaspoon finely minced garlic
Freshly ground pepper to taste
2½ cups ripe tomatoes, cut into ½-inch cubes
1 cup sweet red peppers, cut into small pieces
1 cup green bell peppers, cut into small pieces
1½ cups finely chopped red onion
½ cup finely shredded fresh basil

1. Put the tuna pieces in a skillet and add cloves, parsley, white vinegar, and enough water to almost cover. Add salt and peppercorns and bring to a boil. Let cook about 5 minutes. Remove from heat and let stand 5 minutes.

2. Drain tuna and allow to cool briefly on a plate.

3. Put red wine vinegar in a mixing bowl and gradually add oil, beating with a wire whisk. Add garlic, salt, and pepper. Add tomatoes, red and green peppers, and chopped onion.

4. Cut tuna into 1-inch cubes and add it to the vegetables. Add basil and toss to blend. Serve.

Broiled Sweet Pepper and Snow Pea Salad

◇ ◇

I like to grill sweet peppers on my barbecue grill, but a broiler works just as well. Just make sure to char them evenly all around.

Yield: 4 servings.

2 sweet red peppers (about ¾ pound)

¾ pound snow peas, trimmed

Salt to taste

1 small red onion, peeled, halved, and cut into thin slices

1 tablespoon Dijon-style mustard

2 tablespoons red wine vinegar

½ teaspoon ground cumin

Salt and freshly ground pepper to taste

¼ cup olive oil

¼ cup finely chopped parsley

1. Turn on the broiler. Remove the core and the seeds from the sweet peppers. Place them on the broiling rack about 3 inches from the heat source. Char them on one side, then rotate them. Continue until the peppers are charred all over.

2. Place the peppers in a paper bag and close it. Let sit for 10 minutes. Remove the peppers and peel off the charred skin. Cut them into thin strips.

3. Cook the snow peas in boiling salted water to cover for 2 to 3 minutes—they should be slightly crispy. Drain. Run cold water briefly over the snow peas and drain again. Put snow peas, pepper strips, and onion in a salad bowl.

4. Combine mustard, vinegar, and cumin in a small bowl and add salt and pepper. Beat vigorously with a whisk while adding oil. Stir in the parsley and pour dressing over vegetables. Toss and serve.

WALNUT. *Combine in a bowl ¼ medium onion (minced), 3 tablespoons balsamic vinegar, 3 walnuts (shelled and chopped), 1 tablespoon Dijon mustard. Whisk in ⅓ cup olive oil and ⅓ cup walnut oil. Taste for seasonings.*

Mussel and Farfalle Salad

◇ ◇

We are fortunate to have loads of fresh mussels on Eastern Long Island. I go digging with my son, Jacques, and bring back enough for a big party. Mussels are particularly good in pasta.

Yield: 4 servings.

3 pounds mussels, well scrubbed, with beards and barnacles
    removed
½ cup dry white wine
4 cups water
2 zucchini, cut into ½-inch chunks (about ¾ pound)
½ pound farfalle pasta (bow ties)
1 tablespoon Dijon-style mustard
2 tablespoons red or white wine vinegar
Salt and freshly ground pepper to taste
1 cup olive or corn oil
Pinch of cayenne pepper
4 tablespoons finely chopped shallots or scallions
1 tablespoon finely chopped garlic
2 ripe tomatoes (about ¾ pound), peeled and cut into ½-inch cubes
    (place them in boiling water for 15 seconds to loosen skins)
½ cup coarsely chopped fresh basil leaves or Italian parsley

1. Place the mussels in a saucepan and add the wine. Cover and cook over high heat, shaking the pan occasionally to redistribute the mussels for about 4 minutes or until all the mussels are opened.

2. Remove the mussels with a slotted spoon and set them aside to cool. Strain the liquid and set it aside. There should be about 2 cups. When the mussels are cool enough to handle, remove the meat and discard the shells.

3. Add the reserved broth and the 4 cups water to a pot. Bring to a boil and add the zucchini. Cook 3 minutes and remove the zucchini with a slotted spoon. Let cool.

4. Add the pasta to the pot, stir, and bring to a boil. Cook 15 to 20 minutes or according to package instructions. It should be al dente. Drain well and let cool.

5. Meanwhile, put the mustard, vinegar, salt, and pepper in a mixing bowl. Beat the mixture with a wire whisk while slowly adding the oil a few drops at a time at first, then in a slow drizzle. When all the oil is incorporated, add the cayenne pepper, shallots, and garlic. Blend well.

6. Place the zucchini, tomatoes, pasta, and mussels in a large bowl. Add the sauce and the basil. Toss well. Taste for seasonings and serve.

Soups

◇ ◇ ◇

Black Bean Soup

Fish Soup Marseilles Style

Basic Fish Stock

Garlic Croutons

Homemade Curry Powder

Curried Lentil Soup with Ham

Pumpkin Sage Soup

Country Vegetable Soup

Turkey Vegetable Soup with Coriander

Carrot Soup with Dill

Cold Cucumber and Yogurt Soup with Fresh Mint

Monkfish and Scallop Soup

Butternut Squash Soup with Fresh Goat Cheese
and Spaghetti Squash Crostini

Mussel Soup

Spicy Avocado Soup

Curried Zucchini Soup with Apple Garnish

Potato Leek Soup with Monkfish

Monkfish and Mussel Stew

Veal and Macaroni Soup

Eggplant and Tomato Soup

The first time I tasted tasso, the highly spiced smoked pork sausage, I thought it was too smoky. But in cooking, especially soups, it adds a savory undercurrent of smoke that is not at all overpowering. Tasso generally is found in the Cajun country of southwestern Louisiana, where it is an important ingredient in many dishes. Tasso is available in some specialty shops in the North. If you cannot find it, buy any good smoked pork sausage.

Black Bean Soup

I have found that black bean soup needs to be aggressively seasoned or else the starchy beans will leave it bland. This version gets its richness from the salt pork, and its zest from the ground coriander and cumin.

Yield: 10 servings.

1 pound black beans
12 cups water
Salt and pepper to taste
½ pound lean salt pork, Cajun tasso, or smoked pork sausage, ground very fine
2 cups finely chopped onions
1 tablespoon finely chopped garlic
1 tablespoon chopped fresh oregano or 1 teaspoon dried
1 cup seeded and minced green peppers
1 cup seeded and minced sweet red peppers
2 cups fresh chopped ripe tomatoes or 1 cup crushed canned tomatoes
1 teaspoon ground coriander
1 teaspoon ground cumin
2 tablespoons red wine vinegar
¼ cup dry sherry

1. Place the beans in a bowl, add cold water and rinse well.

2. Place the beans in a pot, add water. Add salt. Bring to a boil and simmer for 30 minutes.

3. Meanwhile, as the beans cook, sauté the salt pork in a pan. When the fat is rendered (most of the fat melted away), add the onions, garlic, oregano, green peppers, red peppers, and cook. Stir until the onions are wilted. Add the tomatoes, coriander, and cumin. Cook briefly.

4. Scrape the mixture into the beans and continue cooking until the beans are tender-cooked, stirring often.

5. Add the vinegar and the sherry. Blend well, bring to a simmer, and serve hot.

NOTE: For garnishing, use chopped hard-cooked eggs and chopped fresh coriander.

Fish Soup Marseilles Style

◇ ◇

In traveling around Europe and America, I have found that there are as many kinds of fish soup as there are fish—from the herb-infused soups of Provence to the chowders of New England. The underpinning of this soup is a good fish stock, which you make with fish heads and bones. Get these from your fish market.

Yield: 8 servings.

2 to 3 pounds fish bones and heads
1 cup diced onions
1 leek (chop the green part and mince the white part; keep them separate)
1 bay leaf
½ teaspoon thyme
1 teaspoon fennel seeds
1 tablespoon black peppercorns
1 cup white wine
6 cups water
1 clove garlic, peeled
6 sprigs parsley
2 tablespoons olive oil
¾ cup minced onions
1 tablespoon minced garlic
½ teaspoon red pepper flakes
½ teaspoon black pepper and salt
4 tomatoes, peeled, seeded, and chopped
¼ cup tomato paste
1 cup white wine
2 pounds monkfish fillet (or any firm white fish like cod, sole, bass, or halibut)

1. Combine in a soup pot all the ingredients up to and including the parsley (not the leek whites yet). Bring to a boil, reduce heat, and simmer for 10 minutes. Strain the liquid and reserve it. You should have about 8 cups.

2. Pour the olive oil into a soup pot and sauté the onions and garlic over medium-high heat just until they are golden. Add the leek whites, pepper flakes, black pepper, salt, tomatoes, and tomato paste. Cook for 3 to 4 minutes.

(Continued on next page)

◇

To make a good fish soup you should have a good fish broth. There is nothing exotic about fish broth. Simply ask your fishmonger for 2 pounds of fresh fish bones, with the heads but with gills removed—gills sometimes contain a little blood, which can give the broth a bitter flavor. There is no need to thoroughly season the broth since there are so many seasonings in the finished soups.

For a little flavor, garlic and onions are sautéed in olive oil, then cooked with leeks, celery, saffron, turmeric, pepper flakes, and salt. Saffron adds a lovely aroma, but it is not necessary. Turmeric, a less expensive substitute, gives the stock a rich reddish color.

Let everything cook for about 1½ hours, skimming the surface foam from time to time. Freeze the stock that you do not use immediately.

3. Add white wine to the pot, bring to a boil and add the fish stock. Bring to a boil, reduce heat and simmer for about 15 minutes.

4. Cut the monkfish into ½-inch cubes and add the pieces to the broth. Cook for 5 minutes, taste for seasoning, and serve with garlic croutons (see recipe below).

Garlic Croutons
◇ ◇

Make a batch of these croutons and use them in soups and salads. Keep them in an airtight container.

Yield: 8 servings.

1 loaf French or Italian bread
2 cloves garlic, peeled
4 tablespoons olive oil
Black pepper to taste

1. Rub the bread all over with the garlic cloves. Slice the bread into ½-inch pieces and sprinkle one side with olive oil. Grind some black pepper over the sliced bread.

2. Place the bread slices on a baking sheet under a broiler until they are golden brown. Turn and broil on the other side.

Homemade Curry Powder

◇ ◇

Here is my recipe for a vibrant homemade curry powder—just mildly spicy. Combine the following in a spice grinder. If you like it hotter, add more white pepper.

Yield: About ¾ cup.

¼ cup turmeric
3 tablespoons ground coriander
2 tablespoons ground cumin
1 tablespoon white peppercorns
1 tablespoon whole cloves
2 tablespoons ground ginger
1 tablespoon ground cardamom
2 teaspoons cayenne pepper
1 tablespoon ground mace
1 tablespoon dried fines herbes
1 tablespoon fenugreek seeds

1. Combine in a spice grinder and grind to a powder.

◇

Indians use curries the way Italians use olive oil. Many American home cooks have shied away from curry dishes for fear that they are too complicated to prepare. That is just not true. Packaged curry powders are available in supermarkets, but they rarely have the finesse of homemade. Moreover, once you have made your own curry powder, it lasts indefinitely in a sealed jar. With your powder ready and dinner ingredients at hand, an exotic meal can be assembled in well under 60 minutes.

Curried Lentil Soup with Ham

◇ ◇

The curried lentil soup here has a mild smoky flavor from the ham. It calls for little green French lentils, but you may substitute other lentils. This is the kind of soup that improves with age.

Yield: 4 servings.

½ pound lean country smoked ham
3 medium-size carrots
½ pound green lentils
2 tablespoons butter
1 cup finely chopped onions
1 tablespoon finely chopped garlic
2 tablespoons curry powder
5 cups fresh or canned chicken broth
2 cups water
1 bay leaf
3 sprigs fresh thyme or 1 teaspoon dried
Salt to taste
1 tablespoon red wine vinegar
2 tablespoons finely chopped coriander

1. Remove most of the fat from the ham and cut it into ½-inch cubes.

2. Trim and scrape the carrots and cut them into roughly ¼-inch cubes.

3. Pick over the lentils for stones, wash them and drain into a colander.

4. Heat 1 tablespoon of the butter in a pot or saucepan. Add the ham, carrots, onions, garlic, and curry powder. Cook briefly over medium heat, stirring, until the onions are wilted.

5. Add the lentils, 4 cups of the chicken broth, water, bay leaf, thyme, and salt. Bring to a boil, and simmer for 25 to 30 minutes, stirring occasionally.

6. Remove 1 cup of the soup, with more lentils than liquid, and set aside. Discard the bay leaf and thyme sprigs.

7. With a potato masher or wire whisk, stir the soup briskly to mash the lentils. Return the soup to a boil. Add the remaining cup of chicken broth, the reserved lentils, the vinegar, and the remaining butter. Check for seasoning and serve, sprinkled with the coriander.

Pumpkin Sage Soup

◇ ◇

I have made this soup for children's parties and the kids love it, especially when I ask them to clean out the baby pumpkins.

Yield: 8 servings.

6 small pumpkins (each about the size of a baseball)
6 sage leaves, slightly crushed
3 tablespoons unsalted butter
1 cup finely chopped onion
2 pounds fresh pumpkin, cut into ½-inch cubes
1 cup water
1 cup fresh or canned chicken broth
Salt and freshly ground pepper
1 cup milk
1 cup half-and-half or heavy cream
¼ teaspoon grated fresh nutmeg
⅛ teaspoon cayenne

1. Cut a circular hole around the top rim of each pumpkin and remove lid. Scrape out fiber and seeds, leaving the inside as smooth as possible. Place crumpled sage leaves in the bottom of each pumpkin.

2. Heat the butter in a pot, and add the onion. Cook over medium heat, stirring, for 1 minute. Add pumpkin, water, chicken broth, salt, and pepper.

3. Bring liquid to a boil, reduce to simmer, and cook for about 20 minutes. Transfer liquid to the bowl of an electric blender or food processor, and purée until smooth. Return mixture to the pot.

4. Add to the pot milk, half-and-half, nutmeg, cayenne, salt, and pepper. Stir well and simmer for 5 to 10 minutes. Taste for seasonings. Serve the soup in the hollowed-out baby pumpkins.

◇

You may notice that in many of these recipes, I call for canned tomatoes. That is because in most parts of the country, the fresh tomato season is short-lived. Canned tomatoes are packed at their peak of flavor. I have found that Italian canned tomatoes are the best.

Country Vegetable Soup

◇ ◇

My vegetable soups usually reflect what is in my garden or, in the off-season, the best produce I can find in the market. If you change some of the ingredients, the seasonings are the same. Garnish it with garlic croutons (page 62).

Yield: About 14 cups.

½ pound leeks
½ pound celery
½ pound green beans
½ pound carrots
1 to 2 zucchini (about ½ pound)
2 tablespoons butter
1 cup finely chopped onions
1 cup crushed ripe tomatoes, or canned (preferably imported)
8 cups beef broth
Salt to taste
Freshly ground pepper to taste
1½ cups fresh corn kernels, scraped from the cob
2 cups freshly shelled green peas
¼ cup chopped fresh basil or parsley

1. Trim off the root end of the leeks. Split the leeks in half and rinse well between the leaves. Pat dry. Cut the leeks into very small dice. There should be about 2 cups.

2. Trim the celery and dice it. There should be about 2 cups.

3. Trim off the ends of the green beans and dice them. There should be about 2 cups.

4. Trim and scrape the carrots. Cut them crosswise into ¼-inch slices. Cut the carrots into ¼-inch dice. There should be about 1½ cups.

5. Trim the zucchini and cut into ½-inch dice. There should be about 2 cups.

6. Heat the butter in a pot and add the onions and leeks. Cook, stirring, about 5 minutes. Add the carrots, celery, and green beans. Cook, stirring, about 3 minutes and stir in the crushed tomatoes.

7. Add the broth, salt, and pepper, and bring to a boil. Let simmer 20 minutes. Add the zucchini, corn, and peas and continue cooking about 10 minutes longer. Serve sprinkled with basil or parsley.

Turkey Vegetable Soup with Coriander

◇ ◇

Fresh coriander, which is used in this recipe for turkey vegetable soup, has a strong flavor that defies indifference. It is far more aromatic than parsley, sage, chives, or sorrel. It has a spiciness and slightly musty flavor that changes the character of any dish.

Once considered exotic, coriander is widely available in supermarkets today. This recipe for vegetable soup has a curry base as well as some sweetness from onions, carrots, leeks, and parsnips. The coriander was an afterthought, and it added a delightful snappy edge. Boneless, skinless turkey breast is added, but you could also use leftover roast turkey.

Yield: 8 servings.

2 tablespoons butter
1 tablespoon curry powder
1 cup chopped onions
4 leeks, trimmed, cleaned, and cut into ¼-inch cubes (about 1 pound)
3 carrots, scraped and cut into ¼-inch cubes (about ½ pound)
1 parsnip, peeled and cut into ¼-inch cubes (about ¼ pound)
3 potatoes, peeled and cut into ¼-inch cubes (about 1 pound)
Salt and freshly ground pepper to taste
4 cups fresh or canned chicken stock
4 cups water
1 boneless, skinless turkey breast, cut into ½-inch cubes (about 1 pound)
3 tablespoons chopped fresh coriander leaves

1. Heat the butter in a saucepan and add the curry powder, onions, leeks, carrots, parsnip, and potatoes. Cook, stirring, until the onions are wilted, about 5 minutes. Add salt, pepper, chicken stock, and water. Bring to a boil and simmer for 30 minutes.

2. Add turkey breast cubes and cook 10 minutes. Garnish each serving with coriander.

Carrot Soup with Dill

◇ ◇

◇

Notice that the carrot soup does not call for cream as a binder. Instead, it is thickened with ricotta cheese, a low-fat alternative that is puréed in a food processor or blender to achieve a creamy consistency. Ricotta can be used in all kinds of soups that call for cream, as well as in many sauces.

Here is a quick and healthful soup that I serve both hot and cold. The foundation is a good chicken stock, either homemade or one of the better commercial varieties. Some sweetness is added in the form of port wine.

Yield: 6 servings.

2 tablespoons butter
¾ cup finely chopped onions
1½ pounds carrots, scraped and sliced crosswise into ½-inch pieces
4 cups fresh or canned chicken stock
Salt and freshly ground pepper to taste
2 cups water
½ cup ricotta cheese
3 tablespoons port
2 tablespoons chopped fresh dill

1. Heat butter in a saucepan and add the onions. Cook, stirring, until they are wilted. Add carrots, stock, salt, pepper, and water. Bring to a boil and simmer for 20 minutes, or until the carrots are soft.

2. Strain the mixture into a pot and reserve the cooking liquid. Purée the solids in a food processor or a food mill along with the cheese and 1 cup of the reserved cooking liquid. Transfer the purée to the saucepan with the remaining cooking liquid. Blend well.

3. Bring the soup to a boil and add the wine and dill. Serve hot or cold.

Cold Cucumber and Yogurt Soup with Fresh Mint

◇ ◇

I love cold summer soups. In the past, I used to bind them with a little cream, but now I use low-fat yogurt, which is just as good. Do not use a yogurt that is presweetened and gelatinous, however. This refreshing summer soup is a cinch to make and looks great at the table.

Yield: 4 servings.

1 tablespoon butter
1 cup chopped onions
1 teaspoon finely chopped garlic
4 cups peeled, seeded, and sliced cucumbers
2 teaspoons curry powder
2 cups fresh or canned chicken stock
Salt and freshly ground pepper
2 cups plain yogurt
1 cup peeled, seeded cucumbers, cut into ¼-inch cubes
2 tablespoons chopped fresh mint

1. Heat the butter in a saucepan and add the onions and garlic. Cook, stirring over medium heat, until wilted; do not brown. Add the sliced cucumbers, curry powder, chicken stock, salt, and pepper. Bring to a simmer and cook for 5 minutes, stirring occasionally.

2. Put the mixture in a food processor or blender and purée to a fine texture. Pour the mixture into a bowl. Chill thoroughly.

3. Stir in the yogurt, cucumber cubes, and mint. Blend well and serve in chilled bowls, garnished with a mint leaf.

Monkfish and Scallop Soup

◇ ◇

Monkfish, a favorite fish of mine, is one of the most uncomely creatures in the sea, with a big, bulbous head, a gaping mouth, and long whiskers.

Just twenty years ago, it was tossed back by commercial fishermen because there was no market for it in the United States. But in Europe it had been a delicacy for decades.

Monkfish goes by other names, including anglerfish, lotte (French), goosefish, and allmouth. The firm, thick fish is reminiscent of lobster, hence it is also called lobster fish. Monkfish is ideal for brochettes and roasting. It is also good in soups because it does not fall apart.

The firm, meaty texture of monkfish is particularly well suited to soups. The delicate scallops provide a lovely counterpoint.

Yield: 6 servings.

1 pound skinless, boneless monkfish fillets
1 pound sea or bay scallops
2 tablespoons olive oil
1½ cups finely chopped onions
1 tablespoon finely chopped garlic
½ cup finely chopped celery
½ cup finely chopped fennel
1 jalapeño pepper, cored, seeded, and finely chopped
6 ripe plum tomatoes, cored and cut into ½-inch cubes
1 cup dry white wine
6 cups water
1 bay leaf
2 sprigs fresh thyme or 1 teaspoon dried
Salt and freshly ground pepper to taste
1 pound mussels, well scrubbed, with beards removed (see page 17)
½ cup chopped parsley or basil

1. Cut the monkfish into 1-inch cubes.
2. If sea scallops are used, cut them in half.
3. Heat the oil in a large pan over medium setting. Add the onions, garlic, celery, and fennel, and cook, stirring, until wilted. Add the jalapeño pepper and tomatoes. Cook, stirring, over high heat for 2 minutes.
4. Add the wine, water, bay leaf, thyme, salt, and pepper. Bring to a boil and simmer for 10 minutes, stirring often.
5. Add the monkfish, scallops, and mussels. Bring to a boil and simmer for 5 minutes. Check the seasonings, then stir in the parsley or basil. Serve immediately with garlic croutons (page 62).

Butternut Squash Soup with Fresh Goat Cheese and Spaghetti Squash Crostini

◇ ◇

This is a fun dish for entertaining, using both spaghetti squash and butternut squash. The recipe comes from Alan Ducasse, the famed French chef who has two three-star restaurants. He came to my kitchen in East Hampton, Long Island, to cook for a day.

Yield: 4 servings.

1 spaghetti squash, halved, seeds removed (about 2 pounds)
Salt and freshly grated black pepper to taste
3 tablespoons butter
1 large butternut squash (about 3 pounds)
2 leeks, trimmed, cleaned, and split from the white tip to the green
7 tablespoons olive oil
1 cup sliced white onions
6 cups fresh or canned chicken broth
4 ounces fresh goat cheese
8 thin slices French baguette, cut on a bias
¼ cup grated Parmesan

1. Preheat oven to 400 degrees.

2. Place the halved spaghetti squash, cut side up, in a baking dish, and dust with salt and pepper. Put 1 tablespoon of butter in the center of each. Bake for 1 hour. Set aside.

3. Cut the butternut squash into 3 pieces. Remove the hard outer skin and the seeds. Cut the flesh into ⅓-inch cubes. You should have 5 cups.

4. Slice the leeks coarsely widthwise. You should have about 1½ cups.

5. Place 2 tablespoons olive oil and 1 tablespoon butter in a pot over medium heat. Add the onions and cook, stirring, until wilted, about 1 minute. Add the leeks and cook, stirring, for 5 minutes.

6. Place the 5 cups of butternut squash in the pot with the onions and leeks. Cook for 5 minutes. Add the chicken broth. Bring to a boil, reduce heat, and simmer for about 20 minutes, or until the butternut squash is just soft.

(Continued on next page)

7. Purée the squash mixture to a fine texture in a blender or food processor. Add 1 tablespoon of olive oil and adjust seasonings. Keep warm.

8. Place the goat cheese in a mixing bowl. Slice the cheese coarsely. Add 2 tablespoons of olive oil and salt and pepper to taste. Chop up the cheese with a spoon to a rough texture.

9. Scrape the flesh from the spaghetti squash, and place in a bowl. Season with salt and freshly ground pepper to taste.

10. Brush the baguette slices with 2 tablespoons of olive oil, and toast until crisp. Sprinkle Parmesan over the toast. Arrange some spaghetti squash over the bread. Season with salt and pepper to taste.

11. Place some of the crumbled goat cheese in the bottom of each soup plate. Ladle the soup over the cheese. Garnish the soup with some of the remaining spaghetti squash.

Mussel Soup

◇ ◇

This is a traditional French mussel soup that I have been making for decades. It is creamy, sweet with shallots, and delicious. If you want to omit the cream, just add ½ cup more white wine and 1 cup of water.

Yield: 4 to 6 servings.

2 pounds mussels
2 tablespoons butter
2 tablespoons finely chopped shallots
¼ cup finely chopped onion
½ teaspoon saffron
2 parsley sprigs
1 bay leaf
1 sprig fresh thyme or ½ teaspoon dried
1 cup dry white wine
2 cups heavy cream
Cayenne pepper to taste
Freshly ground pepper to taste
1 cup chopped fresh, skinless, and seedless tomatoes

1. Scrub mussels under cold running water with a hard brush. Remove beards and drain.

2. Heat butter in a large saucepan. Add shallots and onion and cook briefly, stirring, but do not brown. Add the mussels, saffron, parsley sprigs, bay leaf, thyme, and wine and bring to a boil. Cover and cook over high heat for 4 minutes. Add cream, cayenne, and ground pepper. Bring to a boil and simmer for 2 minutes. Strain the mixture in a fine mesh strainer or cheesecloth. Reserve broth.

3. Remove mussels from shells.

4. Transfer reserved broth to saucepan and add mussels and tomatoes. Bring to a boil. Serve immediately in soup bowls.

Spicy Avocado Soup

◇ ◇

I find that the rich, creamy texture of avocado goes exceptionally well with hot spices. The minced jalapeño peppers give the soup just enough kick.

Yield: 4 to 6 servings.

3 firm, ripe, unblemished avocados (about 1¾ pounds)

2 tablespoons fresh lemon juice

4 tablespoons butter

½ teaspoon finely minced garlic

2 teaspoons seeded and minced jalapeño peppers

2 cups finely chopped onions

¾ cup finely chopped celery

1 tablespoon finely chopped fresh tarragon or half the amount dried

½ teaspoon dried ground cumin

⅛ teaspoon ground mace

2 tablespoons flour

6 cups chicken broth or water

Salt to taste if desired

Freshly ground pepper, preferably white, to taste

1 sweet red pepper, cored, deveined, seeds removed

¼ cup coarsely chopped fresh basil

1 tablespoon chopped fresh mint

1. Peel the avocados and cut them in half. Discard the pits. Drop the halves into a basin of cold water with 1 teaspoon of the lemon juice added.

2. Heat the butter in a large pan. Add the garlic, jalapeño peppers, onions, and celery and cook, stirring often, until the mixture is wilted. Add the tarragon, cumin, and mace and cook, stirring, about 2 minutes.

3. Sprinkle with the flour and stir to blend well. Add the broth, salt, and pepper and bring to the boil. Let simmer about 10 minutes. Remove from the heat and let cool.

4. Select 1 avocado half and cut it into small cubes to be used as a garnish. Set aside.

5. Drain and cut the remaining avocados into large chunks. Add this to the cooled soup.

6. Put the mixture with the avocado chunks into the container of a food processor or electric blender and blend thoroughly. Add the remaining lemon juice, pepper, and salt.

7. Return the soup to the pot. Cut the red pepper into small dice. There should be about 1 cup.

8. Bring the soup to a simmer. Ladle it into 6 or more soup bowls and serve sprinkled with the avocado cubes, red pepper dice, basil, and mint. If desired, this soup may be cooled and chilled well before serving.

Curried Zucchini Soup with Apple Garnish

◇ ◇

When I was a working chef, soups like this required pushing the vegetables through a sieve or using a food mill. Today's food processor makes any kind of puréed soup effortless. This summer soup could not be easier. You just cook the vegetables and toss everything in a food processor or blender. Be sure to taste for seasonings adjustment after you add the sweet apple chunks.

Yield: 4 servings.

1 tablespoon butter
1 cup sliced onion (1 medium white onion)
2 cloves garlic, peeled and chopped
2 teaspoons curry powder (page 63)
Salt to taste
2 medium zucchini, peeled, seeds removed, and chopped
4 cups fresh or canned chicken stock
1 cup plain yogurt
1 Golden Delicious apple
1 bunch fresh mint leaves

1. Place butter and onions in a deep pot over medium heat. Cook, stirring, until the onions are wilted, about 2 minutes. Add the garlic. Cook, stirring, for 1 minute. Add the curry powder. Season with salt to taste. Add the zucchini. Stir for 1 minute.

2. Add the chicken stock. Bring to a boil, reduce heat, cover, and simmer for 10 minutes.

3. Purée the soup in a blender or food processor. Refrigerate.

4. When the soup is cold, stir in the yogurt, reserving a little for garnish. Peel and core the apple; then cut it into small cubes, and stir into the soup. Garnish soup with the reserved dollop of yogurt and some mint leaves.

Potato Leek Soup with Monkfish

◇ ◇

I make this light Mediterranean-style soup with leeks, garlic, potatoes, onions, and bay leaf. A teaspoon of curry adds just the right nuance.

The tradition of putting croutons in soup, or serving steaming soup over croutons, is typically Mediterranean. Make the croutons ahead of time and put them in the bottom of the bowl.

Yield: 4 servings or more.

4 medium leeks
4 large russet potatoes
2 tablespoons butter
1 cup finely chopped onions
1 tablespoon minced garlic
1 teaspoon curry powder
6 cups water
1 bay leaf
Salt and ground white pepper
1 pound skinless, boneless fillets of a white-flesh fish like monkfish
    or cod, cut into 1-inch cubes
¼ cup heavy cream
Garlic croutons (page 62)

1. Trim leeks of roots and all but 2 inches of the greens. Cut in half lengthwise and rinse well. Quarter lengthwise, then cut into 1¼-inch pieces. There should be 3½ to 4 cups. Peel potatoes and cut into ⅓-inch cubes.

2. Melt butter in a large pot. Add onions, leeks, and garlic and cook, stirring, until the onions wilt. Add curry powder and cook, stirring, for 1 minute. Add potatoes, water, bay leaf, and salt and pepper to taste. Bring to a boil and simmer for 20 minutes.

3. Add the fish, bring to a boil. (If monkfish is used, simmer for 3 minutes. If cod is used, simmer for 1 minute.) Add cream and return to a simmer. Remove bay leaf. To serve, arrange croutons on the bottom of each soup bowl. Ladle hot soup over the croutons and serve.

◇

I prepare all sorts of quick and healthful winter soups with many varieties of fish and shellfish, and they can be served as appetizers or as main courses. Monkfish is particularly well suited to soups and stews because of its firm, lean flesh. So are cod, halibut, sea bass, and tilefish.

After choosing the fish, consider the flavors and textures for the soup. If the soup is light and herby, use a subtle-tasting fish. Is it thick and assertive? Creamy and rich? And what herbs do you want to include? Most fish soups are built upon a good fish stock. From there, you embellish the broth as you like.

Monkfish and Mussel Stew

◆ ◇

Yield: 4 servings.

Bouillabaisse, the Provençal seafood stew, has countless variations in this country. While some of the Mediterranean fish that go into the classic version are unavailable in the United States, a perfectly good rendition can be made with native species from the Atlantic, Pacific, and Gulf waters. The version here calls for monkfish, tilefish, or blackfish, in any combination you like.

Monkfish is the firmest of all and works particularly well. Blackfish, which in the East is usually called tautog, is a moderately firm, white-fleshed fish that is relatively inexpensive and excellent for soups and chowders. It is caught along rocky shores from Nova Scotia to Delaware. Tilefish is another widely available and moderately priced species that is less firm than the other two but very tasty in soups. Other firm white-fleshed species could be used, too, but do not use rich, oily fish like mackerel and salmon.

This stew is finished with a dash of an anise-flavored liqueur called Pernod (another brand is Ricard). The French drink this as an apéritif, diluted with water.

1½ pounds boneless, skinless monkfish (tilefish and blackfish also work well)
2 tablespoons olive oil
1 teaspoon finely chopped garlic
1 cup finely chopped onions
1 leek, trimmed, rinsed well, and cut into ¼-inch cubes
½ cup chopped celery
1 teaspoon loosely packed saffron threads (optional)
1 teaspoon turmeric
⅛ teaspoon red hot pepper flakes
Salt and freshly ground pepper to taste
1 cup crushed tomatoes
2 sprigs fresh thyme or ½ teaspoon dried
1 bay leaf
1 cup dry white wine
2 tablespoons Ricard or Pernod or 1 teaspoon aniseed
3 cups fish broth (page 61)
24 mussels, cleaned and well scrubbed
8 Garlic croutons (page 62)
¼ cup coarsely chopped parsley

1. Cut the fish fillets into 1-inch cubes. Set aside. Heat the oil in a pot. Add the garlic and onions. Cook, stirring, until the onions wilt. Do not brown the garlic. Add the leek, celery, saffron, turmeric, pepper flakes, salt, and pepper. Cook, stirring, over medium heat for 2 minutes. Add the tomatoes, thyme, bay leaf, white wine, Ricard, and fish broth. Bring to a boil and simmer for 10 minutes.

2. Add the fish and mussels. Bring to a boil and simmer for 5 minutes.

3. Top each serving with 2 croutons and sprinkle with parsley.

Veal and Macaroni Soup

◇ ◇

I make this soup in the winter and serve it with a salad and thick slabs of bread. It freezes well.

Yield: 4 to 6 servings.

1 pound lean veal
2 tablespoons butter
1 cup finely chopped onions
Salt to taste
Freshly ground pepper to taste
¼ cup flour
3 cups fresh or canned chicken broth
½ cup small tubular macaroni
1 cup heavy cream
1 cup milk
3 egg yolks
½ cup freshly grated Parmesan

1. Cut the veal into small cubes, about ½ inch or slightly smaller. Heat the butter in a heavy saucepan or small pot and add the onions. Cook, stirring, until wilted and add the veal, salt, and pepper.

2. Sprinkle with flour and stir to coat the veal. Add the broth and bring to a boil, stirring. Let simmer uncovered about 30 minutes.

3. Meanwhile, cook the macaroni in boiling salted water until tender, about 10 minutes. Drain. Combine the cream and milk in a mixing bowl. Add the yolks and stir with a wire whisk to blend. Beat thoroughly.

4. Add the cream mixture and cook over very low heat, stirring constantly with a wooden spoon—until the moment the soup starts to boil. Remove from the heat immediately. You must not let this soup boil for more than seconds or the eggs will curdle.

5. Add the macaroni to the soup and stir. Serve immediately with grated Parmesan cheese on the side, to be added as desired.

Eggplant and Tomato Soup

◇ ◇

When I make this soup in summer, I char the eggplant all around on a barbecue grill. It is not necessary, although it adds a nice smoky flavor to the soup.

Yield: About 7 cups or 7 to 8 servings.

1 eggplant (about 1 pound)
¼ cup peanut, corn, or vegetable oil
2 tablespoons butter
1½ cups chopped onions
1 tablespoon finely minced garlic
Salt to taste
Freshly ground pepper to taste
1 bay leaf
½ teaspoon dried thyme
3 cups chopped, canned imported tomatoes
¼ cup raw rice
4 cups fresh or canned chicken broth

1. Trim off the stem end of the eggplant. Peel the eggplant and cut it into 1-inch cubes. There should be about 5 cups.

2. Heat the oil in a large, heavy pan, and when it is hot and almost smoking, add the cubed eggplant. Cook, shaking the pan and stirring, until the cubes are lightly browned. Drain the eggplant on paper towels. There should be about 2¼ cups.

3. Heat the butter in a pan and add the onions and garlic. Cook, stirring, until the mixture is wilted and add the eggplant cubes, salt, and pepper. Add the bay leaf and thyme. Cook, stirring, about 1 minute and add the tomatoes.

4. Add the rice and broth and bring to a boil, stirring. Cook covered about 30 minutes. Remove the bay leaf and pour the mixture into the container of a food processor or electric blender. It may be necessary to do this in two batches. Purée until smooth.

5. Return the soup to the pot and bring to a simmer. Serve.

Poultry

◇ ◇ ◇

Chicken Breasts Florentine

Mushroom Sauce

Turkey Breast with Corn Bread and Sausage Stuffing

Corn Bread and Sausage Stuffing

Corn Bread

Turkey Steaks with Mustard Seeds and Mushrooms

Turkey Breasts with Provençal Herbs

Turkey Breasts with Fresh Tomato Sauce

Turkey Scaloppine with Prosciutto and Cheese

Turkey Patties with Curry Sauce

Curry Sauce

Roasted Turkey with Maple-Corn Sauce

Duck Breasts with Turnips and Asian Spices

Roasted Duck with Figs

Roasted Baby Chickens
with Spicy Mango Barbecue Sauce

◇ ◇

I find that mango gives this zippy barbecue sauce a pleasing undercurrent of sweetness. It can be made in minutes with a food processor or blender. Tabasco and black pepper provide a piquant counterpoint. Adjust the heat to suit your tastes.

Yield: 8 servings.

3 small chickens or Cornish hens (about 2 pounds each, including
    gizzards and necks) or 2 larger ones, trimmed of excess fat
Salt and freshly ground black pepper to taste
3 bay leaves
3 sprigs fresh thyme
3 cloves garlic, peeled
3 tablespoons olive oil
1 large white onion, peeled and halved
½ cup barbecue sauce (see recipe page 86)

1. Preheat oven to 425 degrees.

2. Season the chickens inside and out with salt and pepper. Place bay leaves, a sprig of thyme, and a garlic clove inside each cavity. Brush the chickens with olive oil.

3. Place the chickens in a roasting pan so they are resting on one leg. Add the onion to the pan. Remove fat from gizzards and necks and scatter around the pan.

4. Roast the chickens for 15 minutes, then flip them onto the other leg. Roast another 15 minutes, then place on their backs. Brush the chickens with the homemade barbecue sauce. Roast for another 20 minutes, or longer for larger chickens. Remove and let cool before carving.

5. Carve and serve with a little of the remaining barbecue sauce.

Spicy Mango Barbecue Sauce
◇ ◇

Yield: 2 cups.

1 medium-size ripe mango, peeled and pit removed
2 tablespoons olive oil
½ cup finely chopped onions
1 tablespoon chopped garlic
1 cup ketchup
1 tablespoon Dijon-style mustard
2 tablespoons corn syrup
1 teaspoon Worcestershire sauce
1 teaspoon Tabasco, or to taste
4 slices lemon
Salt and freshly ground black pepper to taste

1. Place the mango in the bowl of a food processor and purée to a coarse texture.

2. In a saucepan, combine the olive oil, onions, and garlic. Sauté briefly over medium-high heat, or until the onions wilt. Add the mango and remaining ingredients; stir and bring to a simmer. Cook for 5 minutes. Remove and let cool. (Surplus sauce can be refrigerated in an airtight jar and used with any barbecued meat or poultry.)

Chicken Breasts Creole Style
◇ ◇

Many people confuse the cooking terms *Cajun* and *Creole*. My friend Paul Prudhomme clarified it for me. In brief, Cajun food, which is from western Louisiana, is based on a darkened roux, which is the foundation of many of their thick, rich sauces. The roux is made by combining flour and butter in a saucepan and cooking, stirring, until it is golden brown. It is the foundation of hearty, rustic cooking—and not necessarily spicy.

Creole food, originating in New Orleans, is more sophisticated fare, and is often based on a tomato sauce of some type. This dish is decidedly Creole in style.

Yield: 4 servings.

4 skinless, boneless chicken breasts, halved (about 1¼ pounds)
1 tablespoon olive oil
¾ cup onion, chopped
¾ cup cored, seeded, and julienned green pepper
¾ cup chopped celery
1 tablespoon finely chopped garlic
1 bay leaf
1 tablespoon paprika
1 cup peeled, diced tomatoes or 1 cup canned crushed tomatoes
Salt and freshly ground pepper to taste
1 teaspoon Worcestershire sauce
1 teaspoon hot pepper sauce (like Tabasco)
1 tablespoon butter
1 tablespoon wine vinegar
4 tablespoons water or chicken broth
4 tablespoons finely chopped parsley

1. Place half a chicken breast (1 fillet) between sheets of plastic wrap. With a mallet or the bottom of a heavy pan, pound lightly to a thickness of ¼ inch. Repeat with the remaining halves.

2. Heat the olive oil in a large skillet. Add the onion, green pepper, celery, garlic, and bay leaf. Cook, stirring, until the onions become transparent. Add the paprika, tomatoes, and salt and pepper to taste. Stir well. Continue cooking for 3 to 4 minutes.

3. Add the Worcestershire sauce and the Tabasco sauce. Simmer until the sauce is reduced by about one-quarter (about 8 minutes). Set aside.

4. Meanwhile, sprinkle the chicken with salt and pepper to taste. Heat the butter in a heavy skillet over medium setting and cook the chicken breasts until golden on one side, about 5 minutes. Turn the pieces and cook for 5 minutes more or until done. Be careful not to over-cook.

5. Add to the pan the vinegar and water and cover. Bring to a boil and simmer for 2 minutes. Remove the bay leaf. Keep warm.

6. To serve, divide the Creole sauce among 4 serving plates. Place the chicken breasts over the sauce and pour the sauce from the skillet over the breasts. Sprinkle with parsley.

Supermarket chickens are sold in clear wrappings, so it is difficult to inspect them for freshness before buying. At home, examine the breastbone—if it is flexible, the chicken is young and tender; if it is hard, the bird is suitable for stewing. The United States Department of Agriculture requires that each chicken be stamped with a date, so at least you have some idea of how fresh it is. One test of freshness is the amount of red juice in the package. If there is a lot, the chicken is old.

Contrary to popular belief, a chicken's color says nothing about its freshness or age. The color has more to do with the bird's diet than anything else. Poultry is extremely perishable and in some cases vulnerable to salmonella bacteria. When you take the chicken home, remove the wrapping and rinse the bird thoroughly under cold tap water. Pat dry, wrap again, and refrigerate. Just to be safe, it's best to use poultry as soon as possible.

If you are watching your calories and fat—and who isn't?—you should learn how to reduce butter and cream in your diet by using low-fat ricotta cheese as a substitute. Ricotta, a

Baked Chicken Breasts with Ricotta-and-Herb Stuffing

So many people write to me asking for flavorful but low-fat meals that I have started to rethink my way of cooking to meet their needs. This dish is a good example. Ricotta cheese is a wonderful, low-fat addition to many dishes. In this recipe, the herbed ricotta filling under the skin helps keep the chicken breasts moist and adds a rich flavor without the fat. It also transforms a chicken breast into a special entrée. Ricotta is also great under the skin of a small game hen.

Yield: 4 servings.

½ cup part-skim-milk ricotta cheese
¼ cup chopped fresh herbs (parsley, thyme, chives, mint, or
    oregano, for example)
¼ teaspoon salt
Freshly ground black pepper
2 whole chicken breasts, split in half
4 sprigs fresh thyme (optional)

1. Preheat oven to 450 degrees.
2. In a small bowl, combine ricotta, herbs, salt, and pepper. Stir until well blended. Taste for seasoning.
3. Loosen chicken skin by sliding two fingers between skin and breast, but leave skin attached along the breastbone side. Spoon a quarter of the cheese mixture under the skin of each breast.
4. Place breasts on a baking sheet. Sprinkle with salt and pepper, and bake for 30 minutes.
5. Garnish each breast with sprig of thyme.

Chicken Breasts with Mustard Sauce

◇ ◇

This is a tasty and quick weekday dish—it takes no more than half an hour. You can make it as mild or as spicy as you like.

Yield: Serves 4.

4 skinless, boneless chicken breast halves (about 1½ pounds)
Salt to taste
Freshly ground black pepper to taste
1 tablespoon butter
4 tablespoons finely chopped onion
¼ teaspoon dried thyme
1 tablespoon red wine vinegar
¼ cup dry white wine
½ cup fresh or canned chicken broth
2 teaspoons tomato paste
¼ cup cream or half-and-half
1 tablespoon Dijon-style mustard
2 teaspoons finely chopped parsley (optional)

1. Sprinkle the chicken breast halves with salt and pepper.

2. Heat the butter in a heavy skillet over medium-high setting and add the breasts, skin side down. Cook until browned, about 6 minutes. Turn the chicken and cook another 6 minutes.

3. Remove the chicken pieces to a warm platter and set aside. Add the onion and thyme to the skillet and cook briefly, stirring, until the onion is wilted. Add the vinegar and wine and bring to a boil. Add the chicken broth and bring to a boil. Stir in the tomato paste. Cook until reduced by half and add the cream. Bring to a full rolling boil and stir in the mustard. There should be about ½ cup.

4. Spoon the sauce over the chicken pieces and garnish, if desired, with chopped parsley.

lean cow's milk cheese (although in Italy they have a sheep's milk version), can be used as a binder in all kinds of sauces. For example, if you want to thicken and enrich a tomato-based pasta sauce, pour it into a blender with a tablespoon or two of ricotta cheese. Add a little more at a time until you reach the desired texture. You will find that the sauce has a rich, creamy texture.

◇

When mustard is called for in this book it is nearly always Dijon-style. There are dozens of mustards in stores, but for making salad dressings, sauces, and the like, Dijon has a nice balance of heat and citrus flavor. Many mustards on the market are sweetened or otherwise flavored, which makes them unsuitable for cooking.

Chicken Breasts with Mushrooms and Pearl Onions

❖ ❖

Here is a quick weeknight recipe that I have made often for my family.

Yield: 6 servings.

24 pearl onions, peeled
4 chicken breast filets, halved widthwise
Salt
Freshly ground black pepper to taste
1½ tablespoons olive oil
½ cup sliced white mushrooms
2 tablespoons chopped basil
½ cup white wine
1 tablespoon butter

1. In a pot half filled with boiling salted water, cook the pearl onions for 2 minutes. Drain and set aside.

2. Season the chicken well with salt and pepper. In a large pan, heat the oil over medium-high setting. Add the chicken and the onions. Cook for 10 minutes and flip. Scatter the mushrooms in the pan. Cook 3 minutes and add the basil, wine, and butter. Cover, and cook for 3 minutes. Serve.

Poached Chicken with Vegetables

◇ ◇

◇

The French dish poule au pot *translates as poached hen or chicken with vegetables. In France, I used to make it with old hens, which have tough meat that needs long stewing. In this country, we use chicken. It is a wonderfully full-flavored meal that can be made a day ahead if desired.*

Yield: 4 servings.

1 3-pound chicken
5 cups fresh or canned chicken stock
3 carrots, scraped and cut into 1½-inch lengths
3 ribs celery, trimmed and cut into 1½-inch lengths
2 or 3 turnips (about ½ pound), trimmed and cut into pieces about
    the same shape as the celery and carrots
1 cup leeks, white section only, cut into 1½-inch lengths
1 fennel bulb, cut into ¼-inch slices
1 zucchini, trimmed, quartered, and cut into 1½-inch lengths
¼ cup rice
Salt and freshly ground pepper to taste
Fresh chervil for garnish

1. Place the chicken in a pot. It should fit snugly or else you will need too much water to cover it and the soup will be weak. Cover the chicken with chicken stock. Add the carrots, celery, turnips, leeks, and fennel. Bring to a boil, and lower to a simmer.

2. Simmer 20 minutes, uncovered. Add zucchini. Simmer 5 minutes longer, skimming foam from top periodically.

3. Add rice, salt, and pepper. Cook until chicken is tender, about 10 minutes.

4. Remove chicken from pot and, when cool enough to handle, cut into serving pieces. Serve in 4 hot soup bowls with equal amounts of vegetables and rice in each bowl. Garnish with fresh chervil and serve.

Poached Chicken with Rice

Yield: 4 servings.

In traditional French cuisine, I have made many recipes based on poached chicken and rice. One of the best is poularde au riz sauce suprême, *in which a whole chicken is cooked in a white stock and combined with cooked rice. The* suprême *sauce is essentially a white roux (cooked flour and butter) combined with reduced chicken stock and cream.*

In the hearty recipe here, a chicken is poached in a well-seasoned stock. A basic white sauce is made with flour, butter, and a little of the chicken cooking liquid. The sauce is finished with cream, cayenne, and lemon juice. Served with rice cooked in the chicken broth, this is a wonderful and relatively easy dinner for 4.

1 chicken (about 3 pounds), cut into 4 pieces (cut in half along the
   backbone, then crosswise in the middle)
2 leeks (whites and 2 inches of green), trimmed and washed well
3 ribs celery
4 parsley sprigs
2 sprigs fresh thyme or 1 teaspoon dried
1 bay leaf
3 medium carrots, scraped and halved widthwise
1 medium onion, peeled, stuck with 2 cloves
6 peppercorns
Salt to taste
2 tablespoons butter
4 tablespoons flour
½ cup cream
½ cup half-and-half
¼ teaspoon freshly grated nutmeg
Pinch of cayenne pepper
2 tablespoons fresh lemon juice

1. Place the chicken in a pot and barely cover with water.

2. Tie the leeks, celery, parsley, and thyme sprigs together with a string to form a bouquet garni. Add it to the pot, then add the bay leaf, carrots, onion with cloves, peppercorns, and salt. Bring to a boil, reduce heat to simmer, and cook until chicken is tender, about 45 minutes. Skim the surface often to remove fat.

3. Remove the chicken from the broth and keep it warm while preparing the sauce. Reserve the broth. Melt the butter in a saucepan, add the flour, and whisk well over medium-low heat. When blended, add 2 cups of the chicken broth and whisk vigorously. Bring to a boil and simmer for 10 minutes.

4. Strain broth through a sieve and return to the saucepan. Add cream, half-and-half, nutmeg, cayenne, and lemon juice. Bring to a boil. Check for seasoning and simmer for 5 minutes.

5. Serve 1 chicken quarter per person. Remove skin if desired. Spoon a little of the sauce over each portion and serve the remainder in a gravy boat. Serve with rice and the poached vegetables.

Boiled Rice

◇ ◇

Yield: 4 servings.

3 cups remaining chicken broth from previous recipe (if not
    enough, add water)
1 cup converted rice
1 tablespoon lemon juice

1. Bring the chicken broth to a boil and add the rice. Return to a boil and stir. Simmer for 17 minutes over low flame, covered. Add the lemon juice, blend well, and serve with the chicken.

BASIC CHICKEN STOCK

◇

Scores of recipes call for chicken stock, from soups and stews to sauces of all kinds. Make chicken stock in big batches and freeze it in plastic containers or ice cube trays. Here is the basic recipe.

3 to 4 chicken carcasses, with
    wings, back, neck, and legs
    (skin removed)
3 quarts water
2 stalks celery, rinsed and halved
    crosswise
2 carrots, scraped, trimmed, and
    halved crosswise
4 sprigs parsley
2 bay leaves
10 black peppercorns
Salt to taste

1. Place all ingredients in a large, deep pot and bring to a boil. Reduce heat to low. Simmer, uncovered, for 2 hours, skimming foam off the surface with a slotted spoon as necessary. Taste the stock and add more salt and pepper if needed.

2. Strain the stock through a large sieve or colander set over a large pot or bowl. Let the strained stock cool slightly and then refrigerate. After the stock is completely chilled, scrape off any fat that has solidified on the surface. Freeze if not using immediately.

YIELD: ABOUT 2 QUARTS.

The exotic and tantalizing dish here was given to me by Jean-Georges Vongerichten, the chef of the acclaimed restaurant Jean-Georges in Manhattan. In his younger days, Mr. Vongerichten spent several years cooking in the Far East and that influence is evident in his light and scintillating creations.

This recipe for Indonesian-style chicken breasts is easy for home cooks to make on short notice. All you need is a supply of ground spices and some garlic. The chicken is marinated for at least 30 minutes or overnight in the spice blend, then sautéed. That's it. A harmonious side dish is curried corn and red peppers. Yogurt makes an excellent binder and absorbs the curry flavor well.

Indonesian-Style Chicken Breasts

Much of Southeast Asian cooking is characterized by the yin-yang taste sensations of sweet and hot. This dish achieves that balance by pairing hot cayenne with honey and lemon.

Yield: 4 servings.

4 skinless, boneless chicken breast halves (about 1¼ pounds total)
Salt and freshly ground pepper to taste
1 tablespoon soy sauce
1 teaspoon honey or brown sugar
2 tablespoons fresh lemon juice
1 tablespoon ground cumin
¼ teaspoon cayenne pepper
½ teaspoon turmeric
1 tablespoon ground coriander
2 teaspoons finely chopped garlic
2 tablespoons vegetable oil

1. Place the chicken in a mixing bowl. Add salt, pepper, soy sauce, honey, lemon juice, cumin, cayenne, turmeric, coriander, and garlic. Blend well and coat the chicken thoroughly. Cover with plastic wrap and refrigerate for at least 2 hours or overnight.

2. Heat the oil in a skillet large enough to hold the pieces in one layer without crowding. Over medium heat, add the pieces of chicken and cook until browned on one side. Turn the pieces and reduce the heat to medium-high. Cook until done. Total cooking time is about 10 minutes. After the chicken pieces are cooked, transfer them to paper towels and keep them in a warm place. Serve hot.

Curried Corn with Red Peppers

◇ ◇

Yield: 4 servings.

4 ears fresh corn
1 medium-size sweet red pepper
2 tablespoons butter
¼ cup finely chopped onion
1 teaspoon finely chopped garlic
1 teaspoon curry powder
Salt and freshly ground pepper
¼ cup plain yogurt

1. Cut and scrape the corn kernels off the cob.

2. Core the pepper and cut it lengthwise. Discard the inner veins and seeds. Cut the pepper in ¼-inch pieces.

3. Heat the butter in a skillet. Add the pepper pieces, onion, and garlic. Cook, stirring, over medium heat until wilted, about 5 minutes. Sprinkle with curry powder and cook, stirring, about 30 seconds. Add the corn, salt, pepper, and yogurt. Cook, stirring, about 2 to 3 minutes. Serve hot.

Arroz con Pollo (Chicken and Rice Casserole)

◇ ◇

This Cuban dish is redolent of different flavors, from earthy cumin to smoky ham and zesty coriander. It is even better the next day.

Yield: 4 servings.

3½- to 4-pound chicken, cut into 10 serving pieces
Salt and freshly ground pepper to taste
½ teaspoon ground cumin
2 teaspoons chopped fresh oregano or 1 teaspoon dried, crumbled
2 tablespoons olive oil
½ cup finely chopped onion
1 tablespoon finely chopped garlic
1 large green pepper, cored, seeded, and cut into 1-inch pieces
¼ pound boneless smoked ham, cut into ¼-inch cubes
1½ cups canned crushed tomatoes
4 ripe plum tomatoes, peeled and cut into small cubes
½ teaspoon saffron threads (optional)
3 cups fresh or canned chicken broth
1 cup converted rice
12 green olives stuffed with pimientos
9-ounce package frozen green peas
¼ cup grated Parmesan cheese
6½-ounce can fancy pimientos, cut into 8 long strips
4 tablespoons coarsely chopped fresh coriander or parsley

1. Preheat the oven to 375 degrees.
2. Season the chicken with salt, pepper, cumin, and oregano.
3. Heat the oil in a large skillet over medium-high setting. Add the chicken pieces and brown on all sides. Remove the pieces to a baking dish and set aside, keeping them warm.
4. Add to the skillet the onion, garlic, green pepper, and ham. Sauté until the vegetables are wilted. Add the crushed tomatoes, tomato cubes, saffron, and broth. Bring to a boil while scraping the bottom of the pan to loosen any sticking particles. Add the rice, olives, and chicken. Stir, cover tightly, and put in the oven. Bake 20 minutes.
5. Stir in the peas and the cheese. Arrange the strips of pimiento on top and bake 5 minutes more. Serve sprinkled with coriander.

Chicken Breasts with Tomatoes and Capers

◇ ◇

This easy-to-make dish combines the sweetness of tomatoes with the briny essence of capers.

Yield: 4 servings.

4 boneless, skinless chicken breasts (about 1¼ pounds)
Salt and freshly ground white pepper to taste
1 tablespoon olive oil
1 tablespoon butter
3 tablespoons finely chopped shallots
1 teaspoon finely chopped garlic
2 teaspoons finely chopped fresh tarragon or 1 teaspoon dried
4 ripe plum tomatoes, cut into small cubes
2 tablespoons red wine vinegar
4 tablespoons drained capers
1 cup dry white wine
1 tablespoon tomato paste
4 tablespoons chopped fresh parsley leaves

1. Sprinkle the chicken well with salt and pepper.

2. Heat the oil and butter in a heavy-bottomed skillet. Add the chicken breasts and sauté over medium-high heat, turning the pieces often until lightly browned, about 5 minutes.

3. Scatter the shallots and garlic around the chicken. Cook briefly; add the tarragon, tomatoes, vinegar, capers, wine, and tomato paste. Stir to dissolve the brown particles adhering to the bottom of the skillet.

4. Blend well. Bring to a boil, cover, reduce heat and simmer for 10 minutes, or until the chicken is cooked. Sprinkle with parsley and serve.

◈

Capers, which I use in many sauces, are the little buds that grow on shrubs in the Mediterranean. They are extremely harsh-tasting when picked but take on a whole different flavor when pickled. They are used in many dishes from the south of Spain and France, and are found here in vinaigrettes, seafood dishes, and sundry sauces.

Chicken Breasts with Fennel Sauce

◇ ◇

This chapter is top-heavy with chicken breast recipes because my mail reveals that people can't get enough of it. This recipe has a lovely anise flavor from fennel.

Yield: 4 servings.

4 skinless, boneless chicken breast halves (about 1¼ pounds total)
Salt and freshly ground white pepper to taste
1 head fennel (about ¾ pound)
2 tablespoons olive oil
4 tablespoons finely chopped shallots
¼ cup dry white wine
¼ cup fresh or canned chicken broth
1 bay leaf
2 sprigs fresh thyme or 1 teaspoon dried
Dash Tabasco sauce
2 tablespoons butter
4 fennel leaves, finely chopped

1. If the chicken breast halves are connected, separate them lengthwise down the middle and trim any membrane or fat. Salt and pepper the breasts generously.

2. Trim the stalk off the fennel and save some green leaves for chopping. Cut the bulb into ¼-inch cubes. There should be about 1½ cups.

3. Heat the oil in a nonstick pan over medium-high setting. Add the chicken breasts and cook until lightly browned, about 4 minutes. Add the shallots.

4. Turn the chicken breasts and scatter the fennel around them. Continue cooking, shaking the skillet and redistributing the fennel, until it is cooked evenly. Cook about 4 minutes. Add the wine, broth, bay leaf, thyme, and Tabasco sauce. Cover tightly and cook over medium heat for 10 minutes. Turn the pieces occasionally.

5. Transfer the chicken to a platter, cover with foil and keep warm.

6. With a slotted spoon, remove about ½ cup of the fennel cubes. Remove the bay leaf and thyme sprig. Pour the remaining fennel mixture into a blender or food processor. Add the butter and blend to a very fine purée. Pour the mixture into a saucepan, season with salt and pepper as needed. Add any liquid that may have accumulated around the chicken. Add the reserved fennel cubes and the chopped fennel leaves. Bring to a simmer and spoon the sauce over the chicken breasts. Serve immediately.

Indian-Style Barbecued Chicken
◇ ◇

I find the combination of spices and textures in Indian cooking fascinating. The coating for this chicken is inspired by northern Indian cuisine, combining yogurt, cardamom, gingerroot, and roasted cumin seeds. The flavors are complex but not necessarily hot.

Yield: 6 servings.

4 tablespoons lemon juice
Salt and freshly ground pepper to taste
1 cup plain yogurt, drained for 15 minutes in a fine sieve or
    cheesecloth
2 teaspoons paprika
2 garlic cloves
½ teaspoon ground cardamom
2 tablespoons chopped fresh gingerroot
1 teaspoon roasted cumin seeds
¼ teaspoon hot red pepper flakes
6 skinless, boneless chicken breasts (about 1¾ pounds)
2 tablespoons oil for broiling

1. Put all the ingredients, except the chicken and oil, into the container of a food processor or blender and purée to a fine texture.

2. Pour the marinade over the breasts of chicken, turning and tossing to coat all the pieces well. Cover with plastic wrap and marinate for 3 to 4 hours or overnight in the refrigerator.

(Continued on next page)

3. Preheat the oven broiler or charcoal grill.

4. If the oven broiler is used, arrange the chicken breasts in one layer on a baking dish. Place the chicken under the broiler about 6 inches from the heat source. Leave the door partly open. Cook about 7 minutes. Shift the pan to the lower rack so that the pieces are about 12 inches from the heat and flip them. Continue broiling for 12 minutes longer with the door partly open. Turn the pieces and broil 5 minutes more on the lower rack.

5. If you use a charcoal grill, brush the grate with oil to prevent the meat from sticking. Place the breasts over the coals and cook for about 7 minutes on one side, turn them and cook about 7 minutes more or until done. They should be turned several times while cooking and brushed with oil.

Sautéed Chicken in Red Wine Sauce with Spaetzle

◇ ◇

Yield: 4 servings.

1 chicken, cut into 6 to 8 serving pieces (3½ pounds)
Salt and freshly ground pepper to taste
2 tablespoons butter
¼ pound mushrooms, left whole if very small, otherwise halved or quartered
16 small white onions, peeled
2 tablespoons finely chopped shallots
2 teaspoons finely chopped garlic
2 tablespoons flour
2 tablespoons cognac or brandy
1½ cups dry red wine
½ cup fresh or canned chicken broth
1 bouquet garni, consisting of 4 parsley sprigs, 2 fresh thyme sprigs or 1 teaspoon dried, 1 bay leaf, and 2 whole cloves (wrapped in cheesecloth and tied)

1. Sprinkle the chicken well with salt and pepper.

2. Heat the butter in a skillet large enough to hold the chicken in one layer without crowding. Add the chicken pieces, skin side down.

3. Cook and brown the pieces over medium-high heat for about 6 minutes. Turn the chicken and cook about 5 minutes longer. Remove chicken and set aside.

4. Over high heat, add to the pan the mushrooms, onions, shallots, and garlic and stir to blend for about 3 minutes.

5. Sprinkle the flour evenly over all. Stir and cook for 1 minute. Add cognac to the pan and ignite it quickly. When the flames die down, add the wine, chicken broth, bouquet garni, salt, and pepper. Stir and bring to a simmer. Return chicken to the pan, cover, and cook 20 minutes or until the vegetables are tender. Remove the cover and simmer to reduce the sauce slightly. Remove the bouquet garni and serve with spaetzle.

◇

Perhaps the first dish I learned from my mother was sautéed chicken à la bourguignonne (chicken in Burgundy wine), made with a simple table wine that French families purchase in bulk from local wine makers. The classic recipe calls for an espagnole sauce (a time-consuming brown sauce) blended with a red wine reduction. Few home cooks have the time or inclination today to make an espagnole sauce. The lighter and quicker recipe here is made with a red wine reduction, cognac, chicken stock, and seasonings. The classic recipe also calls for bacon, which has been omitted here to reduce fat. A glass of good Burgundy rounds out this meal splendidly.

Chicken à la bourguignonne needs a side dish of starch to sop up the sauce. As an alternative to rice or potatoes, you might try serving spaetzle, which is as easy to make as basic noodles.

First, you blend flour, eggs, and milk until they form a loose dough. The mixture is forced through a colander into boiling water. The noodles cook in about a minute. They can be set aside until needed, then sautéed in butter and served hot with a parsley garnish.

Spaetzle

◇ ◇

Yield: 4 *servings.*

2 cups sifted all-purpose flour
2 whole eggs
⅔ cup milk
Salt to taste
½ teaspoon freshly grated nutmeg
2 tablespoons butter
Freshly ground pepper to taste
2 tablespoons finely chopped parsley

1. Place the flour in a mixing bowl. Beat the eggs separately and add them to the flour, stirring with a wire whisk or electric beater. Gradually add the milk, salt, and nutmeg, beating until smooth.

2. Bring a large pot of salted water to a boil. Holding a colander over the boiling water, pour the batter into the colander. Press the batter through the holes of the colander with a rubber spatula or large spoon. As the squiggly spaetzle solidifies, stir gently. They are done when they float on top of the water, in about 1 minute. Drain and transfer them to a clean towel to dry briefly.

3. Heat the butter in a nonstick skillet. When it is bubbling, add the spaetzle with salt and pepper, tossing and stirring for a few minutes. Add the parsley and serve immediately.

Crusty Herbed Chicken Cooked Under Bricks

◇ ◇

This unusual recipe came from my friend Daniel Boulud, owner of the stellar Daniel on Manhattan's East Side. If you like a crispy crust on your chicken, the best way to achieve it is by weighing down the bird while it is cooking—in this case with a brick. Before weighing it down, season the chicken liberally with garlic, rosemary, thyme, and black pepper.

Yield: 4 servings.

1 2½-pound chicken, split in half as for broiling
4 thin slivers of garlic
6 small sprigs fresh rosemary or 2 tablespoons dried
6 small sprigs fresh thyme or 2 tablespoons dried
Salt and freshly ground pepper to taste
2 tablespoons lemon juice
½ cup plus 6 tablespoons olive oil
6 thin lemon slices, seeds removed
1 peeled garlic clove, thinly sliced
¼ teaspoon finely minced rosemary leaves
¼ teaspoon finely minced thyme leaves

1. Cut off the backbone of the chicken (or have your butcher do it). Place each chicken half skin side up on a flat surface and pound all over forcefully with a flat mallet or the bottom of a heavy skillet.

2. Turn the chicken halves skin side down, and with a small paring knife, make one small incision in the breast portion. Make one more small incision in the leg portion. Insert 1 sliver of garlic, 1 small rosemary sprig, and 1 small thyme sprig in each incision.

3. Put the chicken pieces in a flat dish. Sprinkle on all sides with salt and pepper. Sprinkle with 1 tablespoon lemon juice and ½ cup olive oil, turning the pieces to coat well. Arrange the pieces skin side up in the dish and arrange the lemon slices evenly over the skin. Scatter the remaining 2 rosemary sprigs and 2 thyme sprigs over the chicken. Cover with plastic wrap and refrigerate overnight. When ready to cook, preheat the oven to 500 degrees.

4. Pour off and reserve the liquid from around the chicken pieces. Discard lemon slices.

(Continued on next page)

5. Heat a large, heavy skillet, preferably cast iron, until almost smoking.

6. Pour the reserved liquid into the skillet. Immediately add the chicken pieces skin side down. Scatter the garlic slices all around the chicken. Cover the chicken pieces with a heavy skillet that will fit comfortably inside the cooking skillet. Place a heavy brick on it. If necessary, add more weights to make the chicken lie as flat as possible. Cook over high heat about 5 minutes, until the skin is dark golden brown. After 5 minutes, reduce the heat slightly and continue cooking about 1 minute. Remove the weights and turn the chicken pieces. Replace the weights and place the chicken in the oven. Bake 17 minutes. Remove the weights and turn the chicken pieces once more. Continue cooking about 3 minutes, or until the chicken is cooked through.

7. In a small saucepan, combine the remaining 1 tablespoon of lemon juice, 6 tablespoons of olive oil, the minced rosemary and thyme leaves, and salt and pepper to taste. Blend well and heat gently. Cut the chicken into serving pieces and serve the sauce on the side.

Chicken Breasts Florentine

◇ ◇

I like to investigate the origins of famous dishes, in French, Italian, and American cuisine. There are several theories why this dish, which includes spinach, is called Florentine. Some food historians speculate that Florence, in the center of vast agricultural lands, was at one time considered the "spinach capital of Italy." Others say that in 1553, when Catherine de' Médicis married the young man who eventually became Henry II of France, she took with her to France a retinue of Florentine cooks, who introduced many things to her new land, including special dishes made with spinach.

Whatever the case, this tasty dish follows the classic recipe for chicken breast Florentine fairly closely, and it can be assembled in well under an hour.

Yield: 4 servings.

2 large whole chicken breasts, split (so you have 4 pieces on the
    bone), with skin left on
1 pound fresh spinach
1 tablespoon butter
¾ cup finely chopped onion
⅛ teaspoon freshly grated nutmeg
Salt to taste if desired
Freshly ground pepper to taste
½ cup finely grated cheese, preferably Gruyère
Mushroom sauce (see recipe page 106)
2 tablespoons chopped fresh basil (optional)

1. With breast halves skin side down, place a knife in the center of a fillet and make a 3- to 4-inch incision toward the end; repeat in other direction. Do not cut through. Open up the cut portions and flatten with a mallet or bottom of a heavy pan. Pound lightly with smooth mallet without breaking the skin.

2. If bulk spinach is used, pick over to remove tough stems or blemished leaves. Rinse thoroughly and drain well.

3. Heat butter in a skillet and add the onion. Cook, stirring, until wilted. Add spinach and let wilt. Continue cooking, stirring, until the liquid evaporates. Add nutmeg, salt, and pepper. Transfer spinach to a cool plate. Let cool.

4. Place equal amounts of spinach mixture in center of each breast, on the incision. Spoon equal amounts of chopped cheese in center of each mound of spinach. Fold over the edges of chicken to enclose the spinach. (Secure with a toothpick if necessary.)

5. Arrange pieces, skin side up, in the rack of a steamer.

6. Partly fill steamer with water. Cover and bring to a boil. Place the rack over boiling water. Cover closely and let steam 10 minutes.

7. Transfer the chicken to warm serving dishes and spoon on some mushroom sauce. If desired, sprinkle with fresh basil.

Mushroom Sauce

◇ ◇

Yield: About 1¾ cups.

1 tablespoon butter
2 tablespoons finely chopped shallots
½ pound mushrooms of choice, thinly sliced (about 3 cups)
Juice of ½ lemon
Salt and freshly ground pepper to taste
¼ cup dry white wine
1 cup chicken broth
1 cup heavy cream

1. Over medium heat, melt butter in a saucepan and add shallots. Cook briefly until wilted.

2. Add mushrooms and lemon juice and cook, stirring, until the mushrooms give up their liquid. Add salt and pepper and continue cooking until most of the liquid has evaporated.

3. Add wine and broth and cook over high heat until most of the liquid is evaporated. Add cream, reduce heat to medium, and cook 5 minutes.

Turkey Breast with Corn Bread and Sausage Stuffing

◇ ◇

Buying turkey parts, like a whole breast with or without ribs, is a good way to cook for the family without buying an entire bird. This homey recipe calls for serving the breast with a corn bread and sausage dressing seasoned with chopped pecans and fresh sage.

Yield: 6 servings.

Salt and freshly ground white pepper to taste
1 teaspoon ground cumin
1 teaspoon ground coriander
2 teaspoons fresh chopped thyme leaves or 1 teaspoon dried
1 fresh turkey breast with ribs and wings (about 4 pounds)
2 medium-size whole onions, peeled (about ⅓ pound)
2 large garlic cloves, peeled
1 bay leaf
2 tablespoons vegetable oil
1½ cups fresh or canned chicken broth

1. Preheat oven to 450 degrees.

2. In a small bowl, combine salt, pepper, cumin, coriander, and thyme. Blend well. Sprinkle and rub this mixture inside and outside the turkey breast.

3. Place breast, skin side up, in a roasting pan. Put onions on each side, and garlic cloves and bay leaf beneath the breast. Brush outside of turkey with vegetable oil.

4. Put the breast in the oven, and roast 15 minutes. Cover loosely with foil, add chicken broth, and bake 15 minutes, basting a few times.

5. Reduce heat to 425 degrees and remove foil. Continue roasting 15 minutes, basting a few times.

6. Remove turkey breast from the pan and discard fat in the pan. Return the breast, skin side up, to the pan and pour the broth around it. Continue roasting 10 minutes, basting twice.

7. Remove from the oven, cover with foil, and let stand in a warm place 10 minutes before carving. Serve with dressing and pan gravy.

◆

In recent years, I have been experimenting with turkey parts, especially turkey breast steaks, which are widely available in supermarkets. Virtually anything you can do with chicken breasts you can do with turkey cutlets. They cook quickly and go well with all kinds of instant pan sauces— just be careful not to overcook them because they can dry out quickly. Also available are turkey "tenderloins," which are 4- to 6-ounce strips of breast meat from the side of the breastbone. These are exceptionally tender.

A whole turkey breast, with or without bones, can be roasted just like a chicken. The timing is about the same, too. If you prefer dark meat, buy turkey legs and thighs and roast them. Finally, there is ground turkey, which is exceptionally lean. It can be blended with ground beef for meat loaves or hamburgers.

Corn Bread and Sausage Stuffing

◇ ◇

I usually cook stuffings separately from chicken or turkey. For one, the stuffing doesn't complicate the bird's cooking time; secondly, it is easier to serve that way.

Yield: 6 servings.

½ pound ground sweet or hot sausage meat
1 cup finely chopped onions
1 cup finely chopped celery
1 tablespoon finely chopped garlic
3 cups cubed corn bread (see recipe page 109)
½ cup coarsely chopped pecans
Salt and freshly ground pepper to taste
2 tablespoons chopped fresh sage or 1 tablespoon dried
½ cup finely chopped parsley
1 cup fresh or canned chicken broth
1 egg, beaten

1. Put the sausage meat in a 9-inch skillet (cast iron is best) over medium heat. Cook, breaking up lumps, until the meat loses raw look. Drain fat.

2. Add onions, celery, and garlic. Cook, stirring, until wilted. Remove skillet from heat.

3. Add corn bread, pecans, salt, pepper, sage, parsley, broth, and egg. Blend well, and smooth over the top. Cover with foil and bake, along with the turkey, for 30 minutes.

Corn Bread

◇ ◇

Yield: 6 servings.

1 cup yellow cornmeal
1 cup all-purpose flour
4 teaspoons baking powder
Salt and freshly ground pepper to taste
1 teaspoon sugar
1 egg, beaten
1 cup milk
¼ cup melted shortening, plus grease for pan

1. Preheat oven to 425 degrees.

2. In a bowl, combine the cornmeal, flour, baking powder, salt and pepper, sugar, egg, and milk. Blend well with a wire whisk. Stir in shortening.

3. Grease a shallow baking pan (9 by 9 by 2 inches). Pour in the batter and bake for 30 minutes, or until done. (You can do this a day early.)

Turkey Steaks with Mustard Seeds and Mushrooms

◇ ◇

Yield: 4 servings.

I use turkey cutlets as a pinch hitter for veal and chicken in all sorts of recipes. The origin of this recipe—turkey steaks with mustard seeds and mushrooms—was a bottle of mustard seeds that I discovered way in the back of the pantry.

Mustard seeds come in three varieties: black, dark reddish-brown, and yellowish. The yellow seeds are most common in American supermarkets. Indian cuisine employs black seeds extensively, often roasted and ground to a powder. Crushed mustard seeds were used as condiments by ancient Egyptians. The Romans introduced mustard seeds to Gaul, where they were ground and used in sauces. In the Middle Ages, the seeds were prized for their supposed medicinal value.

In this recipe, the turkey steaks are seasoned with salt and ground black pepper, then pressed into mustard seeds on both sides. When the turkey is seared over high heat, the mustard seeds toast. The piquant seeds marry well with the sauce of shallots, tomatoes, vinegar, and chicken broth. The amount of mustard seed used may be varied to taste.

4 tablespoons olive oil
4 slices turkey breast (about ½ pound each)
Salt and freshly ground pepper to taste
3 tablespoons yellow mustard seeds
½ pound mushrooms, sliced
2 tablespoons finely chopped shallots
½ teaspoon finely chopped garlic
¾ cup ripe plum tomatoes, peeled and cut into small cubes
1 tablespoon red wine vinegar
½ cup fresh or canned chicken broth
1 tablespoon butter
2 tablespoons finely chopped parsley or any fresh herb

1. Heat 1 tablespoon of the oil in a nonstick skillet large enough to hold all the turkey pieces in one layer.

2. Sprinkle the turkey slices with salt and pepper and press mustard seeds onto both sides. Add the turkey slices to the skillet and sauté over high heat until lightly browned, about 3 minutes on each side. Transfer the meat to a serving platter and keep it warm.

3. Heat the remaining olive oil in the skillet. Add the mushrooms, salt, and pepper. Stir and cook over high heat until lightly browned. Add the shallots and garlic. Stir briefly and add the tomatoes, vinegar, and broth.

4. Add any liquid that may have accumulated around the turkey. Over high heat, reduce the liquid in the pan by half, stirring in the butter and parsley at the end. Pour the sauce over the turkey slices and serve.

Turkey Breasts with Provençal Herbs

I always keep in my pantry a blend of dried herbs called herbes de Provençe. It is available in most gourmet shops, sold in an earthenware crock. It is a wonderful blend of herbs that can be used with all kinds of dishes. If you have it, use 1 tablespoon instead of the thyme and rosemary in this recipe.

Yield: 6 servings.

2 pieces of boneless turkey breasts (about 1¼ pounds each)
Salt and freshly ground pepper to taste
2 tablespoons olive oil
4 cloves garlic
4 sprigs fresh thyme or 2 teaspoons dried
2 bay leaves
1 tablespoon fresh rosemary or ½ tablespoon dried
¼ cup dry white wine
1 cup fresh or canned chicken broth
2 tablespoons butter
4 tablespoons coarsely chopped fresh basil or parsley

1. Sprinkle the turkey breasts with salt and pepper.

2. Heat the oil in a skillet and add the breasts skin side down. Cook over moderately high heat about 10 minutes. Turn the pieces and add the garlic, thyme, bay leaves, and rosemary. Cook for 10 minutes longer.

3. Pour in the wine, scraping and stirring to dissolve any particles clinging to the pan. Add the broth, cover, and simmer for 15 minutes.

4. Uncover and reduce the liquid by half over high heat. Swirl in the butter and sprinkle with the basil.

When dishes are described as Provençal, they usually have several characteristics in common. For one, they are made with olive oil. In addition, there may be tomatoes, garlic, and olives, as well as a rainbow of herbs that include rosemary, thyme, sage, basil, chervil, oregano, and parsley.

Turkey Breasts with Fresh Tomato Sauce
◇ ◇

Yield: 4 servings.

4 turkey breast steaks (about 1¼ pounds total)
Salt to taste if desired
Freshly ground pepper to taste
3 ripe tomatoes (about 1 pound)
3 tablespoons olive oil
¼ pound mushrooms, thinly sliced (about 2 cups)
2 teaspoons minced garlic
½ teaspoon chopped dried rosemary
¼ cup dry white wine
3 tablespoons butter
2 tablespoons finely chopped basil or parsley
2 tablespoons flour
Juice of ½ lemon
¼ cup finely chopped parsley

1. Sprinkle turkey pieces on both sides with salt and pepper and set aside.

2. Core, peel, and seed the tomatoes. Cut into small cubes. There should be about 2 cups.

3. Heat 2 tablespoons of the oil in a saucepan and add the mushrooms. Cook, stirring, until the mushrooms give up their liquid. Cook further until the liquid in the pan nearly evaporates. Add the garlic and rosemary and stir. Add the wine and cook about 1 minute.

4. Add tomato, salt, and pepper and cook 5 minutes. Add 2 tablespoons of the butter and the basil and stir. There should be about 2¼ cups.

5. Meanwhile, coat turkey pieces with flour and shake off excess.

6. Heat remaining oil and butter in a skillet large enough to hold the pieces in one layer. Put the slices in the skillet and cook on one side until golden brown, about 3 to 4 minutes. Turn slices and continue cooking about 4 to 5 minutes. Sprinkle with lemon juice.

7. Spoon tomato sauce over a warm serving dish and top with the turkey slices. Serve sprinkled with parsley.

Turkey Scaloppine with Prosciutto and Cheese
◇ ◇

I used to make this dish with chicken breasts, but turkey works just as well. The Marsala wine gives it a nice hint of sweetness.

Yield: 4 servings.

4 turkey breast "steaks," sometimes referred to as turkey breast
    tenderloins (about 1¼ pounds total)
Salt to taste if desired
Freshly ground pepper to taste
2 tablespoons flour
2 tablespoons olive oil
2 tablespoons butter
1 tablespoon finely chopped shallots
¼ cup dry Marsala or sherry wine
4 very thin slices prosciutto (about 2 ounces)
4 very thin slices Gruyère or Swiss cheese (about 2 ounces)

1. Put the turkey slices on a flat surface between sheets of plastic wrap. With a mallet or the bottom of a heavy pan, pound the meat lightly. Each slice should be about ¼ inch thick.

2. Sprinkle the turkey pieces on both sides with salt and pepper.

3. Dip the pieces in flour to coat well on both sides. Shake off excess.

4. Preheat the broiler to high.

5. Heat the oil and butter in a skillet and add the turkey pieces. Cook about 1½ minutes or until lightly browned on one side. Turn and cook about 2 minutes longer, turning the pieces occasionally. Scatter the shallots around the turkey pieces. Cook about a minute and add the Marsala. Cook about 1 minute more.

6. Transfer the turkey pieces to a heatproof dish and pour the wine sauce over all. Cover each piece with a slice of prosciutto. Cover the prosciutto neatly with a slice of cheese.

7. Place the covered turkey pieces under the broiler, about 3 inches from the source of heat. Cook until the cheese melts, 45 seconds to 1 minute. Serve immediately.

Turkey Patties with Curry Sauce

◇ ◇

I moistened the turkey in this recipe with chicken broth and seasoned with curry to make delicious patties.

Yield: 4 servings.

1 tablespoon butter
½ cup finely chopped onion
1½ cups fine bread crumbs
½ cup fresh or canned chicken broth
⅛ teaspoon freshly ground nutmeg
2 tablespoons finely chopped parsley
1 egg, lightly beaten
Salt to taste if desired
Freshly ground pepper to taste
1 pound ground turkey
3 tablespoons corn, peanut, or vegetable oil
½ cup blanched, slivered almonds
Curry sauce (see recipe page 115)

1. Heat the butter in a saucepan and add the onion. Cook, stirring occasionally, until wilted.

2. Put 1 cup of the bread crumbs in a mixing bowl and add the broth. Stir. Add the cooked onion, nutmeg, parsley, egg, salt, and pepper. Add the turkey and blend well. Divide the mixture into 8 equal portions.

3. Sprinkle the remaining ½ cup of bread crumbs on a flat surface and roll each turkey patty in them. Flatten each portion into a round patty about ¾ inch thick.

4. Heat about 3 tablespoons oil in 1 or 2 skillets (depending on size). Add the patties and cook about 4 minutes per side, or until nicely browned. Turn often as the patties cook.

5. Meanwhile, put the almonds in another skillet and cook, shaking the skillet and stirring, until the almonds are nicely browned. Remove from the heat and let cool.

6. Spoon the curry sauce over the patties and sprinkle with almonds.

◇

Ground turkey is very lean— about 7 percent fat—so you must take care not to overcook it when used for burgers, meat loaf, and the like. Because its flavor is so mild, you should season it very well. For example, a turkey burger could be enlivened with a little cumin or ground coriander. Or blend in some minced onions and coat with crushed black peppercorns. If you make a ground turkey meat loaf, the egg moistens the meat. Some cooks put a little tomato paste in the mix, too.

Curry Sauce

◇ ◇

Yield: About 1 cup.

1 Golden Delicious apple
1 tablespoon butter
2 tablespoons finely chopped shallots
2 teaspoons curry powder (see page 63 for homemade curry
    powder recipe)
½ cup fresh or canned chicken broth
1 tablespoon tomato purée or crushed tomatoes
¼ cup heavy cream or half-and-half

1. Peel the apple and cut it into quarters. Cut away and discard the stem ends and the core. Cut each quarter into ¼-inch cubes.

2. Heat the butter in a saucepan and add the shallots and curry powder. Cook, stirring, about 1 minute. Add the apple and stir.

3. Add the broth and tomato purée. Cook over moderately high heat for 3 minutes or until reduced to about 1 cup. Add the cream and cook about 2 minutes, stirring. Serve warm or room temperature with turkey patties.

Roasted Turkey with Maple-Corn Sauce

◇ ◇

For some reason, roasted turkey remains primarily a Thanksgiving meal, despite its versatility and bargain price. Most supermarket turkeys weigh anywhere from 10 to 20 pounds, which makes them suitable for entertaining.

When shopping, always look for "fresh" turkeys—although they may have been frozen in transport, their flavor and texture are better than turkeys that are frozen in the supermarket. Most turkeys today are self-basting, but it is still a good idea to baste by hand every 15 minutes or so. Many turkeys have those pop-up gadgets that indicate the bird is done. As for serving, allow about 1 pound of turkey on the bone per person.

There are as many roasting recipes as there are cooks. Some say start in a very hot oven; others say cook turkey in a low oven for a long time. My recipe here calls for a fairly hot oven (450 degrees) throughout.

As I mentioned before, fresh corn was a revelation to me when I first came to America—the French cultivate corn primarily as animal feed. I wanted to add corn to this all-American dish.

Yield: 12 to 16 servings.

12- or 13-pound turkey, with neck
1 onion, peeled and cut into eighths (about ½ pound)
1 tablespoon minced garlic
3 coarsely chopped carrots
Salt to taste if desired
Freshly ground pepper to taste
3 tablespoons corn, peanut, or vegetable oil
3 cups turkey or chicken broth
¼ cup minced onion
2 cups corn kernels freshly scraped from the cob, or use drained, canned, whole-kernel corn
¼ cup bourbon whiskey
2 tablespoons cider vinegar
¼ cup maple syrup
¾ cup heavy cream
1 teaspoon flour
1 tablespoon water

1. Preheat the oven to 450 degrees.

2. Cut off and discard the wing tips of the turkey. Cut off and leave whole the main wing bone and the second wing joint. Set aside. Chop the neck crosswise into 4 pieces of equal length. Set aside.

3. Stuff the cavity of the turkey with the onion pieces, garlic, carrots, salt, and pepper. Sprinkle the outside of the turkey with salt and pepper and rub it all over with 2 tablespoons of the oil.

4. Rub the bottom of a large roasting pan with the remaining oil.

5. Place the turkey on one side in the roasting pan. Scatter the neck pieces and the cut-off wing portions around it. Place in the oven and roast about 40 minutes. Turn the turkey onto its opposite side. Place in the oven and roast another 45 minutes, basting often.

6. Remove the turkey and set aside briefly. Pour off 1 tablespoon of the fat from the pan and set it aside. Pour off and discard the remaining fat.

7. Return the turkey to the pan, breast side up, and pour 2 cups of the broth around it. Bring to a boil on top of the stove and return the turkey to the oven. Roast about 30 minutes. Continue roasting, basting occasionally, about 1 hour and 15 minutes. Remove the turkey from the pan and cover it loosely with aluminum foil.

8. Scoop out the vegetables from the cavity of the turkey and add them to the liquid in the roasting pan. Add the remaining 1 cup of broth and bring to a boil. Cook until the liquid is reduced to about 1⅔ cups. Strain, discarding the solids. Set aside.

9. Heat the reserved tablespoon of fat (or, if desired, you might substitute corn, peanut, or vegetable oil) in a skillet. Add the ¼ cup of finely chopped onion and the corn and cook until the onions are wilted. Add the bourbon, vinegar, and maple syrup and stir, cooking about 2 minutes or until the liquid in the skillet is reduced by half.

10. Add the reserved turkey drippings to the corn mixture and bring to a boil. Cook about 1 minute and add the cream, salt, and pepper to taste. Cook, stirring, and skimming the surface often to remove any foam or scum. Blend the flour with the water and add this to the sauce, stirring until smooth.

11. Carve the turkey and serve the sauce on the side.

Magret *is the term for the breasts of ducks that are raised for foie gras. Because they are force-fed to enlarge their livers, these ducks have unusually large, meaty breasts as well. They are increasingly available in better supermarkets and specialty outlets. If you can't find* magret *breasts, use regular duck breasts.*

Duck Breasts with Turnips and Asian Spices

I have traveled to Asia several times and was intrigued by the blends of spices in the cooking. Asian cooking—Chinese, Japanese, Vietnamese, and more—has had a profound effect on American chefs in the past decade.

Yield: 2 servings.

2 medium white turnips (about ⅓ pound each)
2 duck breasts (*magret,* if possible), skin on (about 8 ounces each)
2 tablespoons coriander seeds
2 whole cloves
2 teaspoons cumin seeds
Salt and freshly ground pepper to taste
4 tablespoons natural honey
3 tablespoons white wine vinegar
1 cup hard cider or ½ cup dry white wine
1 cup fresh chicken broth or good canned version
2 sprigs flat leaf parsley

1. Trim the ends of the turnips and peel them. Cut into ¼-inch slices.

2. Place the duck breasts and the turnips in a large saucepan and cover with boiling water. Cook, simmering, for 1 minute. Remove the duck breasts and cook the turnips 2 minutes longer. Remove the turnips. Place the duck breasts and the turnips into an ice water bath to prevent them from cooking further. When cool, remove the duck and the turnips. Pat the duck dry with a paper towel. Using a sharp knife, remove the thick excess fat, leaving a thin layer of fat underneath. Score the surface of the fat diagonally.

3. Grind the coriander, clove, and cumin by placing them on a cutting board and crushing them with the bottom of a heavy saucepan. This can also be done in a spice mill, but be careful not to grind them too fine—you want a crunchy texture to the spice crust.

4. Meanwhile, season the duck breasts with salt and pepper. Place in a skillet over medium-high heat, skin side down, until lightly browned, about 2 minutes. Add the turnips, turning them from time to time, and continue cooking another 2 minutes. Remove the duck and turnips from

the skillet, and pour off the fat. Pat the skin of the duck with paper towels to absorb any excess fat.

5. In the same skillet, combine the honey and white vinegar. Bring to a boil, stirring constantly, until the mixture begins to caramelize evenly. Add the ground spices while stirring. Be careful not to burn. Remove the skillet from the heat. Return duck breasts to the skillet, fatty side down. Move them around in the pan to coat them with the spice mixture. Remove the duck and keep warm.

6. Return the skillet to medium-high heat and add the cider. Cook, scraping the side and bottom of the pan, until all the brown particles are dissolved. Add the chicken broth and bring to a simmer. Add the duck breasts, fatty side up, and place the turnips around them. Simmer for about 3 to 4 minutes. Remove the duck and keep warm. The meat should be pink in the center.

7. Bring the sauce and the turnips to a boil and cook until the liquid is reduced by more than half—the sauce should have thickened to a syrupy consistency.

8. Cut the breasts on a bias into thin slices. Arrange slices of the breasts in a fan shape on a warm serving plate. Garnish with turnip slices, and spoon the sauce around. Garnish with parsley.

Roasted Duck with Figs

◇ ◇

I always tell people at cooking demonstrations that cooking duck is no more difficult than preparing a chicken. The only difference is that a duck has a lot more fat and less meat—that's why this recipe for 4 calls for 2 ducks. Notice that in this recipe, the duck is seared in a hot pan before it is roasted in a 450-degree oven— this renders off a lot of the fat. Duck is particularly good with sweet accents. Figs and honey are a terrific complement to this rich meat.

Yield: 4 servings.

2 5½-pound ducks, trussed and tied with string
Salt and freshly ground pepper to taste
2 tablespoons vegetable oil
2 cups coarsely sliced onions (about 2 medium onions)
1½ cups coarsely sliced carrots (about 3 medium carrots)
1½ cups coarsely sliced celery (about 3 large stalks)
5 cloves garlic, with skins, halved
1 sprig fresh rosemary or 1 tablespoon dried
2 sprigs fresh thyme or 1 tablespoon dried
¼ cup honey
2 cups port
2 tablespoons butter
12 large fresh figs

1. Preheat oven to 450 degrees.

2. Place a pan over high heat. Sear the ducks all around (about 2 minutes per duck). Place them in a roasting pan.

3. Salt and pepper the ducks all over, including cavities. Brush with oil. Arrange the ducks breast down in a roasting pan. Roast for 15 minutes. Turn the ducks breast side up, and roast for 30 minutes more. Remove them from the oven and pour off any fat.

4. Scatter the onions, carrots, celery, garlic, rosemary, and thyme around the ducks. Increase oven temperature to 500 degrees. Return the ducks to the oven. Cook for 30 minutes more. Brush the duck breasts and legs with honey. Cook for 30 minutes, brushing some more.

5. Remove the ducks from the oven, place on a platter and keep warm. Strain the vegetables, and place them in a saucepan. Add the port, bring to a simmer, and reduce by about one-quarter.

6. Meanwhile, melt the butter in a skillet over medium-high heat. Add the figs and cook about 2 minutes. Add the sauce from the ducks, cover, and simmer for 10 minutes more. Keep warm.

7. To serve, carve the breasts, then remove the legs from the ducks. In the center of 4 large, warm plates, place the breasts and the legs, reserving the rest of the duck for stock. Pour the sauce evenly over the meat.

Beef, Pork, and Veal

◇ ◇ ◇

Classic Boeuf à la Bourguignonne

Puréed Potatoes with Carrots and Onions

Barbecued Medallions of Pork

Brochettes of Pork with Sage

Veal Chops with Raspberry Vinegar

Crown Roast of Pork with Spicy Rice Stuffing

Ham Steaks with Madeira Sauce

Double Veal Chops with Braised Spring Vegetables

Braised Veal Flank with Vegetables

Roasted Vegetables Mirepoix

Veal Patties Stuffed with Ham and Cheese

Veal and Pork Meat Loaf

Fresh Tomato Sauce

Veal and Pork Burgers with Paprika Sauce

Braised Breast of Veal

Veal Shanks with Asian-Style Vegetables

Fillet of Beef in Red Wine Sauce

◇ ◇

When I was the chef at Le Pavillon in Manhattan, filet mignon was our biggest seller, and we prepared it in nearly a dozen ways. To my taste, it is best embellished with a simple red wine sauce like the one here. The shallots add a touch of sweetness and the flavor of the beef comes through.

Yield: 4 servings.

4 filets mignons (about 6 ounces each)
Salt and freshly ground black pepper to taste
3 tablespoons butter
4 tablespoons minced shallots
1½ cups Beaujolais
1 small bay leaf
2 sprigs fresh thyme
1 teaspoon tomato paste

1. Season the fillets with salt and pepper to taste. Place 1 tablespoon of butter in a pan over medium-high heat. When the butter melts, add fillets and cook for 3 to 4 minutes a side, depending on desired doneness. Remove and keep warm.

2. Remove half the fat from the pan and add the shallots. Cook over low heat for about 2 minutes. Add wine, bay leaf, thyme, and tomato paste. Increase heat to medium-high, and stir. Reduce liquid to about ⅓ cup. Strain sauce through a fine sieve into a small saucepan. Bring to a boil, remove from heat, and stir in remaining butter.

3. Place fillets on warm serving plates. Divide the sauce over 4 portions. Sprinkle with freshly ground black pepper to taste.

Poached Fillet of Beef with Winter Vegetables

◇ ◇

Whenever I do this dish at a cooking demonstration, people are amazed that poached beef can be so flavorful. This technique goes back centuries, and it leaves the meat buttery tender. It is important to have a full-flavored beef stock for the sauce and to season it generously.

Yield: 4 servings.

4 large carrots, peeled and trimmed
1 large celery root, peeled
4 medium-size leeks, cleaned and trimmed (white parts only)
Salt to taste
8 cups fresh beef broth (see recipe page 128) or a quality
    commercial broth
Salt and freshly ground black pepper to taste
1 fillet of beef (24 ounces), trimmed of fat and gristle and cut into 8
    equal pieces
Dressing (see recipe page 127)
Sprig of fresh parsley, thyme, or coriander

1. Slice the carrots, celery root, and leeks into sections about 2 inches long and ¼ inch wide. The slices should be the same size so they cook evenly. Place the carrots, celery, and leeks in a pot and cover with the beef broth.

2. Bring the beef broth to a low simmer over medium-high heat. Add salt and pepper, the carrots, celery, and leeks, and simmer 20 to 30 minutes, or until tender. Do not let the broth boil, or it will lose its color.

3. Meanwhile, season the fillets on both sides with salt and pepper. Add to the simmering vegetables, and cook over low heat for 2 to 3 minutes. Do not let the liquid boil. The meat should be served medium-rare.

4. Divide the vegetables in a decorative pattern over 4 warm serving plates. Place the beef pieces next to the vegetables. Spoon over the dressing. Season if necessary. Garnish with fresh herbs. The broth can be served on the side in a consommé cup.

Dressing for Poached Beef

◇ ◇

In recent years, I have been experimenting with the briny and complex-tasting Vietnamese *nuoc mam*. It is a fermented fish sauce and adds a real zing to all kinds of dishes. *Nuoc mam* is widely available in Asian groceries.

Yield: About ⅓ cup.

¼ teaspoon finely chopped garlic
¾ teaspoon freshly squeezed lemon juice
½ teaspoon *nuoc mam*
½ teaspoon soy sauce
Freshly ground white pepper to taste
⅓ cup virgin olive oil
½ teaspoon whole coriander seeds

1. Combine the garlic, lemon juice, *nuoc mam*, soy sauce, and pepper in a mixing bowl.
2. Add the olive oil slowly, whisking briskly to emulsify the dressing.
3. Add the coriander seeds, and mix well.

Beef Broth

◆ ◆

Many of my recipes call for beef broth. Broths, or stocks, are the soul of fine French cooking. Beef broth is not difficult to make, and it freezes well. Put it in individual plastic containers or ice cube trays.

Yield: 3 quarts.

2 pounds lean beef chuck
3 pounds beef bones
10 quarts water
2 large carrots, scraped and quartered
1 large onion, peeled and pierced with 4 cloves
Greens of 2 leeks, washed and cut into large chunks
4 ribs celery, trimmed and quartered
2 bay leaves
4 sprigs fresh thyme
10 peppercorns

1. Place the beef and the bones in a deep pot. Cover with 5 quarts water and bring to a boil. Remove and discard water. Return beef and bones to the heat, and add 5 quarts water and the remaining ingredients. Bring to a boil.

2. Simmer 3½ to 4 hours. Skim off surface foam periodically. When cooked, strain and set aside.

◆

Leeks, which add flavor to all kinds of broths and sauces, originated in the Mediterranean area. A member of the onion and garlic family, they resemble giant scallions. You usually trim off the root end and use all but a little of the green part (which should be saved for stocks). Rinse well to remove sand.

Broiled Skirt Steak Cajun Style

◇ ◇

My friend Paul Prudhomme has taught me a lot about the Cajun technique of seasoning. Note how all of these dried spices interact to create a dynamic sensation on the palate, but without overpowering the steak.

Yield: 4 servings.

4 skirt steaks (½ pound each)
Salt to taste
2 tablespoons olive oil
1 teaspoon chili powder
½ teaspoon ground cumin
¼ teaspoon cayenne pepper
¼ teaspoon freshly ground black pepper
1 teaspoon dried thyme
2 tablespoons butter
2 tablespoons finely chopped parsley

1. A half hour before broiling or grilling, sprinkle the steaks with salt. In a bowl, blend well the oil, chili powder, cumin, cayenne, black pepper, and thyme. Brush this mixture on all sides of the steaks. Cover the steaks with plastic wrap but do not refrigerate.

2. Preheat the broiler to high or preheat the outdoor grill.

3. If broiling, arrange the steaks on a rack and place under the broiler about 6 inches from the source of heat. Broil for 4 minutes with the door partly open. Turn the steaks and continue broiling, leaving the door partly open. Broil about 4 minutes more, or until done.

4. If grilling, place the steaks over very hot coals and cover. Cook for 4 minutes. Turn the steaks, cover, and cook about 4 minutes more, or to the desired degree of doneness.

5. Transfer the steaks to a hot platter and dot with butter. Let them stand in a warm place for 5 minutes to redistribute the internal juices, which will accumulate as the steaks stand. Sprinkle with parsley and serve.

Skirt steak is one of my favorite cuts of meat, something I used to eat early in the morning with workers at the Paris food market Les Halles. The skirt steak goes by many names, including hanger steak, oyster steak, and butcher steak. The last arose because butchers traditionally kept these sinewy yet exceptionally juicy cuts for themselves.

If you know how to cook a skirt steak, it can be delicious, and less expensive than sirloins or fillets. The skirt steak comes from the pad of muscle that runs from the rib cage toward the loin. It is usually sold in sections of about 12 ounces each, and has a thin, silvery membrane that should be removed by the butcher.

Because skirt steak contains a lot of moisture, it should be cooked very quickly over high heat to sear. Let the steak reach room temperature before broiling or grilling.

When finished, let the steak sit for 5 minutes before carving, so the juices can settle. Cut the steak on a bias across the fibrous muscle, over a cutting board that can catch the runoff. Pour the juice back over the steak when serving, or use it in your sauce.

Seared Top Round of Beef with Fresh Horseradish Sauce

◇ ◇

Yield: 4 servings.

◆

I use fresh horseradish with boiled meats, cold cuts, and in certain sauces. Fresh horseradish bears no resemblance to the preserved version in jars. The bottled type is pickled either in vinegar or in a combination of vinegar and beet juice. To use fresh horseradish, which is milder than the commercial version, trim the brown skin with a paring knife. Run the pulp over the small holes of a kitchen grater. When buying fresh horseradish, look for stalks that are firm and unblemished. Roll leftover stalks in plastic wrap and refrigerate.

1½ pounds top round of beef, about 1½ inches thick
2 teaspoons black peppercorns, crushed
2 tablespoons vegetable oil
4 ounces fresh horseradish, grated
1 tablespoon white vinegar
4 tablespoons heavy cream
Salt and freshly ground black pepper to taste
2 tablespoons butter

1. Place the meat in a roasting pan, and coat it with the crushed peppercorns. Press the peppercorns to make them adhere. Drizzle the vegetable oil over the steak on both sides. Set aside.

2. Put the horseradish, vinegar, and cream in a saucepan over medium-high heat. Bring to a boil. Remove from heat. Add salt and pepper to taste, cover and set aside.

3. Transfer the steak to a pan, preferably cast iron, that has been heated over medium-high heat. Sear for 2 minutes and flip. Season with salt to taste. Sear for 2 minutes more and reduce heat to medium. Continue cooking, flipping occasionally, for 15 to 20 minutes, depending on degree of doneness desired. When done, transfer the meat to a warm dish, and place 2 tablespoons of butter over it. Let the meat rest for 5 minutes.

4. Slice the beef crosswise on a wide bias. Serve on warm plates moistened with the pan juices, along with the horseradish sauce.

Sautéed Medallions of Pork with Prunes

◇ ◇

Prunes and pork are a heavenly combination. I have added a bit of cumin here to counterbalance the sweet prunes. A quick sauce can be made by removing fat from the skillet in which the pork cooks and adding onions and garlic, then port, vinegar, tomato paste, and chicken broth.

Yield: 4 servings.

The term deglaze refers to pouring wine or stock into a pan that has just been used to cook meat or fish. The surface of the pan is then scraped with a spatula to release all of the flavor-packed particles clinging to the bottom.

8 slices boneless pork tenderloin, trimmed of excess fat (about 3 ounces each)
Salt and freshly ground black pepper to taste
2 teaspoons ground cumin
2 tablespoons vegetable oil
2 sprigs fresh rosemary or 1 teaspoon dried
½ cup finely chopped onions
1 teaspoon chopped garlic
¼ cup port
1 tablespoon red wine vinegar
1 tablespoon tomato paste
½ cup fresh or canned chicken broth
24 pitted prunes
2 tablespoons butter
2 tablespoons finely chopped fresh coriander or parsley

1. Place pork slices in a flat dish. Combine salt, pepper, and cumin, and blend well. Season pork slices with this mixture.

2. Heat the oil in a nonstick skillet large enough to hold the slices in one layer. When the oil is hot, add meat and rosemary and cook over medium heat for 5 minutes or until browned.

3. Turn the meat slices over and cook for 5 minutes more. Reduce heat and continue cooking for a few minutes longer or until done. Transfer meat to a warm platter.

4. Remove fat from skillet, add onions and garlic, and stir until wilted. Add port, vinegar, tomato paste, and chicken broth. Stir to dissolve brown particles that cling to the bottom. Add prunes, and cook until reduced by half.

5. Add pork slices and any accumulated juices. Add butter; bring to a simmer, shaking the pan to blend butter. Sprinkle with coriander or parsley. Serve immediately.

Pork Cutlets Parmigiana

◇ ◇

When I first came to this country, veal parmigiana was considered a classy dish. Years of dreary interpretations have made the term seem terribly outdated. Yet there is no reason why this traditional dish has to be stodgy, for the combination of ingredients is quite tasty.

The recipe below uses less expensive loin of pork, which is lean yet moist if cooked properly. Often veal parmigiana has a sauce that is thick, pulpy, and supercharged with oregano. In this updated version, the ingredients are cooked for a relatively short time, which yields a brighter and lighter sauce.

Yield: 4 servings.

8 thin slices lean boneless loin of pork (about 2 ounces each)
1 egg, beaten
3 tablespoons water
1 teaspoon ground cumin
2 teaspoons finely chopped fresh rosemary or 1 teaspoon dried
Salt and freshly ground black pepper to taste
1½ cups fine fresh bread crumbs
1 tablespoon olive oil
1 tablespoon finely chopped garlic
2 tablespoons finely chopped onion
2 cups canned crushed tomatoes
1 teaspoon chopped fresh oregano or ½ teaspoon dried, crumbled
4 tablespoons vegetable oil
4 thin slices mozzarella cheese, sliced in half
4 tablespoons grated Parmesan or Romano cheese

1. Place each piece of pork between sheets of plastic wrap and pound with a meat pounder or a mallet. (It should look like veal scaloppine.)

2. Place the egg, water, cumin, rosemary, and salt and pepper in a mixing bowl and beat well. Place the bread crumbs on a flat dish.

3. Dip the pork slices in the egg mixture to coat and then dip in the bread crumbs. Pat lightly with the flat side of a kitchen knife to help the crumbs to adhere.

4. Meanwhile, heat the olive oil in a saucepan and add the garlic and onion. Cook, stirring, for 1 minute. Do not brown. Add the tomatoes, oregano, salt, and pepper to taste. Bring to a boil and simmer for 5 minutes.

5. In a large nonstick skillet over medium heat, heat 2 tablespoons of vegetable oil and place as many cutlets as possible in one layer. When the slices are golden brown on one side, about 3 minutes, cook on the other side for 3 minutes. As the pieces are done, transfer them to a heated platter. Add more oil, if necessary, to the skillet, and continue cooking the rest of the slices in the same manner.

6. Preheat oven to 400 degrees.

7. Spoon a little sauce over the bottom of a baking dish large enough to hold the cutlets in one layer. Add the cutlets, spoon more tomato sauce on top, and cover each cutlet with mozzarella cheese. Add the remaining sauce. Sprinkle the Parmesan cheese over the dish and bake until piping hot and cheese is melted, about 10 minutes.

Escoffier's classic recipe for
steak au poivre notes, "If the
sauce is allowed to cook too long
after the eight peppercorns are
added, the dominating
flavor of the pepper will become
detrimental to the taste." With
today's asbestos palates, cooks
are making combustible sauces
that would wilt Escoffier's
mustache.

The steak au poivre here
has a substantial coating of
black pepper, but it is still only
moderately spicy.

The cut of meat normally
called a shell steak goes by
several other names, including
New York steak and club steak.
It comes from the short loin, one
of the most tender parts of beef.
Shell steak can be prepared in
many ways; one of my favorite
quick recipes is shell steak with a
snappy black pepper sauce.

Ask your butcher for 4
boneless shell steaks that weigh
about 8 ounces each after excess
fat is trimmed. The steaks should
be coated lightly and evenly
with the crushed pepper. When
they are cooked, remove them
from the pan, pour off any
excess fat, and make the sauce
with some butter, shallots, wine,
beef broth, tomato paste, and
thyme.

Sirloin Steak with Crushed Peppercorns

I like to serve this steak with a lusty side dish of sautéed wild mushrooms with shallots and garlic (see recipe page 135). This aromatic dish should be prepared as close to serving time as possible.

Yield: 4 servings.

4 boneless sirloin steaks, about 8 ounces each, with the excess fat removed
Salt to taste
4 tablespoons cracked peppercorns, white or black
1 tablespoon vegetable oil
2 tablespoons finely chopped shallots
½ cup dry red wine
½ cup beef broth, fresh or canned
2 teaspoons tomato paste
2 sprigs fresh thyme or 1 teaspoon dried
2 tablespoons butter
2 tablespoons finely chopped parsley

1. Sprinkle the steaks with salt.

2. Use a mallet, meat pounder, or bottom of a pan to crush the peppercorns, but not too fine. Sprinkle the peppercorns evenly over the steaks on both sides. Press down with your hands to help the peppercorns adhere to the meat.

3. Heat the oil in a cast-iron skillet large enough to hold the steaks in one layer. When the skillet is hot and almost smoking, add the steaks, cook about 3 minutes until browned, then turn. Cook about 2 to 3 minutes more for medium-rare. Remove to a warm platter.

4. Pour the fat out of the skillet, add the shallots and cook, stirring, until they are wilted. Do not brown. Add the wine, broth, tomato paste, and thyme. Reduce to half a cup. Add any liquid that may have accumulated around the steaks. Bring to a simmer. Remove from heat and swirl in the butter.

5. Remove the thyme sprigs and pour the sauce over the steaks. Sprinkle with parsley.

Sautéed Wild Mushrooms with Shallots and Garlic

◇ ◇

Yield: 4 servings.

1 pound fresh wild mushrooms, like chanterelles, morels, porcini,
    or any cultivated mushrooms of your choice
2 tablespoons olive oil
Salt and freshly ground black pepper to taste
1 tablespoon butter
2 tablespoons fine bread crumbs
1 tablespoon finely chopped shallots
1 teaspoon finely chopped garlic
2 tablespoons finely chopped parsley

1. Trim the mushrooms, wash them in cold water and drain well.

2. If the mushrooms are large, slice them or cut them in halves or quarters.

3. Heat a large, heavy skillet and add the olive oil. When it is very hot and almost smoking, add the mushrooms, salt, and pepper. Cook over high heat, shaking and tossing the skillet so that the mushrooms brown evenly. They should be almost mahogany in color.

4. Add the butter, and quickly sprinkle in the bread crumbs, shallots, and garlic, and toss well for 10 seconds. Add the parsley and serve immediately.

◇

I am amazed how supermarkets have changed in the past twenty years. Take mushrooms, for example. Supermarkets that once carried only white button mushrooms now display all kinds of seasonal wild mushrooms. Here is a sampler.

WHITE BUTTON. *Very mild-flavored and delicate.*

PORCINI. *Thick and sometimes quite large, these very flavorful mushrooms are well suited to grilling (brush with olive oil and season with salt and pepper). They have thick stalks and a red-tinted cap.*

OYSTER MUSHROOMS. *Both cultivated and wild, they have a smooth, creamy texture and relatively mild earthy flavor. Oyster mushrooms have small, fan-shaped caps.*

ENOKI. *Popular in Japanese cooking, these are the size of bean sprouts. You find them in soups, salads, and stir-frys. They have a lovely delicate flavor.*

CHANTERELLES. *A favorite of French chefs, they have a trumpet shape and orange-tan color. They are great in sauces, soups, and pasta.*

(continued on next page)

SHIITAKES. *These flat-domed cultivated mushrooms have a meaty texture and subtle flavor.*

MORELS. *Very distinctive-looking with a stout stem and beehivelike top, these intensely flavored mushrooms are used most often in sauces.*

PORTOBELLOS. *Another cultivated mushroom, portobellos have a potent, woodsy flavor and meaty texture. They can be used in sauce or grilled.*

◆

The most coveted cut of beef is the long strip of meat underneath the sirloin and short loin, called the tenderloin. The slightly tapered ends are used for tournedos and filets mignons, while the thick, buttery center is the most coveted cut of all. This is the section used for châteaubriand, a dish popular in my days as a chef, but rarely seen today. It is simply a grilled fillet served with château potatoes (potatoes cut into strips and cooked in butter) and accompanied by béarnaise sauce. It is sometimes more economical to purchase the whole fillet and freeze the end pieces for later use than to buy the premium-priced center cut.

Roast Fillet of Beef with Madeira-Mushroom Sauce

◇ ◇

The recipe here calls for a fillet of about 1¾ pounds. It should be well trimmed of fat and tied with kitchen twine every 2 to 3 inches. Tying the beef helps it maintain its shape and cook evenly. The fillet is seasoned well with salt and pepper and placed in a 450-degree oven for about 25 minutes (for rare).

The sauce is made on top of the stove with mushrooms, shallots, Madeira, beef stock, tomato paste, and butter. To get the most flavor from the mushrooms, it is essential to brown them well and extract all the moisture.

Yield: 4 to 6 servings.

1 center-cut fillet of beef, well trimmed and tied (about 1¾ pounds)
Salt and freshly ground black pepper to taste
1 tablespoon olive oil
1½ cups thinly sliced mushrooms (white button mushrooms or wild mushrooms of choice)
2 tablespoons finely chopped shallots
½ cup Madeira wine
½ cup fresh or canned beef stock
1 teaspoon tomato paste
2 tablespoons butter
1 tablespoon finely chopped parsley

1. Preheat the oven to 450 degrees.

2. Sprinkle the meat on all sides with salt and pepper. Rub with oil.

3. Place the beef in a shallow roasting pan; place the pan on the bottom rack of the oven. Roast for 25 minutes for rare, turning and basting once or twice as the beef roasts.

4. Transfer meat to a warm platter; cover loosely with foil to keep warm.

5. Pour off the fat from the pan. Place the pan on top of the stove and add the mushrooms, salt, and pepper. Cook, stirring, over medium heat until lightly browned. Add the shallots, and cook briefly, stirring. Add the wine and cook, stirring and scraping the bottom to dissolve the browned particles. Reduce by half and add the stock, tomato paste, and

any juices that have accumulated around the roast. Cook over high heat for about 5 minutes or until the sauce is reduced to ¾ cup. Swirl in the butter and add the parsley.

6. Transfer the meat to a warm serving platter. Slice the beef on the bias, and serve with the sauce.

Pork Tenderloin with Apples

◇ ◇

I grew up near apple and peach orchards, and my mother often used those fruits in cooking. This recipe here for pork tenderloin seasoned with cumin and served with apples is my interpretation of one of her dishes. It can be prepared in well under an hour. The quick sauce is made by combining apples and onions in the pan, then adding vinegar, chicken broth, honey, and tomato paste. The sweetness of the apples is counterbalanced nicely by the tart vinegar.

Yield: 4 servings.

2 boneless pork tenderloins (about 2 pounds total)

Salt and freshly ground black pepper to taste

2 medium-size Granny Smith apples

3 tablespoons flour

1 teaspoon ground cumin

1 tablespoon vegetable oil

4 tablespoons finely chopped onion

2 tablespoons red wine vinegar

½ cup fresh or canned chicken broth

2 tablespoons honey

1 tablespoon tomato paste

1. Sprinkle the pork tenderloins with salt and pepper. Cut each apple into quarters. Peel quarters and core them.

2. Blend the flour with the cumin and dredge the tenderloins in the mixture. Heat the oil over medium-high setting in a heavy skillet and add the tenderloins. Cook, turning the pieces so they brown evenly on all sides, about 5 minutes.

(Continued on next page)

◆

In recent years, I have cooked a lot more with pork, often as a substitute for expensive veal. As the pork industry tells you in its advertising campaign, pork tenderloin is an exceptionally healthful and versatile cut of meat. The tenderloin is the choice cut of any meat because it comes from muscle that gets very little exercise, in contrast to, say, the leg or shoulder.

Well-trimmed meat cut from the tenderloin of pork is less fatty than tenderloin of beef, and nearly as lean as skinless chicken breast. A 3½-ounce portion of trimmed pork has 4.8 grams of fat; beef tenderloin has 9.6 grams and chicken breast has 3.6. The same portion of pork has 166 calories, compared with 207 for beef and 165 for chicken. Of course, cooks must keep in mind that the leaner the meat, the more prone it is to drying out if overcooked.

◈

As much as I enjoy hamburgers made from freshly ground sirloin, it's fun to experiment with other types of burgers.

Lamb and veal are a fine combination. Ground pork works well, too. Or you can try combining meats, like lamb, beef, and pork in equal proportions.

The recipe here uses lean ground pork. Scallions, fresh coriander, ginger, soy sauce, garlic, bread crumbs, chicken broth, and hot sauce give it an Asian flavor.

An à la minute sauce can be made by combining orange juice, lemon juice, butter, soy sauce, and fresh coriander in a saucepan. If you have any other favorite fresh herbs on hand, they can be added.

3. Pour off fat from the pan and add apples and onion around the meat. Cook and stir for about 3 minutes. Add vinegar, broth, honey, and tomato paste. Bring to a simmer, stirring, and cover tightly. Cook about 20 minutes.

4. To serve, slice the meat on the bias and spoon some apple-onion sauce over each serving.

Pork Burgers Asian Style
◈ ◈

Yield: 4 servings.

1½ pounds lean ground pork
½ cup chopped onion
3 tablespoons freshly chopped coriander (optional)
1 tablespoon freshly grated ginger
2 tablespoons light soy sauce
2 teaspoons finely chopped garlic
½ cup fresh bread crumbs
¼ cup fresh or canned chicken broth
Salt and freshly ground black pepper to taste
¼ teaspoon Tabasco
1 teaspoon vegetable oil
½ cup fresh orange juice
2 tablespoons fresh lemon juice
2 tablespoons butter

1. Place the pork in a mixing bowl and add the onion, 2 tablespoons of the coriander, ginger, 1 tablespoon of the soy sauce, garlic, bread crumbs, broth, salt, pepper, and Tabasco. Blend well.

2. Divide the mixture into 8 equal portions and form them into hamburger shapes about 1 inch thick. Heat the oil in a large pan (cast iron is best) over medium heat. Add the burgers and cook for 7 to 8 minutes. Turn burgers and cook 8 minutes or until done. Transfer them to a serving plate and keep warm.

3. In a small saucepan, combine the orange and lemon juices and remaining soy sauce. Reduce by half. Add butter and remaining coriander. Blend well and pour over burgers.

Grilled Pork Medallions with Herb Marinade
◇ ◇

Yield: 4 servings.

8 boneless pork loin slices, trimmed of excess fat (about 3 ounces each)
2 tablespoons olive oil
3 tablespoons fresh lemon juice
4 tablespoons dry white wine or fresh chicken broth
1 tablespoon dry mustard
2 teaspoons finely chopped garlic
1 teaspoon ground cumin
1 tablespoon chopped fresh rosemary or 2 teaspoons dried
1 tablespoon chopped fresh sage or 2 teaspoons dried
Salt and freshly ground black pepper to taste
2 tablespoons butter

1. Preheat a charcoal or gas grill.

2. Place each pork loin slice on a flat surface and pound slightly with a mallet or meat pounder.

3. In a large, flat dish blend the oil, lemon juice, wine, mustard, garlic, cumin, rosemary, sage, salt, and pepper. Blend well.

4. Add pork slices and turn them in the marinade. Cover with foil and set aside until ready to cook.

5. Remove meat from the marinade, reserving the marinade. Cook on the grill for 3 to 4 minutes on one side. Turn and cook 2 to 3 minutes on the second side. Continue cooking, turning them often, for a total of 10 minutes.

6. Meanwhile, heat the marinade in a saucepan for 2 minutes until it begins to boil. Add the butter and blend well. Transfer pork slices to the marinade and cover with foil. Let the meat sit in a warm place for 5 minutes before serving.

Pork Chops with Sweet Peppers

◇ ◇

In summer, when my garden is colored with all kinds of sweet peppers, I like to make this quick and delicious dish.

Yield: 4 servings.

4 lean center-cut pork chops (about 1½ pounds)
Salt and freshly ground black pepper to taste
1 small red pepper
1 small green pepper
1 small yellow pepper
2 teaspoons vegetable oil
½ cup finely chopped onion
2 teaspoons minced garlic
1 teaspoon ground cumin
2 tablespoons red wine vinegar
½ cup fresh or canned chicken broth
½ cup canned Italian crushed tomatoes
1 bay leaf
1 teaspoon fresh rosemary or ½ teaspoon dried
4 tablespoons chopped Italian parsley

1. Sprinkle the chops with salt and pepper.

2. Core and seed the peppers. Cut the flesh into thin strips about 1½ inches long.

3. Heat the oil in a nonstick skillet large enough to hold the chops in one layer. When very hot, add the chops. Cook them until well browned, about 4 minutes on each side.

4. Pour off the fat from the skillet. Add the onion and garlic to the pan. Stir well and cook until the vegetables are wilted. Add the peppers and cumin and cook, stirring, for 1 minute. Add the vinegar, chicken broth, tomatoes, bay leaf, and rosemary. Cover and cook over low flame for 20 minutes.

5. Uncover and reduce the liquid if necessary to produce a thick sauce. Just before serving, sprinkle with chopped parsley.

Bitochki with Stroganoff Sauce (Russian Chicken Burgers)

◇ ◇

Yield: 4 servings.

1½ pounds skinless, boneless breast of chicken (see note below)
1 cup fine bread crumbs
⅓ cup heavy cream
Pinch of cayenne pepper
Salt to taste
Freshly ground black pepper to taste
⅛ teaspoon freshly grated nutmeg
2 tablespoons corn, peanut, or vegetable oil
Stroganoff sauce (see recipe page 142)
Dill sprigs for garnish

1. Cut away and discard any fat, tissues, and soft cartilage from chicken breasts. Cut chicken meat into 1-inch cubes. Put cubes into container of food processor or electric blender and blend to fairly fine purée. Do not overblend; the meat should be the least bit coarse for texture.

2. Spoon and scrape the meat into a mixing bowl. Blend ½ cup of bread crumbs and cream, and add to chicken. Add cayenne, salt, pepper, and nutmeg. Blend thoroughly with your hands.

3. Divide the mixture into 4 equal portions. Shape each portion into a ball. Roll each ball in the remaining bread crumbs to coat thoroughly.

4. Press down to flatten the balls into large patty or hamburger shape. Pat top and bottom and around the sides to make crumbs adhere.

5. Heat the oil in a large pan. Add patties (in batches if necessary) and cook until nicely browned on one side, 2 or 3 minutes. Turn and cook 10 minutes more. Serve with stroganoff sauce; garnish with dill sprigs.

NOTE: Lean veal free of connecting tissues and bone or a combination of chicken and veal may be used.

◇

The intermingling of French and Russian cuisines goes back at least to the time of Catherine the Great, when noble Russian families took great pride in employing French or Swiss chefs. Lavish feasts usually began with a zakuska, an array of tidbits including caviar, herring, pâtés, cold fish, vegetables, and breads—all accompanied by prodigious amounts of vodka.

One item that came into the French cooking lexicon from the zakuska is a highly seasoned meat patty called bitok. The Russian version, according to historical accounts, was zestily seasoned with paprika, pepper, cumin, and other spices. Of course, the variations are endless. The seasonings are nutmeg, cumin, black pepper, and paprika. You could experiment with favorite herbs and spices. These patties are lightly breaded and browned, which takes only about 6 minutes.

(continued on next page)

The classic Russian sauce for a bitok or bitochki is stroganoff, of which there are many versions. The one I prefer is made with sour cream and a touch of paprika and onion. You could make a lighter sauce by combining sautéed chopped onions with pepper-flavored vodka, vinegar, chicken broth, sour cream, and tomato.

Stroganoff Sauce
◇ ◇

Yield: About ½ cup.

1 tablespoon butter
¼ cup finely chopped onion
½ teaspoon paprika
1 tablespoon red wine vinegar
¼ teaspoon dried thyme
⅓ cup cream
¼ cup sour cream
Salt to taste
Freshly ground black pepper to taste

1. Melt butter in a saucepan and add onion and paprika. Cook, stirring, until onion is wilted.

2. Add vinegar and thyme and cook, stirring, until the vinegar is almost evaporated.

3. Add cream and cook until mixture is reduced by almost half. Add the sour cream, salt, and pepper and heat to just boiling. It is not essential, but the sauce is smoother if strained through a sieve, pressing to extract most of the liquid from the solids. Reheat briefly and serve.

Classic Boeuf à la Bourguignonne

◇ ◇

Being from Burgundy, I have a particular fondness for this classic French dish. It uses inexpensive shoulder of beef, which tenderizes over long cooking. This is a fine recipe for entertaining. Serve it with egg noodles.

Yield: 10 servings.

1 6-pound lean boneless shoulder of beef
¾ pound carrots, scraped and cut into 2-inch lengths
12 or more small white onions, peeled (about ¾ pound)
¾ pound white turnips, peeled and quartered (or cut into eighths,
    depending on size)
4 whole cloves garlic, peeled
1 sprig fresh rosemary or 1 teaspoon dried
2 sprigs fresh thyme or 1 teaspoon dried
2 bay leaves
6 sprigs fresh parsley
¼ teaspoon grated nutmeg
1 bottle red Burgundy wine or any dry red
Salt and freshly ground black pepper to taste
½ pound lean salt pork or bacon, cut into thin slices
4 tablespoons vegetable oil
⅓ cup flour
1 tablespoon butter
¾ pound button mushrooms, thinly sliced

1. Cut the meat into 1½-inch cubes.

2. Place the meat in a deep bowl and add the carrots, onions, turnips, garlic, rosemary, thyme, bay leaves, parsley, nutmeg, wine, salt, and pepper. Cover and let stand overnight in the refrigerator, stirring occasionally.

3. Preheat the oven to 375 degrees.

4. Drain the meat, vegetables, and herbs, but reserve the marinating liquid. Separate the meat and vegetables. Tie the herbs in cheesecloth.

5. Drop the salt pork slices into cold water and bring to a boil. Blanch for 3 minutes and drain. *(Continued on next page)*

6. In a heavy, wide, and deep casserole or Dutch oven, heat the vegetable oil and add the meat, salt pork, onions, and garlic. Stir and cook over high heat for about 15 minutes.

7. Sprinkle the meat with flour and stir thoroughly so that the flour coats the meat and other ingredients. Add the marinating liquid and stir. Add the herbs in cheesecloth, then the carrots. Cover and bring to a boil on top of the stove. As soon as the liquid boils, place the casserole in the preheated oven.

8. Heat the butter in a saucepan and add the sliced mushrooms. Cook until lightly browned. Add them to the stew. Cook about 45 minutes and add the turnips. Continue baking about 1 hour longer. The total baking time once the kettle is placed in the oven is 2 hours.

9. Remove the casserole and uncover. Carefully spoon off and discard all the fat from the top of the stew. Serve hot with potato purée (see recipe below).

Puréed Potatoes with Carrots and Onions

◇ ◇

I have found that there is no end to the vegetables that can be blended into a potato purée—celery, garlic, fennel, shallots, sweet peppers. You should use a potato ricer or hand masher, however, because food processors make the potatoes gummy.

Yield: 4 servings.

3 potatoes (about 1¼ pounds)
4 carrots, trimmed, scraped, and cut into 1-inch lengths
  (about 2 cups)
½ cup sliced onions
Salt to taste
2 tablespoons butter
Freshly ground black pepper to taste
⅛ teaspoon freshly grated nutmeg
½ cup hot milk
2 tablespoons chopped parsley (optional)

1. Peel the potatoes and cut them into eighths. Place the carrots, onions, and potatoes in a saucepan. Add cold water to cover and salt to taste. Bring to a boil and simmer about 20 minutes or until the vegetables are tender. Do not overcook or they will become mushy.

2. Put the vegetables through a food mill or potato ricer. Blend until smooth, but no more. Return to a clean saucepan.

3. Add more salt (if necessary), the butter, pepper, and nutmeg and blend well. Place over low heat and stir in the milk, then the parsley. Serve.

Barbecued Medallions of Pork

◇ ◇

This recipe for broiled medallions of marinated pork loin requires only 10 minutes' cooking time. The marinade is made with cider vinegar, olive oil (or vegetable oil), chili powder, cumin, dry mustard, and black pepper. This is a fairly spicy combination, so a teaspoon of honey is added to tame the heat.

A well-trimmed pork loin does not need much marinating. In fact, too much will break down the protein and leave it mushy, so let it sit for only about 15 minutes. That is just enough time for the flavors to penetrate.

Yield: 4 servings.

Salt to taste
8 boneless pork loin slices, trimmed of fat (about 3 ounces each)
2 tablespoons olive or vegetable oil
¼ cup cider vinegar
2 teaspoons finely chopped garlic
1 tablespoon chili powder
1 teaspoon ground cumin
1 teaspoon dry mustard
1 teaspoon honey
½ teaspoon freshly ground black pepper

1. Preheat a charcoal grill or oven broiler.

2. Sprinkle salt over medallions of pork. Combine the remaining ingredients in a mixing bowl and blend well. Place pork in the marinade and coat well on both sides. Cover with plastic wrap and let stand in a cool place (not in the refrigerator) for 15 minutes.

3. Place medallions on the heated grill or on the tray of the oven broiler. Cook about 5 minutes on one side, basting often. Turn and continue cooking, basting often, on second side for about 5 minutes more or until done.

Brochettes of Pork with Sage

◇ ◇

In the recipe below for brochettes of pork, the meat is cubed and marinated in olive oil, red wine vinegar, garlic, sage (fresh or dry), turmeric, cumin, salt, and hot pepper. I have found that cumin reacts nicely with sage. Turmeric also gives the pork an appetizing caramel color.

Yield: 4 servings.

1¼ pounds lean loin of pork
2 tablespoons olive oil
1 tablespoon red wine vinegar
1 teaspoon finely chopped garlic
2 tablespoons chopped fresh sage or 2 teaspoons dried
1 teaspoon turmeric
1 teaspoon cumin
¼ teaspoon hot red pepper flakes
Salt and freshly ground black pepper to taste

1. Preheat the broiler or prepare a charcoal fire.

2. Cut the pork into 1-inch cubes and place in a mixing bowl. Add the remaining ingredients and stir until well mixed. Cover with plastic wrap and marinate for at least 15 minutes.

3. Arrange the pork cubes on 4 skewers. If wooden skewers are used, it is best to soak them first for half an hour in cold water and cover the tips with foil to prevent burning.

4. Place the meat on a broiler rack about 6 to 8 inches from the source of the heat and cook, turning as necessary, until done, 20 minutes or longer.

5. If grilling, prepare a charcoal fire. When the coals and grill are properly hot, brush the grill lightly with oil. Arrange the skewered pork on the grill and cook, turning as necessary, until done, 20 minutes or longer.

VARIATION: You can add cut-up vegetables to the skewers: sweet peppers, small onions, leeks, eggplant, and more.

◇

Sage is one of those herbs that practically grows before your eyes, and if you don't watch out, it will take over a large chunk of your garden. Fresh sage has a delightful woodsy aroma with a touch of citric sharpness that interacts particularly well with mild-flavored meats like veal, chicken, and pork. In French cuisine, especially in Provence, sage is found in many stews, soups, and roasts.

In northern Italian cooking, sage is a prominent ingredient in many veal dishes; in Tuscany, pane alla salvia is flavored with sage and sautéed in olive oil. In the south, focaccia, the herbed flatbread, often has a good dose of it.

Dried sage is much stronger than fresh, so it is crucial that you scale down when using it.

Veal Chops with Raspberry Vinegar

◇ ◇

Just a generation ago, vinegar was considered little more than a modest kitchen staple, like baking powder or salt—and just about as interesting. No one really knew much about it except that it came in two colors, red and white, and when mixed with oil, it made a basic salad dressing.

The acidity of vinegar, when used judiciously, adds a sharp, clean dimension to sauces. Flavored vinegars can be sublime, for they penetrate ingredients during the marination process, adding a deep, lingering nuance.

While we now have dozens of vinegars to choose from in supermarkets and specialty stores, some of the flavored varieties, especially those made with herbs, are exceedingly expensive considering how easy they are to make. I make my own tarragon vinegar, for example, by combining fresh tarragon, both the stem and leaves, with white wine or cider vinegar. A raspberry vinegar is made by combining roughly a quart of berries with a quart of vinegar and letting it stand for several days. If you want the vinegar to be clean, strain well—otherwise just leave the berries to settle in the bottom of the bottle.

Here is a dish I came up with one evening when the only vinegar I had in the house was flavored with raspberries. This unlikely sounding but surprisingly harmonious combination is a delight. A sautéed veal chop is finished in a broth tinged with raspberry vinegar. Be cautious, though, for the flavor of fruit vinegar intensifies in the cooking process.

Yield: 4 servings.

4 loin veal chops (about ½ pound each)
Salt and freshly ground black pepper
2 tablespoons butter
4 whole cloves garlic, peeled
1 large bay leaf
4 sprigs fresh thyme or 1 teaspoon dried
3 tablespoons raspberry vinegar
½ cup fresh or canned chicken broth
2 tablespoons coarsely chopped fresh chervil or parsley

1. Sprinkle the chops on both sides with salt and pepper.

2. Heat the butter in a heavy skillet and add the chops. Brown on both sides over medium-high setting, turning once or twice. They should be cooked about 5 minutes on each side.

3. Add the garlic, bay leaf, and thyme. Cook about 3 minutes. Pour the vinegar around the chops. Add the broth. Cover closely and simmer for 15 minutes, or until the meat is tender.

4. Remove the garlic cloves and crush or mash them into a paste. Return the garlic to the pan and blend with the sauce. Cover tightly and cook for 5 minutes more. Remove the thyme and bay leaf. Sprinkle with the chervil or parsley and serve.

Crown Roast of Pork with Spicy Rice Stuffing
◇ ◇

I like to serve this regal-looking dish when entertaining. Buy the pork trimmed and ready for roasting. The spicy rice stuffing adds a little zing.

Yield: 12 to 14 servings.

The Stuffing

1 cup converted rice (yields 2½ cups cooked rice)
2 tablespoons unsalted butter
¾ cup coarsely chopped onions
1 tablespoon chopped garlic
½ pound beef or pork sausage meat
1 sweet red pepper, diced
1 cup coarsely chopped fennel
¼ teaspoon ground cumin
⅛ teaspoon ground cloves
1 whole egg, beaten
½ cup chopped parsley
¾ cup pistachio nuts (pretoasted or toasted in a dry skillet)
    (optional)
Salt and freshly ground black pepper to taste

1. Bring 4 cups of lightly salted water to a boil. Add rice, return to a boil while stirring, and simmer 17 minutes. Stir occasionally. Drain well and set aside.

2. In a large saucepan over medium heat, melt butter and add onions and garlic. Stir 5 minutes. Add sausage meat and break it up with a fork. Add red pepper, fennel, cumin, and cloves. Cook about 10 minutes while stirring.

3. Preheat oven to 375 degrees.

4. In a large mixing bowl, combine rice with sausage mixture. Add egg, parsley, pistachio nuts, salt, and pepper. Blend well.

(Continued on next page)

The Pork

> 8-pound crown roast of pork, trimmed by a butcher
> Vegetable oil for coating roast
> Salt and freshly ground black pepper to taste
> 1 tablespoon dried rosemary
> 2 white onions, chopped
> 1½ cups chicken stock
> ½ cup water

1. Cut a circle of aluminum foil roughly the shape of the crown roast and place in center of roasting pan. Put the pork on it. Fill inside of roast with stuffing, packing it firmly as you go. The filling should reach the top; smooth it over with a spatula and cover stuffing (but not meat) with aluminum foil.

2. Coat meat with vegetable oil and dust lightly with salt; season generously with pepper. Press dried rosemary sprigs around the exterior. Scatter onions around roast and cook about 2 hours in the preheated oven. Baste occasionally.

3. Transfer pork to a serving platter, covering loosely with aluminum foil, and keep warm. Pour off fat from roasting pan and remove circular piece of foil from pan. Leave onions in pan and place pan over medium-high flame. Add chicken stock and water. Bring to a boil while scraping bottom of pan to remove clinging particles. Simmer 5 minutes. Strain the liquid and serve it as gravy with pork.

Ham Steaks with Madeira Sauce
◇ ◇

Some foods have natural affinities for one another, including this marriage of ham steaks and Madeira wine. There is something about the faint saltiness of ham that is enhanced by the pleasant sweetness of the wine.

Ham in a Madeira wine sauce is an uncommonly easy dish to prepare. As a main course, it can be made even more substantial with the addition of quartered, peeled apples and a touch of mustard.

The recipe involves simply cooking ham steaks in a small amount of butter and scattering the apple quarters all around with Madeira wine sprinkled over all. The meat is removed, a bit of tomato paste and mustard is added to the sauce, and the sauce, reduced for a brief moment, is poured over all. The total cooking time is about 10 minutes or less.

Yield: 4 servings.

2 ham steaks (about 1¾ pounds total weight)
2 apples, preferably McIntosh (about 1 pound total weight)
3 tablespoons butter
2 tablespoons finely chopped shallots
4 tablespoons Madeira wine
1 teaspoon tomato paste
1 teaspoon Dijon-style mustard

1. Remove any excess fat from each ham steak.
2. Cut the apples into quarters. Cut away and discard the cores. Peel the quarters.
3. Use 2 skillets, preferably nonstick, each large enough to hold a ham piece. Heat 1 tablespoon of butter in each skillet. Add 1 tablespoon of shallots to each skillet. Cook briefly, stirring, and add 1 ham steak to each skillet.
4. Arrange 1 quartered apple around each steak. Spoon half the Madeira over the apples in each skillet. Cover closely and cook 5 minutes. Transfer the ham steaks to a hot platter and arrange the partly cooked apples around or over the pieces of meat.
5. Pour the cooking liquid from one skillet into the other skillet. Add the remaining 2 tablespoons of wine, the tomato paste, and mustard, and stir to blend. Bring to a simmer, swirl in the remaining 1 tablespoon butter and pour the sauce over the ham and apples.

Double Veal Chops
with Braised Spring Vegetables
◇ ◇

Sometimes I like to splurge and buy thick, juicy veal chops, which can be prepared in many ways. This seasonal dish, colored with spring vegetables, is good for entertaining.

Yield: 4 servings.

4 tablespoons olive oil
2 tablespoons butter
½ pound lean veal trimmings for stew, cubed
2 thick loin veal chops (1½ pounds each)
10 garlic cloves, unpeeled
Salt and freshly ground black pepper to taste
1½ cups homemade or canned chicken broth
4 ounces pancetta or lean bacon, cut into 4 pieces
1 pound small new potatoes, halved
4 large carrots, peeled and trimmed, halved on a bias
    (about ½ pound)
20 pearl onions, peeled
4 scallions, cleaned and trimmed
8 asparagus spears, peeled and trimmed
1 bunch broccoli rape, hard stems removed

1. In a heavy skillet large enough to hold the veal chops in one layer, heat 2 tablespoons of olive oil and 1 tablespoon butter over medium-high setting. Add the veal trimmings. Brown for 5 minutes, stirring. Add the veal chops and garlic. Season well with salt and pepper. Cook the veal chops for about 10 minutes a side, moving the chops around the pan periodically. Remove the veal chops, leaving the garlic and the veal trimmings in the pan. Drain all fat from the skillet.

2. Add the chicken broth to the pan. Deglaze over high heat, reducing by half. Check seasonings. Return the veal chops to the pan with their accumulated juices. Remove from the heat and keep warm in an oven set on very low.

3. Meanwhile, in a large skillet, preferably cast iron, brown the pancetta over medium heat in 2 tablespoons olive oil. Cook for 2 minutes, stirring, and add the potatoes, carrots, onions, and scallions. Reduce heat to medium-low. Cook, stirring, for 30 minutes.

4. Bring 4 cups of salted water to a boil. Add the asparagus and broccoli rape. Return to a boil and cook for 1 minute. Drain well.

5. Add remaining butter to the vegetable skillet. Add the drained green vegetables. Check for seasonings.

6. Slice the veal thin off the bones and serve with vegetables and reduced pan juices. Include garlic cloves if desired.

Braised Veal Flank with Vegetables
◇ ◇

Yield: 8 servings.

6 pounds veal flank, trimmed and cut into strips 6 inches long and
    2 inches wide
    (or boneless breast of veal cut the same way); there should be
    8 strips
Flour for dredging veal
Salt and freshly ground black pepper to taste
⅓ cup vegetable oil
1 cup sliced onions
1 cup chopped leek whites
¾ cup diced carrots
2 ribs celery, sliced
2 cloves garlic, minced
2 cups dry white wine
1 cup canned crushed tomatoes
4 sprigs thyme
1 bay leaf
3 whole cloves

1. Preheat oven to 375 degrees.

2. Trim the veal strips to square off the edges. Roll each piece and tie with twine. Dredge the veal rolls lightly in flour seasoned with salt and pepper.

3. In an ovenproof skillet large enough to hold all the veal rounds in one layer, heat the oil over medium-high flame and sear the veal on all

(Continued on next page)

sides, about 15 minutes. Add the onions, leeks, carrots, celery, and garlic. Cook for another 5 minutes. When the meat is browned, drain off the fat.

4. Add the white wine; bring to a boil. Add the tomatoes, thyme, bay leaf, cloves, and 4 cups of water. Bring to a boil. Remove from the heat and place in the oven, covered. Cook for 1½ hours. Remove the cover, reduce oven to 350 degrees, and cook for another 30 minutes. Remove bay leaf and thyme and serve with roasted vegetables *mirepoix* (see recipe below) and Savoy cabbage.

Roasted Vegetables Mirepoix
◇ ◇

A *mirepoix* is a French term that refers to sautéeing onions, carrots, and celery in butter. It is the base of many sauces and soups.

Yield: 8 servings.

2 to 3 tablespoons vegetable oil
2 cups celery, sliced into ¼-inch pieces on the bias
2 cups carrots, peeled and sliced into ¼-inch pieces on the bias
2 cups onions, peeled and sliced into ¼-inch pieces on the bias
1 tablespoon butter
Salt and freshly ground black pepper to taste

1. In a nonstick sauté pan, heat 1 tablespoon of the oil, and cook the celery over medium-high heat, stirring, until it browns lightly. Remove the celery with a slotted spoon.

2. Add the carrots to the same pan along with a little more oil if necessary. Cook over medium heat until they brown lightly. Remove the carrots with a slotted spoon.

3. Add the onions to the same skillet with more oil if necessary. Brown lightly over medium heat for 4 minutes, or until the carrots are soft; add the celery and carrots. Cook for another 4 minutes. Remove to paper towels with a slotted spoon. Drain well.

4. Return the vegetables to the pan with the butter. Toss over medium heat, season with salt and pepper, and keep warm.

Veal Patties Stuffed with Ham and Cheese

◇ ◇

My grandchildren love this dish, crispy outside and oozing with cheese. The flavor-packed recipe below has many ingredients, but it is easy and quick to make. Moreover, you can assemble the meat mixture in advance and refrigerate it.

Yield: Serves 4.

1¼ pounds ground lean veal or chicken or turkey
2 tablespoons finely grated onion
½ cup fine fresh bread crumbs
4 tablespoons chopped fresh parsley
½ teaspoon chopped garlic
2 teaspoons finely chopped fresh rosemary or 1 teaspoon dried
¼ cup milk
¼ teaspoon freshly grated nutmeg
Salt and freshly ground black pepper to taste
8 squares thinly sliced country ham or prosciutto, each about 1½ inches square
8 thin slices of Gruyère or Swiss cheese, each about 1½ inches square
1 tablespoon corn or vegetable oil
4 tablespoons butter
2 small plum tomatoes, cored and cut into small cubes
2 tablespoons fresh lemon juice

1. In a bowl, mix the ground veal, onion, bread crumbs, parsley, garlic, rosemary, milk, nutmeg, salt and pepper to taste. Blend well.

2. Divide the mixture into 8 portions of equal weight. Shape each portion into a thin patty about 3 inches across.

3. Arrange one layer of ham in the center of each of 4 of the patties. Cover the ham with a square of cheese, then another slice of ham, and then the remaining slice of cheese. Leave a clear margin of meat around the ham and cheese. Cover each ham-and-cheese patty with one of the remaining plain patties. Seal the edges firmly.

4. Using a nonstick skillet large enough to hold the patties in one layer, heat the oil. When hot, add the veal patties. Cook over medium

(Continued on next page)

heat on one side, covered, until lightly browned, about 3 minutes, and then turn. Continue cooking and turning the patties carefully so they will cook evenly, about 10 minutes. Transfer to a warm platter. Keep warm.

5. Wipe out skillet and add butter, swirling until it is hazelnut brown. Add tomatoes, and salt and pepper. Cook over high heat for 1 minute. Add lemon juice and blend well. Pour mixture over patties and serve immediately.

Veal and Pork Meat Loaf
◇ ◇

I have been making meat terrines for decades, so to my taste there is no reason why American meat loaf has to be boring. Combining various ground meats and spices turns a prosaic dish into a dynamic one. Combining meats offers a more interesting texture and flavor. My experimentation reveals that beef gives the loaf texture, pork gives it flavor, and the veal adds subtlety. Lamb is commonly used in Middle Eastern and Indian dishes. Any meat you use should be relatively lean, although a little fat is needed to keep the loaf moist.

In the recipe here, finely chopped mushrooms are added for flavor. Home cooks often overseason meat loaf, so be careful. A quick, fresh tomato sauce is a nice touch. If you cannot find some good-looking ripe tomatoes, use canned ones.

Yield: 6 servings.

1 tablespoon butter
4 tablespoons finely chopped onion
1 teaspoon finely chopped garlic
¼ pound mushrooms, finely chopped
¾ pound ground lean veal
¾ pound ground lean pork
Salt and freshly ground black pepper to taste
½ cup fresh bread crumbs
½ cup crushed fresh or canned tomatoes
1 egg
¼ teaspoon freshly grated nutmeg
¼ teaspoon ground cumin

1. Preheat oven to 450 degrees.

2. Melt butter in a pan. When hot, add onion, garlic, and mushrooms. Cook, stirring, over medium heat, for 8 minutes. Let cool.

3. Place veal and pork in a mixing bowl and add onion-and-mushroom mixture. Add remaining ingredients and blend well.

4. Spoon mixture into a loaf pan measuring 9 by 5 by 3 inches. Place the pan in a larger heatproof dish and pour boiling water around the pan.

5. Cover lightly with foil and bake for 45 minutes. For the last 15 minutes, remove the foil and bake uncovered. Serve with fresh tomato sauce (see recipe below) or cold with a salad.

Fresh Tomato Sauce
◇ ◇

Yield: About 2 cups.

1½ pounds fresh ripe tomatoes or 3 cups canned crushed tomatoes
2 tablespoons olive oil
4 tablespoons finely chopped onion
1 tablespoon finely chopped garlic
1 tablespoon chopped fresh rosemary or 1 teaspoon dried
⅛ teaspoon hot red pepper flakes
Salt and freshly ground black pepper to taste

1. If fresh tomatoes are used, cut out and discard the core and cut the flesh into ¾-inch cubes. There should be about 3½ cups.

2. Heat oil in a saucepan and add the onion and garlic. Cook briefly, stirring. Do not brown the garlic. Add tomatoes. Bring to a boil and add rosemary, pepper flakes, salt, and pepper. Simmer, stirring occasionally, for 10 minutes.

3. Place mixture into a food processor or blender and blend thoroughly. Pour the sauce through a sieve or strainer, discarding any solids that will not pass through. There should be about 2 cups. Return to the saucepan and bring to a simmer.

Veal and Pork Burgers with Paprika Sauce

◇ ◇

I like to combine several meats in burgers, meat loaves, and terrines, which gives them more complex flavors and different textures. This combination works particularly well.

Yield: 4 servings.

1 pound lean ground veal
½ pound lean ground pork
1 tablespoon olive oil
1 cup finely chopped onions
¼ teaspoon paprika
1½ cups fresh bread crumbs
1 cup fresh or canned chicken broth
⅛ teaspoon freshly grated nutmeg
¼ teaspoon ground cumin
Salt and freshly ground black pepper to taste
1 tablespoon corn or vegetable oil
1 tablespoon butter
2 teaspoons pepper-flavored vodka (optional)
1 tablespoon red wine vinegar
¼ cup sour cream
2 teaspoons tomato paste
1 tablespoon finely chopped fresh dill
1 tablespoon lemon juice

1. Place the veal and pork in a mixing bowl.

2. Heat the olive oil in a small saucepan and add ¾ cup chopped onion and the paprika. Cook over medium heat, stirring often, about 3 minutes without browning. Let cool.

3. Combine in a bowl the ground meats, cooked onions, 1 cup of the bread crumbs, ½ cup of chicken broth, nutmeg, cumin, salt and pepper. Blend well with your hands.

4. Divide the mixture into 8 portions of equal weight. Shape each portion into a ball. Flatten each into a patty and coat the patties with the remaining ½ cup bread crumbs.

5. Heat the corn oil in a nonstick skillet large enough to hold the patties in one layer. Cook the patties until lightly browned on one side, about 3 minutes. Turn and cook about 3 minutes on the second side or until done. Transfer the patties to a warm platter and keep them warm.

6. Meanwhile, heat a smaller skillet and add the butter and the remaining ¼ cup chopped onions. Cook, stirring, over medium heat until the onions wilt. Add the vodka, vinegar, remaining ½ cup broth, and bring to a boil. Add the sour cream and tomato paste. Cook about 2 minutes. Add the dill and lemon juice, blend well with a wire whisk, and pour over the patties. Serve immediately.

Braised Breast of Veal

◇ ◇

I have noticed that a classic bistro dish, *tendrons de veau braisés* (braised veal breast), is reappearing in homey French bistros around this country. It is made from inexpensive breast of veal that is browned well, then braised for about 2 hours along with onions, celery, garlic, and carrots. The meat is cooked on the bone, lending extra flavor.

Yield: 6 to 10 servings.

1 7-pound breast of veal (have the butcher cut it to make 6 strips of
    equal width)
½ cup flour
Salt and freshly ground black pepper to taste
¼ cup vegetable oil
½ cup chopped onions
1 tablespoon chopped celery
1 tablespoon chopped garlic
1 cup diced carrots
1 cup dry white wine
1 bay leaf
4 sprigs fresh thyme or 1 teaspoon dried
3 cups chicken stock
½ cup canned crushed tomatoes

1. Halve each of the veal strips crosswise.
2. Season the flour with salt and pepper and dredge the breast sections.

(Continued on next page)

3. Heat the oil in a large pan (cast iron is best) over a medium flame. Add the veal pieces, turning often to brown all over. This should take about 10 minutes.

4. Drain the fat from the skillet and add the onions, celery, garlic, and carrots. Cook, stirring, for 2 minutes. Add the wine, bay leaf, thyme, chicken stock, and tomatoes. Stir, bringing to a boil. Cover, reduce heat, and simmer for 2 hours, or until the meat is well cooked. Taste for seasonings.

5. Remove the excess fat if necessary. Remove the bay leaf. Serve with buttered noodles, rice, or mashed potatoes.

Veal Shanks with Asian-Style Vegetables
◇ ◇

To my taste, veal shank on the bone is one of the most succulent cuts of meat. Slow cooking leaves the meat falling off the bone.

Yield: 6 servings.

4 large veal shanks (roughly 4 pounds total)
4 cloves garlic, each cut into 3 strips
Freshly ground black pepper to taste
4 cups fresh or canned chicken broth
2 cups water
¼ cup soy sauce
2 whole cloves
1 teaspoon aniseed
1 cup dry white wine
1½ cups scallions, cut into 1-inch lengths
5 cups coarsely chopped kale
½ head Chinese cabbage, coarsely chopped (about 5 cups)
12 baby carrots, peeled
½ cup chopped fresh coriander (optional)
1½ cups bean sprouts

1. Make small incisions around the veal shanks and insert the strips of garlic. Rub the shanks with pepper.

2. In a large pot, combine the shanks, broth, water, soy sauce, cloves, aniseed, and wine. Bring to a boil, cover, and simmer for 1½ hours, or until the veal is tender. Add the scallions, kale, Chinese cabbage, and carrots. Cook for 15 minutes. Add the coriander and bean sprouts. Cook for 5 minutes. Taste for seasonings and serve.

Lamb

◇ ◇ ◇

Marinated Brochettes of Lamb with Honey

Roasted Lamb Chops with Potatoes and Onions

Lamb Chili with Lentils

Lamb Patties with Mushroom Sauce

Marinated Grilled Butterflied Leg of Lamb

Lamb Chops Provençal

Lamb Patties Moroccan Style with Harissa Sauce

Harissa Sauce

Couscous with Yellow Squash

Medallions of Lamb with Shallot Sauce

Lentils with Balsamic Vinegar

Lamb Stew

Lamb Burgers with Feta Cheese

Lamb Shanks with Lentils

Stuffed Saddle of Lamb with Pan Gravy

Spicy Lamb Loaf

Medallions of Lamb with Leek-and-Tarragon Sauce

Lamb and White Beans with Vegetables

Grilled Lamb Chops with Cabernet-and-Caper Butter

Cabernet-and-Caper Butter Sauce

Roasted Rack of Lamb with Herbs

Grilled Rack of Lamb with Rosemary-Lemon Sauce

Curried Lamb Chops

Marinated Brochettes of Lamb with Honey
◇ ◇

Yield: *4 servings.*

1½ pounds skinless, boneless loin or leg of lamb

4 tablespoons fresh lemon juice

4 tablespoons olive oil

½ cup dry red wine

⅓ cup honey

1 tablespoon chopped fresh rosemary or 2 teaspoons dried

1 tablespoon finely chopped garlic

2 teaspoons ground cumin

Salt and freshly ground pepper to taste

2 large red peppers, cored, seeded, and cut into 16 2-inch squares

2 large white onions, cut into 16 2-inch squares

1 medium-size eggplant, cut into 16 2-inch squares, ½ inch thick

8 tablespoons coarsely chopped fresh coriander or parsley

1. Cut the lamb into sixteen 2-inch cubes.

2. Combine the lamb with lemon juice, olive oil, wine, honey, rosemary, garlic, cumin, salt, and pepper. Blend well, cover with plastic wrap, and marinate for 1 hour.

3. Preheat the oven broiler or a charcoal grill. If wooden skewers are used, soak them in cold water until ready to use.

4. Drain the meat, reserving the marinade, and arrange the meat on 4 skewers, alternating with red pepper, onion, and eggplant squares.

5. Broil under high heat—about 4 minutes on each side for rare—while brushing with the reserved marinade.

NOTE: This recipe also works well with pork or chicken.

◇

When making marinades, I like to experiment with different flavors and various combinations of oils, vinegars, fruits, and herbs. Vinegar and oil, the common marinade base, can be brightened with lemon or lime, salted with soy sauce, thickened with mustard, and flavored with all kinds of fresh herbs. We recommend marination time of about 1 or 2 hours for most meats because the acid in marinades can make the meat mushy on the outside.

When I was a young cook, part of my duties involved "breaking down," or butchering, beef and lamb on the hoof. The art of butchering is just about gone today, and restaurants now receive the meat in vacuum-packed plastic packages. Still, it behooves the home cook to be familiar with different cuts of meat, in this case, lamb.

LEG. *This is probably the most popular cut of lamb. It comes two ways: the American style (with the shank removed) and the French style (with the shank bone). If you want to grill the leg of lamb, you can ask for it deboned and butterflied (flattened so it sits evenly on the grill).*

RIB. *Among the most tender cuts of lamb, ribs can be cut individually or presented connected (a crown roast). These ribs are best broiled, sautéed, or roasted.*

SHOULDER. *Not as tender as chops or the leg, the shoulder is best long cooked, usually braised. You can buy it with or without the bone—without is easier to slice and serve. It is extremely flavorful.*

Roasted Lamb Chops with Potatoes and Onions

Côtes d'agneau Champvallon, a homey bistro-style dish of lamb, potatoes, and onions, was one of the house specials I cooked at the old Le Pavillon in Manhattan in the 1950s. The restaurant was a particular favorite of steady customers like J. Edgar Hoover and Cole Porter. Sometimes, they didn't even look at the menu and simply asked the captain if *Champvallon* was available.

It is indeed a wonderful assemblage, and easy to make. In the old days, many cooks made it with mutton chops. This version calls for more delicate rib lamb chops.

Yield: 6 servings.

12 rib lamb chops (about 2½ pounds total weight)
Salt and freshly ground pepper to taste
6 medium-sized Idaho or Washington potatoes (about 2¼ pounds)
2 medium-sized white onions (about ½ pound), peeled
2 tablespoons butter
2 garlic cloves, crushed
1½ cups fresh or canned chicken broth
2 sprigs fresh thyme or 1 teaspoon dried
1 bay leaf

1. Preheat oven to 375 degrees.
2. Trim off all the fat from the chops. Sprinkle the chops with salt and pepper.
3. Peel the potatoes and cut them into slices about ⅛ inch thick. There should be about 4 to 5 cups. Drop the slices immediately in cold water to avoid discoloration. Drain.
4. Cut the onions in half and slice them as thin as possible. There should be about 2½ cups. Set aside.
5. Heat the butter in a heavy pan and brown the chops lightly on one side. Do not cook through. Turn them and cook until they are lightly browned on the other side.
6. Place all the lamb chops in a large baking dish or casserole. Scatter onions over the chops and add the crushed garlic in the center. Lay the sliced potatoes over the chops evenly. Sprinkle with salt and pepper to taste, pour the chicken broth over everything and add the thyme and bay leaf. Cover with aluminum foil.

7. Bring the liquid to a boil on top of the stove and place the dish on the bottom rack of the oven. Bake about 20 minutes, remove the foil and continue cooking, basting often, for 50 minutes or 1 hour or until the chops are fork tender and the potatoes are lightly browned. If you want the potatoes browned further, place the dish under the broiler for a minute or so.

Lamb Chili with Lentils
◇ ◇

Lamb is perhaps my favorite meat. I substitute it for beef and pork in many recipes, such as this one for chili.

Yield: 8 servings or more.

1 tablespoon olive oil
2 pounds lean lamb, preferably from the leg, cut into ¼-inch cubes
2 cups finely chopped onions
2 tablespoons finely chopped garlic
1 cup finely chopped celery
1 cup finely chopped sweet red pepper
1 jalapeño pepper, cored, seeded, and chopped fine
1 teaspoon ground cumin
3 tablespoons chili powder
1 teaspoon crumbled fresh oregano or 2 teaspoons dried
2 bay leaves
3 cups canned crushed tomatoes
1 cup fresh or canned chicken broth
Salt and freshly ground pepper to taste
1 cup green lentils
Sour cream for garnishing
Limes for garnishing

1. Heat the oil in a large, heavy pot and add the meat. Cook over medium-high heat for 3 or 4 minutes, stirring with a large wooden spoon until it is browned all over.

2. Add the onions, garlic, celery, red pepper, jalapeño pepper, cumin, and chili powder. Stir to blend well. Cook until the onions are translucent.

(Continued on next page)

LOIN. *This cut runs from the ribs to the legs, and averages about 6 pounds untrimmed, but half that trimmed. It is delicious seasoned with salt, pepper, and herbs, and roasted.*

BREAST. *This fatty cut needs a lot of trimming, so have your butcher do it. It is not terribly tender, so braising is the best cooking method.*

SHANKS. *These succulent cuts are wonderful seasoned and roasted, or braised with chopped vegetables, red wine, and herbs.*

3. Add the oregano, bay leaves, tomatoes, and chicken broth along with 1 cup of water and salt and pepper. Bring to a boil, stirring often. Cook for 20 minutes.

4. Place the lentils in a saucepan with 3 cups of water and salt to taste. Bring to a boil, and simmer for 15 minutes, stirring often. Drain.

5. Add the lentils to the meat mixture. Cook for 10 minutes, stirring often. Remove bay leaves. Serve in warm bowls with a dollop of sour cream and wedges of lime.

Lamb Patties with Mushroom Sauce
◇ ◇

Whenever I want a milder-tasting meat patty, I mix some ground veal or ground pork into the ground lamb.

Yield: 4 servings.

1¼ pounds ground lean lamb
3 tablespoons olive oil
1½ cups finely chopped onions
1 teaspoon finely chopped garlic
1 teaspoon ground cumin
½ cup finely chopped coriander or parsley
½ cup fine fresh bread crumbs
1 egg, lightly beaten
Salt and freshly ground pepper to taste
1 tablespoon butter
1 pound fresh mushrooms, thinly sliced (about 2 cups)
¼ cup dry white wine
½ cup chopped peeled fresh tomatoes or canned crushed tomatoes
¾ cup fresh or canned chicken broth
1 teaspoon chopped fresh tarragon or ½ teaspoon dried
2 teaspoons arrowroot or cornstarch
1 tablespoon water

1. Place the lamb in a mixing bowl.

2. Heat 2 tablespoons of the oil in a pan over medium-high setting and add the onions and garlic. Cook briefly, stirring, until wilted. Sprinkle with cumin and stir, blending well. Remove from heat and set aside.

3. Scrape the onion mixture into the lamb. Add the coriander, bread crumbs, egg, salt, and pepper. Blend well with fingers and shape the mixture into 20 small patties. Set aside.

4. For the mushroom sauce, heat the butter in a saucepan and add the mushrooms, salt, and pepper. Cook over medium-high heat until all the moisture from the mushrooms has evaporated.

5. Add the wine and simmer briefly over high heat. Add the tomatoes, broth, and tarragon. Cook about 5 minutes, stirring occasionally.

6. Blend the arrowroot with the water. Stir into the sauce and cook briefly.

7. Meanwhile, heat the remaining olive oil in a large nonstick pan (if you cannot fit all of the patties in at once, cook them in batches). Add the patties and turn them so they brown evenly, about 5 minutes. Drain the fat.

8. Add the patties to the sauce, cover, and simmer about 10 minutes.

Marinated Grilled Butterflied Leg of Lamb

Yield: 6 to 8 servings.

Whenever I grill a leg of lamb I first "butterfly" it. This allows the meat to lie flat on the grill and cook more evenly. Your butcher can do it in a few minutes. If you have to do it at home, begin by removing most of the outer fat. With the tip of a boning knife, find the big hipbone (it runs at about a 45-degree angle from the leg bone). Run the knife along the hipbone on all sides to sever the meat. At this point, you will see the ball joint and socket that connects the leg to the hip. Cut through the tendons that join the ball joint and socket and remove the hipbone. To remove the leg bone, flip the lamb over and slice deeply from the socket to the narrow end of the leg. Continue cutting all around the leg bone to sever the meat. Remove the bone, cut the meat open, and pound it flat into a butterfly pattern.

1 leg of American lamb (8 to 9 pounds)
Salt and freshly ground pepper to taste
¼ cup olive oil
1 cup dry red wine
2 tablespoons Dijon mustard
2 tablespoons fennel seeds
2 tablespoons finely chopped garlic
4 sprigs fresh thyme or 2 teaspoons dried
2 teaspoons cumin
1 bay leaf, crumbled
2 tablespoons butter

1. Have the butcher butterfly the leg of lamb or do it at home (see sidebar). Cut the meat, leaving it in one piece so that it will lie flat on a grill. If necessary, pound it with a mallet so it lies flat.

2. Preheat broiler or charcoal grill.

3. Prepare the lamb for grilling; lay it out flat and sprinkle it on all sides with salt and a generous quantity of pepper.

4. Combine in a bowl all of the remaining ingredients except the butter and blend them well.

5. Place the lamb in a baking dish large enough to hold it. Pour the marinade over the meat, and turn and rub the lamb so it is evenly coated. Marinate for about 1 hour. It is not essential to refrigerate before cooking; if it has been refrigerated, let it return to room temperature.

6. Remove lamb from the marinade and place it flat on the grill, or if an oven broiler is used, place the lamb 4 to 5 inches from the source of heat. Reserve the marinade. Cook the lamb on the grill or under the broiler about 15 minutes. Turn and cook another 15 minutes for rare meat; for medium or well done, cook longer according to taste. Meanwhile, transfer the marinade to a saucepan, simmer for about 3 minutes, and add the butter.

7. Transfer the lamb to a baking dish and pour the marinade over it. Cover loosely with aluminum foil and let the meat rest in a warm place for 10 to 15 minutes. Slice the meat thinly and serve with the pan gravy.

Lamb Chops Provençal

◇ ◇

Yield: 4 servings.

4 lamb chops, with most of the fat removed (about ½ pound each)
Salt and freshly ground pepper to taste
1 tablespoon olive oil
2 teaspoons chopped fresh rosemary or 1 teaspoon dried
4 sprigs fresh thyme or 1 teaspoon dried
2 tablespoons chopped onion
2 teaspoons finely chopped garlic
1 tablespoon red wine vinegar
2 cups fresh tomatoes, cored, peeled, and cut into ½-inch cubes
1 bay leaf
¼ cup pitted black olives
¼ cup pitted green olives
4 tablespoons chopped fresh basil or parsley

1. Sprinkle the chops with salt and pepper.

2. Heat the oil in a large, heavy pan, preferably cast iron. Cook the chops until brown on one side, about 5 minutes. Turn and sprinkle with rosemary and thyme. Cook 5 minutes more for rare, longer for medium-rare or well-done. Remove the chops to a warm platter and keep warm.

3. Pour off most of the fat from the pan and add the onion and garlic. Cook and stir until wilted. Add the vinegar, tomatoes, bay leaf, black and green olives, salt and pepper. Simmer for 5 minutes, stirring occasionally. Add any juices that have accumulated around the lamb chops.

4. Remove the bay leaf and pour the mixture over the lamb chops; sprinkle with basil.

◇

Whenever I travel, I bring back in my culinary luggage ideas for new recipes. The dish below I picked up on a trip to Provençe. The lamb chops are cooked quickly in a hot pan, preferably cast iron, and when they are done, a quick sauce is made in the same pan. This is done simply by adding the garlic, onions, vinegar, tomatoes, black and green olives, and seasoning. Provençal cooking is more sensory than calculated, so you must taste for seasonings periodically—and always before serving.

When I traveled around the Middle East, I found that lamb, a staple there, is prepared in many wonderful ways. It is not always easy to identify a particular dish as being, say, Moroccan as opposed to Tunisian. These lamb patties are called Moroccan style because they include cumin, garlic, black pepper, and parsley, flavors usually associated with that country.

❖

Harissa sauce, which usually is identified as a Tunisian hot condiment, is found on tables throughout North Africa and parts of the Middle East. It adds fire to everything from couscous and tagine (roughly defined as a meat stew) to kebabs and meat patties. Hot peppers, caraway seeds, garlic, olive oil, and cumin are almost always included in the formula. Just combine the ingredients in a blender or food processor and purée well. Harissa sauce lasts indefinitely if covered tightly and refrigerated.

Lamb Patties Moroccan Style with Harissa Sauce

❖ ❖

I like the spicy harissa with lamb. It also goes well with grilled chicken. The trick to making moist, tender ground meat dishes, whether kebabs, meatballs or even hamburgers, is to bind them loosely. Ground meat that is pressed too tightly tends to be tough and dry.

Couscous is an appropriate side dish for these Moroccan patties. This recipe calls for the precooked grain, which can be quite good if you use a flavorful broth and stir well to keep the grains fluffy. It has been enlivened with onions, garlic, yellow squash, and coriander.

Yield: 4 servings.

1½ pounds ground lean lamb
1 teaspoon paprika
¼ teaspoon crushed dried red hot pepper flakes
¼ teaspoon freshly ground black pepper
1 teaspoon ground cumin
2 teaspoons finely chopped garlic
2 tablespoons grated onion
4 tablespoons finely chopped parsley
Salt to taste
1 tablespoon vegetable oil
Harissa sauce (see page 173)

1. Put the lamb in a mixing bowl and add all the ingredients except the vegetable oil and harissa sauce. Blend the mixture thoroughly by hand.

2. Shape the mixture into 8 equal-size patties similar to hamburgers.

3. Heat the oil in a nonstick pan large enough to hold all the patties. Two pans may be necessary.

4. Add the patties to the pan. Cook them over medium-high heat about 3 to 4 minutes on each side, depending on the degree of doneness desired. Drain on paper towels and serve with the harissa sauce on the side.

Harissa Sauce
◇ ◇

Yield: ½ cup.

12 jalapeño peppers
3 cloves garlic, peeled
1 teaspoon caraway seeds
¼ teaspoon ground cumin
½ teaspoon ground coriander
¼ cup olive oil

1. Cut off the stems of the jalapeño peppers. Slice them open and cut off and discard the veins and seeds. Chop the peppers coarsely.

2. Put the peppers and all of the remaining ingredients in a food processor or blender. Blend to a fine liquid texture.

Couscous with Yellow Squash
◇ ◇

I often serve couscous as a substitute for rice. Its faintly nutty flavor and its ability to soak up sauces make it ideal for this dish.

Yield: 4 servings.

1 tablespoon butter
1 tablespoon olive oil
¼ cup finely chopped onion
1 teaspoon finely chopped garlic
¾ cup diced yellow squash, cut into ¼-inch cubes
Salt and freshly ground pepper to taste
1¼ cups fresh or canned chicken broth
1 cup precooked (fast-cooking) couscous
¼ cup coarsely chopped fresh coriander (optional)

1. Heat the butter and oil in a saucepan. Add the onion, garlic, squash, salt, and pepper. Cook, stirring, until wilted, but do not brown.

2. Add the chicken broth and bring to a boil. Add the couscous and blend well. Cover tightly, remove from the heat and let stand 5 minutes. Add the coriander and blend well with a fork.

Medallions of Lamb with Shallot Sauce

Yield: 4 servings.

Some recipes here call for shallots instead of onions. The major difference between the two is that shallots are milder in flavor, and slightly sweet. Shallots have bulbs shaped like garlic, with a head comprised of multiple cloves. Just peel them and slice them as you would onions. They should be firm and without any green sprouts. Chefs often use shallots in delicate sauces. If you cannot find shallots—supermarkets usually carry them—use red onion.

2 skinless, boneless loins of lamb (about 1½ pounds total)
Salt and freshly ground pepper to taste
1 tablespoon olive oil
4 cloves garlic, peeled
1 tablespoon chopped fresh rosemary or 2 teaspoons dried
2 tablespoons finely chopped shallots
¼ cup dry white wine
¼ cup fresh or canned chicken broth
1 tablespoon butter
Lentils with balsamic vinegar (see page 175)
2 tablespoons coarsely chopped parsley

1. Cut the lamb into 12 pieces of equal size. Sprinkle with salt and pepper.

2. Heat the oil in a nonstick pan large enough to hold the lamb pieces in one layer. Add the lamb, garlic, and rosemary. Brown the lamb quickly on all sides and cook, turning, over fairly high heat—about 4 minutes for rare. Remove lamb pieces to a platter and keep warm.

3. Add the shallots to the pan and cook briefly, stirring, until wilted. Add the wine and chicken broth. Cook and reduce to about ½ cup. Swirl in the butter and any juices that have accumulated around the lamb. Blend well, taste for seasoning, and remove the garlic cloves if desired. Keep warm.

4. To serve, divide the lentils equally on 4 warm plates. Place 3 pieces of lamb over the lentils and spoon some shallot sauce over the lamb pieces. Sprinkle with parsley and serve immediately.

Lentils with Balsamic Vinegar

◇ ◇

I started cooking with balsamic vinegar about fifteen years ago, when it started flooding the American market. Its sweetness, combined with a touch of acid, makes it suitable for salad dressings, sauces, and bean dishes like this one.

Yield: 4 servings.

2 cups lentils
4 cups water
Salt to taste
2 cloves
1 medium-size onion
1 bay leaf
2 sprigs fresh thyme or ½ teaspoon dried
1 tablespoon butter
1 teaspoon finely chopped garlic
½ cup finely chopped onion
½ cup finely diced carrots
1 tablespoon balsamic vinegar
Freshly ground pepper to taste

1. Pick over the lentils and discard any foreign particles. Rinse the lentils well and drain.

2. Put the lentils in a saucepan and add the water and salt. Bring to a boil. Stick the cloves into the onion and add it to the saucepan with the bay leaf and thyme. Cover and let simmer 20 minutes, until tender. Drain, remove the bay leaf, and reserve ½ cup of the cooking liquid.

3. Meanwhile, heat the butter in a pan and add the garlic, chopped onion, and carrots. Cook, stirring, until wilted. Do not brown. Add the vinegar and reserved ½ cup cooking liquid. Cover and simmer 5 minutes.

4. Add the lentils to the carrot mixture and bring to a boil. Simmer 2 minutes. Serve lentils with the lamb.

◇

Lentils are appearing more frequently in both restaurant and home cooking. The French have several varieties; the most common are the dark green ones associated with the Loire region and the clay-colored ones from northern Burgundy. American lentils are fatter but tasty, and much less expensive. Lentils are excellent sources of protein (½ cup of dry lentils has 24.7 grams of protein, versus 23.4 for a 3½-ounce serving of skinless white chicken meat) and fiber (1.7 grams in ½ cup).

While lentils are most often associated with cold-weather cooking, they make wonderful cold salads when combined with summer vegetables, poultry, or even certain seafood (fresh salmon and tuna, and even canned tuna, can be combined to make fine quick summer salads).

The lentils in the accompanying recipe are cooked in water seasoned with cloves, onion, bay leaf, and thyme. They are then combined with some sautéed garlic, more onion, and carrots. Balsamic vinegar adds a lovely sharp-sweet nuance in the final minutes of cooking.

◆

Other vegetables can be substituted for the ones listed in this lamb stew, depending on what is in season. Among those I use are scallions, cut into 1-inch pieces; asparagus, cut up lengthwise; and spring onions, blanched in unsalted water for 1 minute. Midsummer substitutions might include green, red, and yellow peppers, cut into strips; eggplant, cut into ½-inch dice; and zucchini, cut into 1- by ¼-inch sticks, all blanched for 1 minute. You could also try adding shallots, roasted on a tray in their skins for ½ hour at 400 degrees, then peeled. For late summer, in addition to the vegetables suggested here, you might use cauliflower and broccoli, cut into florets and blanched for 1 minute, or summer squash, cut into 1- by ¼-inch sticks. Add whatever combination you desire to the stew and cook until the vegetables are tender.

Lamb Stew

◆ ◆

When entertaining, I like to do as much as possible in advance so I don't spend the entire evening in the kitchen. Here is a time-saver. The base of this lamb stew can be prepared and frozen. On the day you want to serve it, you defrost it and add fresh seasonal vegetables to the base.

For the lamb stew here, braise the meat with some onions, garlic, and celery, then add tomato paste, herbs, and white wine. This base easily keeps for a month in the freezer. You don't add other vegetables until it is thawed.

A word about the defrosted stew base: Before adding fresh ingredients, bring it to a rolling boil, which will restore its texture if it has separated in the freezer.

Yield: 8 to 10 servings.

The Lamb Base

2 tablespoons vegetable oil
1 5-pound boneless lean leg of lamb, cut into 1½-inch cubes
Salt to taste
Freshly ground pepper to taste
1 cup finely chopped onions
1 tablespoon finely minced garlic
½ cup finely diced celery
4 tablespoons all-purpose flour
1 cup dry white wine
5 cups chicken stock, lamb stock, or water
3 tablespoons tomato paste
Bouquet garni, consisting of 1 bay leaf, 4 sprigs thyme, 6 sprigs parsley, the green of 1 leek (tied together in cheesecloth)

The Vegetables

4 turnips (about 1 pound)
12 small red potatoes (about 1½ pounds)
24 baby carrots (about 8 ounces)
½ pound string beans, trimmed and cut into 3-inch pieces

3 ears shucked corn, with kernels cut from the cob, about 2 cups
   (or frozen corn)
1 cup shelled peas

1. In a large pan (cast iron is best), heat the oil over high setting and add the meat cubes. Sprinkle with salt and pepper. Brown well on all sides, turning. If the pan is not large enough to hold all the meat in one layer, sauté the meat in several batches. The browning will take from 10 to 15 minutes total.

2. Pour off fat from the pan, add the onions, garlic, and celery, and stir well. Add the flour and cook over medium heat for 3 minutes, stirring occasionally. Add the wine, stock, tomato paste, and bouquet garni. Stir to loosen the brown particles that may cling to the bottom of the pan. Bring to a boil, cover, and simmer for 1 hour and 15 minutes or until the lamb is tender.

3. Remove the bouquet garni. Transfer the stew base to a freezer container and cool for about 2 hours. Then place in the freezer.

4. The day before serving, remove the stew base from the freezer and defrost it in the refrigerator for 24 hours. Or if you have a microwave oven, you can defrost the stew the day you want to serve it.

5. When ready to reheat the defrosted stew, trim and peel the turnips, potatoes, and baby carrots. Cut the peeled turnips and potatoes lengthwise into approximately 1½-inch wedges, so that all are roughly the same thickness. This makes cooking time uniform and adds to the visual appeal.

6. In a pot, add the turnips, potatoes, carrots, string beans, corn, and peas. Cover with cold water. Bring to a rolling boil and blanch for 1 minute. Drain and set aside until ready to use.

7. Pour the defrosted lamb stew into a large kettle and bring to a boil over medium-low heat. Add the vegetables and simmer gently for 10 minutes. Taste for seasoning and serve.

Lamb Burgers with Feta Cheese

◇ ◇

You may substitute goat cheese for the feta cheese.

Yield: 4 servings.

1½ pounds lean lamb, ground
Salt to taste if desired
Freshly ground pepper to taste
¼ teaspoon ground cumin
2 teaspoons finely chopped fresh rosemary or half that amount
    dried
¾ cup crumbled feta cheese
4 teaspoons finely chopped parsley

1. Divide lamb into 8 portions of equal size. Shape each into a patty and sprinkle on both sides with salt and pepper.

2. Sprinkle the top of each patty with an equal amount of cumin and rosemary. Pat to help them adhere.

3. The patties may be broiled or cooked in a pan. If broiled, preheat broiler to high. Place patties on a baking sheet and place about 3 inches from source of heat. Broil them 3 minutes if you want them rare, 4 to 5 minutes for well-done. Turn patties and cook 2 minute if you wish them rare, about 4 minutes for well-done.

4. If patties are cooked in a pan, select one large enough to hold them in one layer. Brush pan with a little oil and heat thoroughly on stove. Cook patties over moderately high heat for 3 minutes if you wish them rare, 4 to 5 minutes for well-done. Turn patties and continue cooking 2 minutes for rare, 4 minutes for well-done.

5. Top each with a portion of feta cheese. Place under broiler, preheated to high, about 3 inches from the source of heat. Let broil about 1 minute. Dot center of each patty with ½ teaspoon of finely chopped parsley.

Lamb Shanks with Lentils

◇ ◇

Whenever I see good lamb shanks in the supermarket, I buy them. If I don't use them that evening, I freeze them for another time. Rosemary is a natural combination with lamb.

Yield: 6 servings.

1 pound dried lentils

4 cloves garlic

3 tablespoons minced fresh rosemary or 2 tablespoons dried

6 lamb shanks, trimmed of excess fat (about 7 pounds)

Salt and freshly ground black pepper to taste

1 tablespoon olive oil

7 cups water

1 bay leaf

4 tablespoons unsalted butter

1 cup chopped onions

1 tablespoon chopped garlic mixed with ½ teaspoon thyme

1½ cups chopped leeks (optional)

2 cups canned crushed tomatoes with paste added

2 cups water

Chopped parsley for garnish

1. Preheat oven to 425 degrees. Inspect lentils for small stones or spoiled beans. Rinse thoroughly in cold water.

2. Mince the garlic and combine with the rosemary. Rub mixture over lamb shanks. Salt and pepper well. Rub olive oil over shanks. Place in roasting pan and cook for 1 hour.

3. Place lentils in a deep pot with 7 cups water, bay leaf, and salt. Bring to a boil, reduce to a simmer, and cook about 30 minutes, or until lentils are soft.

4. In a frying pan, melt the butter over medium heat and sauté the onions and garlic-thyme mixture for 5 minutes, or until the onions wilt. Add leeks to pan. Salt and pepper to taste. Add tomatoes, stir well, and cook for 2 minutes at medium-low heat.

5. Drain lentils, remove bay leaf, and add lentils to tomato mixture. Simmer 15 to 20 minutes more.

(Continued on next page)

The lamb you buy in
supermarkets is anywhere from
6 months to 1 year old. Baby
lamb is only 3 to 4 months old.
Mutton, which is not consumed
much in this country, comes
from an animal more than a
year old. Whenever possible,
buy fresh American lamb, which
is much more tender and subtly
flavored than frozen imports
from New Zealand or other
countries.

6. After the shanks have cooked, remove the pan from the oven and pour off accumulated fat. Add 2 cups of water to pan and cover shanks loosely with aluminum foil. Reduce oven to 350 degrees and cook 30 minutes more.

7. Serve the shanks with lentils and a sprinkling of chopped parsley.

Stuffed Saddle of Lamb with Pan Gravy

Saddle of lamb is a wonderfully delicate and flavorful cut, and it demands subtlety in cooking. In this recipe, you roll it around a stuffing of spinach, pine nuts, and mushrooms. When the roast is carved, each slice presents an attractive tableau on the plate.

Yield: 8 to 10 servings.

The Stuffing

1 egg
¼ teaspoon cream
¾ pound white mushrooms
Juice of ½ lemon
2 tablespoons unsalted butter
6 tablespoons chopped shallots
2 teaspoons minced garlic
1 10-ounce package of fresh spinach, cleaned and with large
    stems removed (about 8 cups)
Salt and freshly ground black pepper
⅛ teaspoon grated nutmeg
½ cup pine nuts, lightly toasted in a pan

1. In a small bowl, combine the egg and cream and stir well. Set aside.

2. Chop the mushrooms coarsely and place in a bowl. Sprinkle with lemon juice, coat well, and set aside. Melt butter in a large pan over medium-high heat and add the shallots and garlic. Sauté, stirring, for several minutes. Do not let the garlic brown. Add mushrooms and turn heat to high. Stir well for several minutes until moisture evaporates from mushrooms.

3. Add spinach and stir to wilt. Season with salt and pepper to taste. Add nutmeg. Cook several minutes, stirring, to remove the moisture. Add pine nuts, pour in egg and cream mixture, and blend well. Cook approximately 2 minutes over high heat while stirring. Remove the mixture to a bowl and let it cool.

The Lamb and Gravy

> 4- to 4½-pound saddle of lamb (ask butcher to trim excess fat and debone it, keeping it in one piece so it can be stuffed and rolled; after deboning, saddle should weigh about 3¾ to 4 pounds; have butcher chop bones for use in gravy)
> 2 medium onions, peeled and quartered
> 1 cup homemade (page 93) or canned chicken stock
> ¼ cup water

1. Preheat oven to 425 degrees.
2. Lay saddle of lamb flat on a counter, fat side down. Distribute the stuffing evenly over the meaty center section. Fold the left flap over the filling, then fold the right flap all the way over the first flap. Tie the rolled lamb in about five places with kitchen twine. Place lamb over a double sheet of aluminum foil and fold up the sides of the foil so they reach halfway up the meat. Secure with kitchen twine, to help keep stuffing inside during cooking.
3. Place the lamb in a roasting pan and scatter the chopped-up pieces of bone and onions around it. Roast about ½ hour. Remove foil. Cook about ½ hour more. Check lamb with meat thermometer—rare is 130 degrees, medium 140. Transfer to serving platter, cover loosely with foil, and let stand in a warm place for 15 minutes before carving.
4. To make gravy, pour off all fat from the roasting pan. Place pan, containing bones and onions, on stovetop over medium-high flame. Add chicken stock and water and scrape bottom of pan with wooden spatula to remove clinging particles. Bring to a boil and simmer several minutes while scraping. Strain into a bowl. Makes about 1 cup gravy.

Spicy Lamb Loaf
◇ ◇

This lamb loaf is a tasty twist on beef meat loaf. Sometimes I add some ground veal for a more subtle flavor.

Yield: 6 or more servings.

2 pounds ground lean lamb
1 tablespoon corn, peanut, or vegetable oil
1 cup finely chopped onion
1 cup finely diced celery
1 cup finely chopped green pepper
1 teaspoon finely minced garlic
Salt to taste
Freshly ground black pepper to taste
⅛ teaspoon freshly grated nutmeg
1 teaspoon ground cumin
2 teaspoons Worcestershire sauce
⅛ teaspoon Tabasco sauce (or more if desired)
1 tablespoon Dijon-style mustard
½ cup fine fresh bread crumbs
1 egg, lightly beaten

1. Preheat oven to 400 degrees.
2. Put meat in a mixing bowl and set aside.
3. Heat oil in a pan and add onion, celery, green pepper, and garlic. Cook, stirring, until vegetables are wilted. Set aside to cool briefly.
4. Add cooked vegetables to meat. Add salt, pepper, nutmeg, cumin, Worcestershire sauce, Tabasco sauce, mustard, bread crumbs, and egg. Blend well with the fingers.
5. Pack mixture into a 6-cup loaf pan. Smooth the top.
6. Place the pan in the oven and bake 50 minutes. Remove from the oven and let stand 10 minutes. Slice and serve.

Medallions of Lamb
with Leek-and-Tarragon Sauce
◇ ◇

I rarely see lamb steaks in restaurants—most menus carry rack of lamb, lamb chops, or braised shoulder of lamb. This recipe should make you a convert to delicious lamb steaks.

Yield: 4 servings.

2 boneless, skinless loins of lamb (about 1½ pounds trimmed
    weight)
Salt to taste
Freshly ground pepper to taste
1 or 2 leeks (about ¾ pound)
3 tablespoons butter
¾ cup fresh or canned chicken broth
3 tablespoons cream
2 tablespoons olive oil
3 tablespoons finely chopped shallots
3 tablespoons dry white wine
1 teaspoon tomato paste
1 tablespoon finely chopped fresh tarragon or ½ tablespoon dried
    tarragon

1. If any fat remains on the loin of lamb pieces after they are trimmed, carefully cut it away. Place each loin of lamb on a flat surface and cut crosswise into 4 pieces of equal size.

2. Place each piece upright (grain side up) and pound lightly with a flat mallet. The flattened pieces will measure about ½ inch thick. Sprinkle with salt and pepper.

3. Trim off the stems of the leeks. Cut leeks crosswise into 1½-inch pieces. Cut each piece lengthwise into very thin shreds (julienne). Put leeks in a pan and add 2 tablespoons of the butter and salt and pepper.

4. Cook leeks over moderate heat, stirring occasionally, about 1 minute. Add ¼ cup of the chicken broth and cover. Continue cooking about 10 minutes. Add cream and cook, uncovered, about 3 minutes.

5. Meanwhile, heat olive oil in a heavy pan and add medallions of lamb. Cook about 4 to 5 minutes over relatively high heat until browned.

(Continued on next page)

Turn pieces and continue cooking about 4 to 5 minutes to the desired degree of doneness. Transfer pieces to a warm platter.

6. Pour off fat from the pan and wipe pan with paper towels. Add remaining tablespoon of butter to the pan. When it is hot, add shallots and cook briefly, stirring. Add wine, remainder of chicken broth, and tomato paste. Stir. Add any liquid that may have accumulated around the lamb pieces. Cook the sauce, stirring, until it is reduced to ½ cup. Stir in tarragon.

7. Spoon sauce over meat. Serve with leeks in cream sauce on the side.

Lamb and White Beans with Vegetables
◇ ◇

I use dried beans often, particularly in cold weather. In this recipe, they add needed starch, and a hearty character reminiscent of cassoulet.

Yield: 8 to 10 servings.

1 tablespoon vegetable oil
4 pounds lamb stew meat from the leg or shoulder, cubed
Salt and pepper to taste
2 cups coarsely chopped carrots
2 cups coarsely chopped onions
1 tablespoon chopped garlic
2 bay leaves
1 teaspoon dried thyme
1 cup white wine
1 cup crushed canned tomatoes
1 tablespoon tomato paste
3 cups chicken stock
8 cups water
1 pound white beans, soaked in water overnight
1 carrot, peeled
1 whole onion pierced with a clove
1 garlic clove, peeled
1 cup water
½ cup chopped parsley

1. Preheat the oven to 350 degrees.

2. Heat the oil in a heavy cast-iron pot over high heat and add half of the meat to the pot and brown on all sides. Season with salt and pepper. Remove the browned meat cubes from the pot, set aside, and brown the rest. When that is browned, add the cooked lamb to the pot along with the chopped carrots, onions, and garlic. Season with 1 bay leaf and thyme and cover with the white wine, tomatoes, tomato paste, chicken stock, and water. Bring to a boil, cover, and simmer in the oven for 1 hour.

3. Meanwhile, place the beans in a large pot, add the carrot, the onion pierced with a clove, the remaining bay leaf, and the garlic clove. Cover with water and season with salt. Bring to a boil, cover, and simmer for about 1 hour or until soft.

4. Drain the beans and reserve 1 cup of the cooking liquid, the carrot, and the onion. Add the beans, carrot, and onion to the lamb with the reserved cooking liquid. Return the pot to the oven and cook 15 minutes longer. Remove the pot from the oven and check for salt and pepper. Sprinkle with chopped parsley and serve.

Grilled Lamb Chops with Cabernet-and-Caper Butter

◇ ◇

This recipe comes from Albert Portale, chef of Gotham Bar and Grill in Manhattan. "Cabernet and lamb are wonderful together," he says. "You use one glass of wine to prepare the butter, and serve the rest of the bottle with the meal."

Chef Portale has the right idea about cooking with wine. In cooking, always use a wine that you would drink. Never use so-called "cooking wine." I usually buy magnums of inexpensive white and red wines for cooking.

Yield: 4 servings.

8 loin lamb chops, about 10 ounces each (a total weight of 5½ pounds)
Salt to taste if desired
Freshly ground pepper to taste
4 large sprigs fresh rosemary
4 large sprigs fresh thyme
⅔ cup Cabernet-and-caper butter sauce (see page 187)
1 bunch watercress

1. Neatly trim off and discard most of the triangle of fat on the lamb.

2. Sprinkle each chop with salt and pepper. Place the rosemary and thyme sprigs over the grilling grate. Place lamb chops over the herbs. Cook 5 minutes. Turn and cook to the desired degree of doneness, about 5 to 7 minutes longer, for a total cooking time of 13 to 15 minutes. Spoon the sauce over the chops and garnish with watercress.

Cabernet-and-Caper Butter Sauce

◇ ◇

Yield: About 9 tablespoons.

¾ cup full-bodied dry red wine, preferably Cabernet Sauvignon
3 tablespoons finely chopped shallots
8 tablespoons unsalted butter, at room temperature
2 tablespoons drained capers
2 tablespoons finely chopped parsley
Salt to taste if desired
Freshly ground pepper to taste

1. Combine the wine and shallots in a saucepan, and cook until the wine is almost completely evaporated, 10 to 15 minutes. Do not let the shallots become dry or burned. Set aside until thoroughly cooled.

2. Put the butter in the saucepan over medium heat and start beating with a wire whisk while adding the capers, parsley, salt and pepper to taste. Serve hot over the lamb.

Roasted Rack of Lamb with Herbs

◇ ◇

An American rack of lamb, trimmed, generally weighs between 7 and 8 pounds, enough for 4 people. New Zealand lambs are small and feed only 2 to 3. Unless you are deft with a knife, when buying rack of lamb, make sure it is well trimmed of fat and that the back bone has been removed.

Yield: Serves 6 to 8.

2 racks of lamb with the shinbones (the flat continuous bone on top
    of the ribs) and fat removed
Salt and freshly ground pepper to taste
2 tablespoons olive oil
½ cup fine fresh bread crumbs
2 tablespoons chopped parsley
2 teaspoons finely chopped garlic
2 tablespoons finely chopped shallots
2 teaspoons chopped fresh thyme leaves or 1 teaspoon dried
2 tablespoons melted butter
2 tablespoons dry white wine
⅓ cup fresh or canned chicken broth

1. Preheat the oven to 500 degrees or more.

2. If necessary, remove the top thick layer of fat from the rack. The loins and the rib should be almost clean of fat. Hack off the ends of the rib bones, leaving about 2 inches of the ribs intact. Sprinkle with salt and pepper.

3. The baking pan should be large enough to hold the racks in one layer side by side. Place the racks, meat side down, in the pan and brush with 1 tablespoon of olive oil.

4. Meanwhile, combine the bread crumbs, parsley, garlic, shallots, fresh thyme, and 1 tablespoon of olive oil in a bowl. Set aside.

5. Place the racks of lamb on the bottom rack of the oven. Cook for 15 minutes, turning and basting occasionally.

6. Remove meat from the oven and sprinkle the meaty side of the ribs with the bread crumb mixture. Pour the melted butter over the mixture. Place in the oven and bake for 8 to 10 minutes for medium-rare. The bread crumb mixture should be lightly browned. Remove the racks onto a platter and keep warm.

7. Remove any melted fat from the pan. If there is any bread crumb mixture in the pan, leave it. Add the white wine and the broth. Place the pan on top of the stove, bring to a boil, scraping the bottom to remove the brown particles from the pan. Add any juices that accumulate around the racks. Bring to a simmer and cook for 2 to 3 minutes. Serve with the carved racks.

Grilled Rack of Lamb
with Rosemary-Lemon Sauce
◇ ◇

I love the aroma and flavor of fresh rosemary, and it goes especially well with lamb. It can be used in all sorts of dishes, from soups and salads to dressings, egg dishes, and roasted meats.

Yield: 4 to 6 servings.

2 racks of lamb, 8 ribs per rack (about 3½ pounds total)
Salt and freshly ground pepper to taste
2 teaspoons dried rosemary or 1 tablespoon fresh
2 tablespoons olive oil
4 tablespoons unsalted butter
2 tablespoons minced shallots
2 tablespoons fresh lemon juice
¼ cup diced parsley

1. If necessary, peel the thick layer of fat off the back of the racks of lamb. Trim all other fat with a knife and discard. Using a heavy cleaver, chop off the rib bones nearly all the way to the meat. This allows the meat to lie on the grill more easily; the ribs should be grilled separately and served as well.

2. Place all the meat in a roasting pan. Season generously with salt and pepper. Sprinkle with rosemary and rub with olive oil. Cover and let sit refrigerated for several hours.

3. Place the base of the racks over hot coals and grill for about 10 minutes, covered, turning occasionally. Add the rib sections during the last 5 minutes.

(Continued on next page)

4. When the meat is cooked, place all pieces in an ovenproof roasting pan and let rest on the side of the grill grate where heat is least intense. Add the butter and shallots to the pan. When the butter has melted, add the lemon juice and the parsley. Let all this mix with the meat drippings for about 5 minutes.

5. Carve the rack into serving portions in the roasting pan to catch the juices. Place the meat and some of the ribs on each serving plate. Stir the sauce well over the heat and spoon some over the meat. Serve immediately.

Curried Lamb Chops

◇ ◇

Moghul meat cuisine is built around lamb. Whenever I go to an Indian restaurant, I study the composition of flavors and adapt them to French and American cuisine. This dish is one example.

Yield: 4 servings.

8 lamb chops, preferably taken from the rack (about 2 pounds)
Salt to taste
Freshly ground pepper to taste
1 tablespoon curry powder
1 tablespoon corn, peanut, or vegetable oil
2 tablespoons butter
2 tablespoons finely chopped shallots
½ cup dry white wine
½ cup fresh or canned chicken broth
1 teaspoon tomato paste
1 tablespoon finely chopped parsley

1. Sprinkle the chops on both sides with salt and pepper. Rub them on both sides with curry powder to coat evenly.

2. Heat the oil in a pan large enough to hold the chops in one layer. Add the chops and cook until browned on one side, about 2 minutes. Turn the chops and brown on the second side, about 2 minutes. Turn the chops onto their fatty rims and continue cooking until the rims are rendered of fat, about 2 minutes.

3. Turn the chops flat side down and cook, turning them occasionally. The total cooking time for the chops should be about 15 minutes.

4. Transfer the chops to a dish and pour off all the fat from the pan. Add 1 tablespoon of the butter to the pan and heat. Add the shallots and cook, stirring, about 15 seconds. Add the wine and bring to a boil. Cook about 1 minute and then add the chicken broth and tomato paste. Cook over moderately high heat until reduced to about ½ cup. Swirl in the remaining 1 tablespoon butter and pour the sauce over the chops. Serve sprinkled with parsley.

Seafood

◇ ◇ ◇

Salmon with Sorrel Sauce

Salmon Fillets with Sweet Red Pepper Sauce

Roasted Salmon Fillets with Goat Cheese and Coriander

Steamed Salmon Fillets with Herb Vinaigrette

Sautéed Scallops with Snow Peas

Grilled Sea Scallops with Tomatoes and Onions

Shrimp in Paprika-Yogurt Sauce

Rice with Raisins and Pine Nuts

Shrimp with Snow Peas and Tomatoes

Shrimp in Curry Sauce

Escabeche with Summer Vegetables

Sichuan-Style Poached Sea Bass with Hot Bean Sauce

Sautéed Striped Bass with Wild Mushrooms

Curried Mussels

Sautéed Trout with Orange

Pan-Fried Skate Wings with Capers

Marinated Broiled Tuna Steaks with Sauce Niçoise

Tuna Steaks Moroccan Style

Couscous with Raisins and Red Peppers

Rolled Fillets of Sole à la Nage

Sautéed Fillet of Sole with Fresh Tomatoes and Ginger Sauce

Snapper Fillets Provençal Style

Saffron Rice

Steamed Halibut Fillets with Scallion-Ginger Vinaigrette

Poached Halibut Steaks with Lemon Sauce

Flounder with Chervil Butter Sauce

Flounder Fillets with Mushrooms and Tomatoes

Monkfish Stew with Red Wine (Matelote)

Marinated Monkfish Brochettes

Poached Lobsters with Basil Sauce

Salmon with Sorrel Sauce

◇ ◇

This sumptuous dish was made famous by my longtime friend Pierre Troisgros at the restaurant Troisgros in Roanne, France. I have enjoyed it many times, most recently with a TV crew when I was doing a food documentary in France. The combination of acidity from the sorrel and richness of the salmon is a delight.

Yield: 4 servings.

4 tablespoons finely minced shallots
1 cup dry white wine, preferably Chardonnay
⅓ cup dry vermouth
1 cup heavy cream
4 cups fresh sorrel, washed, stemmed, and center veins removed
1 tablespoon fresh lemon juice
Salt and freshly ground black pepper to taste
1 12-ounce center-cut salmon fillet, boneless

1. In a saucepan over high heat combine the shallots, wine, and vermouth. Cook until the mixture is almost evaporated. It should have a syrupy consistency. Add cream and bring mixture to a simmer. Cook, stirring frequently, for 30 minutes. Remove from heat and strain sauce through a fine sieve into a clean saucepan.

2. Tear the sorrel into thumb-size pieces and drop them into the sauce. Add lemon juice, salt and pepper to taste, and cook briefly, stirring. Remove from heat and keep warm.

3. Cut the salmon in half widthwise. Then halve each piece, leaving 4 portions. Pound each piece lightly with the back of a saucepan to make the surface even.

4. Season the salmon on the skin side with salt and pepper. Cook fillets, skin side down, in a nonstick pan over medium-high heat for 1 minute. Flip and cook another minute. Check for doneness (it should lose its red color in the center).

5. Distribute sorrel sauce evenly over center of 4 warm serving plates. Place a salmon fillet over each, arranging some sorrel strands around them. Serve immediately.

The two principal types of
salmon on the American market
are the Pacific and the Atlantic.
Atlantic salmon has the superior
flavor and more delicate texture.
The best Pacific salmon are
called chinook (or king salmon)
The most prized salmon are from
Ireland and Scotland—and are
also the most costly. Farm-raised
Norwegian salmon, which many
chefs prefer today, is also good.

Salmon Fillets with Sweet Red Pepper Sauce

Like so many recipes, this one was born of necessity. I had so many sweet peppers in my garden I had to start using them. The sweetness of the peppers complements the salmon quite well.

Yield: 4 servings.

2 medium sweet red peppers
2 tablespoons butter
4 skinless, boneless salmon steaks (about 4 to 6 ounces each)
Salt and freshly ground pepper to taste
4 tablespoons finely chopped shallots
¼ cup dry white wine
½ cup heavy cream
2 tablespoons finely chopped dill and some dill sprigs for
    garnishing

1. Core and remove the seeds from the red peppers. Cut them into ¼-inch cubes or strips.

2. Heat the butter in a large nonstick skillet over high setting.

3. Season both sides of the fillets with salt and pepper to taste. Place the steaks in the pan and cook until they are lightly browned, about 2 minutes per side. The time will vary, depending on the thickness of the fish and the doneness desired.

4. Transfer the steaks to a warm platter. Leave the cooking butter in the skillet. Add the shallots and the red peppers. Cook, stirring, until wilted.

5. Add the wine, reduce by half, add the cream and cook, stirring over medium-high heat, until reduced again by half. Check the seasonings.

6. Add the salmon steaks, the chopped dill, and any juices that have accumulated around the fillets, and bring to a simmer. Cook 1 minute. Do not overcook. Serve immediately with some sauce and the dill for decoration.

Roasted Salmon Fillets with Goat Cheese and Coriander

◇ ◇

As a chef, I like to challenge myself by coming up with flavor and texture combinations that at first seem improbable. Fish with goat cheese is just such a notion. Delicate fish like sole, grouper, bass, and halibut would be overpowered, but salmon, with its rich, flavorful flesh and moist texture, works very well.

The recipe here (bluefish could be substituted) is highly seasoned and the cheese is crumbled and spread over the fish at the end. Its tart flavor counteracts the sauce's sweet onions, tomatoes, and herbs. Fresh coriander is a zesty contribution, and the Ricard (an anise-flavored liquor) lends a Provençal accent.

Use a relatively young goat cheese, one that is slightly firm to the touch but not hard—the older it is, the harder it becomes.

Yield: 4 servings.

4 tablespoons olive oil
½ cup chopped onion
1 tablespoon finely chopped garlic
½ cup dry red wine
4 tablespoons capers
1 tablespoon chopped fresh rosemary or 1 teaspoon dried
1 teaspoon chopped fresh oregano or ½ teaspoon dried
⅛ teaspoon hot red pepper flakes
½ cup canned crushed tomatoes
Salt and freshly ground pepper to taste
12 pitted black olives
4 boneless salmon fillets (about 6 ounces each)
⅓ pound goat cheese, crumbled
2 tablespoons anise-flavored liquor, like Ricard (optional)
4 tablespoons chopped fresh coriander (optional)

1. Heat 2 tablespoons of the olive oil in a saucepan. Add the onion and garlic, and cook briefly while stirring. Add the wine, capers, rosemary, oregano, pepper flakes, tomatoes, salt, pepper, and olives. Bring to a boil and simmer 5 minutes.

2. Preheat the oven to 475 degrees.

(Continued on next page)

3. Pour 1 tablespoon of the oil in a baking dish large enough to hold the fish in one layer. Arrange the fish skin side down, sprinkle with salt and pepper. Pour the crushed tomato sauce around the fish fillets; brush the top of the fillets with the remaining 1 tablespoon oil and the cheese.

4. Bake for 5 minutes and sprinkle with Ricard. Switch to the broiler and broil for 5 minutes. Do not overcook the fish. Sprinkle with the coriander and serve immediately.

Steamed Salmon Fillets with Herb Vinaigrette
◇ ◇

I have made this recipe with many different fish—tuna and bluefish are particularly good. It is a healthful summer dish with no cream or butter. The basic sauce is made by combining fresh herbs, scallions, chives, tarragon, garlic, oil, vinegar, and mustard. Mix them briefly in a food processor or blender, not so long that you destroy the texture.

This dish can be served hot as a main course or cold as an appetizer. The herb dressing should be at room temperature or slightly cool.

Yield: 4 servings.

½ cup chopped fresh chervil, parsley, or coriander
½ cup coarsely chopped scallions, including green part
4 tablespoons coarsely chopped chives
1 tablespoon chopped fresh tarragon or ½ tablespoon dried
1 teaspoon minced garlic
6 tablespoons olive oil
2 tablespoons red wine vinegar
1 tablespoon Dijon mustard
Salt and freshly ground pepper to taste
4 boneless, skinless salmon fillets (about 6 ounces each)
16 large basil leaves, plus additional leaves for garnish

1. Combine the chopped chervil with the scallions, chives, tarragon, garlic, oil, vinegar, mustard, salt, and pepper in the bowl of a food processor or blender. Process until the mixture is chopped fine, but overblending will harm the texture.

2. Pour water into the bottom of a steamer. Season the fillets with salt and pepper and place them on a steamer rack. Lay 4 basil leaves over each fillet and cover. Bring the water to a boil and steam for 4 to 5 minutes. Do not overcook. The fish can be served hot or cold.

3. Transfer the fish to a serving plate. Spoon the vinaigrette over the fillets and garnish with fresh basil leaves.

Sautéed Scallops with Snow Peas
◇ ◇

I make this dish with both sea scallops and bay scallops. If using large sea scallops, cut them in half.

Yield: 4 servings.

½ pound snow peas, trimmed and washed

Salt to taste

2 tablespoons olive oil

2 teaspoons finely chopped garlic

2 plum tomatoes, peeled and cut into ¼-inch cubes (about ¼ pound)

1 teaspoon chopped fresh thyme or ½ teaspoon dried

Freshly ground pepper to taste

1 tablespoon butter

1¼ pounds sea scallops, cool but not icy from refrigerator (cut in half if too large)

4 tablespoons chopped fresh coriander or parsley

Juice of 1 lemon

1. In a small pot, bring enough water to a boil to cover the snow peas and add salt to taste. Add peas, bring to a boil, cook for 1 minute, and drain.

2. Heat oil in a nonstick skillet. Over medium-high setting, add the garlic and tomatoes, and toss for 1 minute. Add snow peas, thyme, salt and pepper, then cook and stir for 1 minute more.

3. Using a nonstick skillet large enough to hold the scallops in one layer, heat butter over high setting. Add scallops, season with salt and pepper, and cook, shaking so that the scallops cook evenly and quickly, for about 2 minutes. Be careful not to overcook them.

4. Add the tomato–snow pea mixture, coriander, and lemon juice. Cook, stirring, for 1 minute. Serve immediately.

Grilled Sea Scallops with Tomatoes and Onions

As their names imply, sea scallops come from the deep ocean bottom, while bay scallops grow in estuaries and more shallow water. Sea scallops are larger—measuring as much as 5 inches across. They are deliciously sweet and briny. Cut them in half if they are too big.

Bay scallops, measuring only up to 3 inches across, have an incredibly buttery texture and sweet flavor. They are considerably more expensive because they are seasonal and limited.

Another kind of scallop is called a calico, which also comes from deep ocean waters. These do not have the flavor of bay and sea scallops, and can be tough. All three can be cooked in similar ways.

When I have very fresh sea scallops, I usually make a quick, fresh tomato sauce. Anything more assertive would mask the scallops' flavor.

Yield: 4 servings.

1½ pounds jumbo sea scallops
5 tablespoons olive oil
2 large ripe tomatoes, seeded and cut in eighths
1 medium red onion, cut in eighths
2 cloves garlic, crushed
1 cup dry white wine
2 tablespoons salted capers, rinsed and drained
1 tablespoon chopped niçoise olives
1 teaspoon chopped fresh thyme leaves or ½ teaspoon dried
1 teaspoon chopped fresh rosemary leaves or ½ teaspoon dried
Coarse salt and freshly ground pepper to taste
2 tablespoons extra-virgin olive oil

1. Preheat a grill. Wipe the scallops dry with paper towels and brush them with a tablespoon of olive oil. Grill over very high heat just enough to make crosshatch marks on both sides. Do not cook any longer.

2. Heat 1 tablespoon of olive oil in a saucepan. Add the tomato and onion and sauté for 5 minutes. Add the garlic and wine and cook 2 minutes more. Stir in the capers, olives, thyme, half of the rosemary, the remaining 3 tablespoons of olive oil, and salt and pepper.

3. Pour the mixture into a baking dish and arrange scallops on top. Bake for 5 minutes. Remove from the oven and cool. Sprinkle with the extra-virgin olive oil and remaining rosemary and serve at room temperature.

Shrimp in Paprika-Yogurt Sauce

◇ ◇

This Indian dish, using yogurt, coriander, and paprika, is typical of Moghul cuisine of the north. Keep an eye on the shrimp, which cook very quickly.

Yield: 4 servings.

1½ pounds medium-size raw shrimp
1 large sweet red pepper, cored and seeded
1 large green pepper, cored and seeded
2 tablespoons butter
Salt and freshly ground pepper to taste
2 teaspoons paprika
1 tablespoon finely chopped shallots
1 teaspoon finely chopped garlic
2 tablespoons cognac (optional)
½ cup sour cream
1 cup drained plain yogurt
4 tablespoons chopped fresh coriander

1. Shell and devein the shrimp (page 9).
2. Cut the red pepper into ½-inch cubes.
3. Slice the green pepper into 1½-inch-long strips.
4. Heat the butter in a large nonstick skillet. Add the shrimp, salt, pepper, and paprika. Stir with a wooden spatula. When the shrimp become pink (in 2 to 3 minutes), remove them with a slotted spoon, leaving any cooking liquid in the pan.
5. In the same skillet, add the red and green peppers, shallots, garlic, salt, and pepper. Cook, stirring, about 3 to 4 minutes over medium-high heat. Add the cognac, shrimp, and any juices that have accumulated. Cook over medium heat for 2 minutes more.
6. Add the sour cream and yogurt. Blend well and check for seasonings. Add the chopped coriander and bring to a simmer for about 30 seconds. Do not boil or the sauce will separate. Serve with rice with raisins and pine nuts.

◇

I have learned a lot from Indian cuisine about using yogurt in sauces instead of cream. Yogurt can be just as smooth and creamy, and it binds seasonings very well. Often a yogurt sauce is mixed with a little sour cream, which keeps it from breaking down.

When buying yogurt for cooking, get plain low-fat yogurt, one without a lot of gelatin (that gives it the texture of pudding). Brands like Dannon and Colombo are good. Plain low-fat or no-fat yogurt has about 150 calories per cup. Nonfat yogurts have no saturated fat, while low-fat has about 1 to 2 percent. Drain yogurt through cheesecloth before cooking to remove excess water, which makes a smoother sauce.

Rice with Raisins and Pine Nuts
◇ ◇

Yield: 4 servings.

1 tablespoon olive oil
2 tablespoons finely chopped onion
1 teaspoon finely chopped garlic
1 cup converted rice
1 cup raisins
¼ cup pine nuts
1½ cups water
Salt and pepper to taste

1. Add the olive oil to a saucepan, then the onion and garlic. Cook over medium heat, stirring, until wilted. Add the rice, raisins, and the pine nuts.

2. Add the water, salt, and pepper. Bring to a boil, stirring; cover, and simmer for exactly 17 minutes.

3. Stir to fluff the rice and blend well.

Shrimp with Snow Peas and Tomatoes

◇ ◇

I add a little black currant vodka to this dish, which contributes a very faint fruity flavor. You could also use lemon vodka.

Yield: 4 servings.

1¼ pounds medium-size shrimp, peeled and deveined (page 9)

3 tablespoons fresh lemon juice

1 tablespoon grated fresh ginger

2 tablespoons black currant vodka or other flavored vodka

¼ teaspoon red hot pepper flakes

Salt and freshly ground pepper to taste

½ pound snow peas

4 ripe plum tomatoes

2 tablespoons butter

2 tablespoons olive oil

1 tablespoon finely chopped garlic

2 tablespoons finely chopped coriander or parsley

1. In a bowl, combine shrimp, lemon juice, ginger, vodka, pepper flakes, salt and pepper to taste. Blend well. Cover with plastic wrap; let stand for at least 15 minutes.

2. Pluck off and discard the ends of each snow pea.

3. Drop tomatoes into a pot of boiling water, let stand about 10 seconds. Remove and peel. Cut away cores, then cut tomatoes into ½-inch cubes.

4. Melt butter and olive oil in a large nonstick skillet over high heat. Add snow peas. Cook, stirring occasionally, for 30 seconds. Add tomatoes, cook for 1 minute, continuing to stir. Add garlic, shrimp, and marinade. Cook about 3 minutes—do not overcook. Check for seasoning. Add coriander, blend well, and serve immediately.

To reduce fat and calories in the shrimp in curry sauce, some of the sour cream used to thicken the sauce has been replaced by yogurt. As I mentioned earlier, eight ounces of unsweetened yogurt has only about 150 calories and 7 grams of fat, as against 493 calories and 9.8 grams of fat for sour cream. Some sour cream is necessary, however, because yogurt alone tends to break down in cooking. In this recipe, the proportion is 1 cup of plain yogurt to ½ cup of sour cream. This quick sauce would also work well with scallops, lobster, chicken, or lamb.

Shrimp in Curry Sauce

I started experimenting with my own blends of curry powder some years ago. Finally, I found a blend that balances heat and spiciness. If you prefer to buy curry powder, take care to keep it sealed tightly—it can go flat quickly.

Shrimp are ideal for time-pressed cooks since they can be prepared in just minutes. With an *à la minute* sauce, like the quick curry described here, dinner can be on the table in well under 60 minutes. This sauce is made with a good homemade curry powder (page 63). Piquant curry counterbalances the sweet ingredients—in this case, onions and apples. Rice is the traditional side dish to curries.

Yield: 4 servings.

1½ pounds medium-size shrimp
1 tablespoon olive oil
½ cup finely chopped onions
¼ pound finely chopped celery
½ cup diced apple, cut into ¼-inch cubes
1 teaspoon finely chopped garlic
Salt and freshly ground pepper to taste
1 bay leaf
1 tablespoon curry powder
1 tablespoon lemon juice
½ cup sour cream
1 cup plain yogurt
¼ cup chopped fresh coriander

1. Peel and devein the shrimp. Rinse well.
2. Heat the oil in a nonstick skillet large enough to hold the shrimp in one layer. Add the onions, celery, apple, and garlic. Add salt and pepper. Cook over medium heat until wilted. Do not brown.
3. Add the shrimp, bay leaf, and curry powder. Cook, stirring often, for about 3 minutes over high heat. Add the lemon juice, sour cream, and yogurt. Gently bring the mixture to a boil while stirring. Sprinkle with coriander and serve immediately with rice or couscous.

Escabeche with Summer Vegetables

❖ ❖

I love visiting Spain and sampling their wonderful cold seafood platters, like the *escabeche* here. Many of their seafood salads have vinegar in them because they sit out on the bar for several hours. This refreshing combination would make a fine brunch entrée or dinner appetizer. It is best if prepared a day ahead and refrigerated.

Yield: 9 servings.

❖

Escabeche *is a Spanish term for a salad that comprises seafood or shellfish that is cooked, then marinated in a spicy mixture. It is usually served cold.*

1 pound mussels, well scrubbed with beards removed (see page 17)

⅓ cup white wine

½ cup olive oil

2 large leeks, cleaned, trimmed, and cut coarsely (about 2 cups)

2 cups cubed onions

2 tablespoons finely chopped garlic

2 small eggplants, trimmed, washed, and cut into ¾-inch cubes (about ¾ pound)

3 large sweet red peppers, cored, seeded, and cut into large cubes

2 medium-size zucchini, trimmed, washed, and cut into ¾-inch cubes (about ¾ pound)

6 plum tomatoes, cored and cut into ½-inch cubes

Salt and freshly ground pepper to taste

½ teaspoon red pepper flakes

1 teaspoon dried oregano

6 sprigs fresh thyme or ½ teaspoon dried

2 bay leaves

24 cured black niçoise or Moroccan olives

4 tablespoons red wine vinegar

1 tablespoon balsamic vinegar

¼ cup drained capers

1 lemon, cut into 12 thin slices, seeds removed

¾ pound mahi-mahi fillets, skinless, cut into 1-inch cubes

1 pound medium-size shrimp, peeled and cleaned

½ cup chopped parsley or coriander

1. Place the mussels and wine in a deep pan, cover tightly, and cook over medium heat for about 2 minutes or until they open. Set aside and let cool. Strain the liquid and reserve ½ cup. Remove meat from the shells and set aside.

(Continued on next page)

2. In a large heavy pan or casserole, heat the olive oil over medium-high flame. Add the leeks, onions, and garlic, and cook, stirring, until wilted. Add the eggplant, and increase heat to high. Cook briefly, stirring. Do not let the garlic brown.

3. Add to the pan the sweet peppers, zucchini, tomatoes, salt, and pepper. Stir. Add the pepper flakes, oregano, thyme, bay leaves, olives, red wine vinegar, balsamic vinegar, capers, lemon, and the reserved cooking liquid. Cook, stirring, for about 10 minutes. Check seasonings.

4. Add the fish fillets, shrimp, and cooked mussels. Cover, and cook for about 4 minutes, stirring gently. Let cool and refrigerate, covered. Serve cold, garnished with sprinkled parsley.

Sichuan-Style Poached Sea Bass with Hot Bean Sauce
◇ ◇

This is a variation of a dish I have had many times at Shun Lee restaurant in Manhattan. My friend Michael Tong, the restaurant's owner, gave me the basic recipe and I have been making it for guests ever since.

Both hot chili sauce and hot bean paste are available in specialty groceries and Asian markets. Taste them for heat level before adding them to the recipe.

Yield: 4 servings.

1 sea bass, cleaned, head and tail left on (1½ to 2 pounds)
6 cups fish or chicken stock
2 tablespoons vegetable oil
1 tablespoon minced ginger
1½ cups finely chopped scallions (white and green sections)
1 tablespoon chili sauce
1 tablespoon hot bean paste
6 tablespoons sweet rice wine (like Shaoxing wine, available in Asian groceries)
1½ teaspoons sugar
½ teaspoon salt

1. Place the fish on its side and, using a sharp knife, make three deep parallel cuts crosswise, about 2 inches apart. Flip the fish and repeat.

2. Bring the stock to a boil in a wok. Leave the heat at high and add the fish. When the liquid returns to a boil, lower the heat to simmer. Cook about 6 minutes or until the fish is barely cooked through. Gently remove the fish to a strainer, discarding the stock but reserving any liquids that drip through the strainer.

3. Wipe out the wok and place over high heat. When it is hot, add the vegetable oil. When the oil is hot, add the ginger and the scallions. Cook, stirring, for 10 seconds, then add the chili sauce, hot bean paste, and sweet rice wine. Cook, stirring, for 20 seconds, then add any reserved poaching liquid, along with the sugar and salt. Bring the sauce to a boil.

4. Place the fish in the boiling sauce and spoon some sauce over it. Continue cooking and spooning the sauce over the fish for 2 minutes. Remove from the heat.

5. Carefully transfer the fish to a platter. Check the sauce for seasoning, pour sauce over the fish, and serve.

Sautéed Striped Bass with Wild Mushrooms

◇ ◇

Unfortunately, I cannot eat the sea bass I catch near my home on Eastern Long Island (because of pollution in their Hudson River breeding grounds). To my taste, sea bass is one of the finest fish for cooking. Sea bass from other waters are on the market, though, and I served this one with a mildly seasoned wild mushroom sauce.

Yield: 4 servings.

3 large Idaho or Washington potatoes, peeled and cut into ovals ⅛ inch thick
6 tablespoons vegetable oil, plus more if needed
Salt to taste
3 cups coarsely sliced cèpes or porcini (about 1 pound)
1 cup coarsely sliced chanterelles (about ⅓ pound)
Freshly ground pepper to taste
4 tablespoons finely chopped shallots
1 teaspoon finely chopped garlic
4 tablespoons finely chopped parsley
4 striped bass fillets, with skin removed (about 6 ounces each)
¼ cup flour for dredging
4 tablespoons butter
1 tablespoon lemon juice
4 tablespoons chopped chives

1. Rinse the potato slices under cold running water, drain well and pat dry.

2. Heat 2 tablespoons of oil in a large, nonstick skillet over high heat. Add potatoes, salt to taste, and cook until lightly browned on both sides. Remove from skillet; keep warm.

3. Add a little more oil to the pan if necessary, and add the cèpes and chanterelles. Salt and pepper to taste. Cook over high heat until the mushrooms wilt. Add the shallots, garlic, and parsley. Cook for about 1 minute, stirring gently; set aside. Keep warm.

4. Dredge the fish in flour, and shake off the excess. Set aside.

5. In another large, nonstick skillet, add the 4 remaining tablespoons of vegetable oil over medium heat. Add the fillets. Season well. Cook until lightly browned, about 3 or 4 minutes. Reduce the heat to

medium, gently flip the fish and cook 3 to 4 minutes more, or until done. Do not overcook. Remove and keep warm.

6. Divide the potatoes evenly over 4 plates in a ring pattern. Place the fish over the center, and put the mushroom mixture over the fish.

7. In a saucepan over medium-high heat, melt the butter and cook, swirling the butter occasionally, until lightly browned. Add lemon juice, then pour lemon butter equally over each serving. Sprinkle with chives and serve.

Curried Mussels

◇ ◇

This is an elegant, and absolutely delicious, first course. You can make it in well under half an hour.

Yield: 4 servings.

1 cup heavy cream
1 tablespoon mild curry powder (page 63)
1 tablespoon freshly squeezed lemon juice
3 tablespoons butter
¼ cup shallots, sliced thin
4 sprigs fresh thyme or 1 teaspoon dried
1 bay leaf
1 cup dry white wine
9 cups mussels, cleaned (page 17) (about 3 pounds)
2 tablespoons flour
Salt to taste

1. Combine the cream, curry powder, and lemon juice in a small bowl and mix well. (This step enables the curry flavor to develop.)

2. Melt 1 tablespoon of the butter in a large pot over high heat. Add the shallots, thyme, and bay leaf. Stir until wilted. Add the white wine and bring to a simmer. Add the mussels, cover, and cook for 2 to 3 minutes, or just until the mussels open. Stir from time to time to assure even cooking. As soon as the mussels are opened, remove them from heat, and strain cooking liquid through a fine sieve into a bowl. Reserve 2 cups of the juice.

(Continued on next page)

Rainbow trout, a freshwater fish, has a fairly rich flesh. For that reason, it goes well with sauces high in acid, such as a vinaigrette, or in this case, an orange sauce. Lemon butter is also good with trout.

3. Remove the top shell from each mussel and discard it, leaving the mussel meat attached to its bottom shell. Arrange decoratively on a serving platter and keep warm.

4. In a large saucepan over medium heat, melt the remaining butter and whisk in the flour, stirring until the mixture is smooth. Cook briefly; do not brown. Slowly add the 2 cups of reserved cooking juice, whisking constantly. Bring to a rolling boil. Add the cream-and-curry mixture, and combine well. Strain the sauce through a fine sieve. Add salt, and check for seasoning. Ladle the sauce over the mussels, and serve immediately.

Sautéed Trout with Orange

I am an avid fisherman, but primarily I fish in saltwater bays and the ocean. I love rainbow trout, however, and when I see really fresh ones in the market, I buy them. Their rich flesh goes beautifully with this acidic-sweet orange sauce.

Yield: 4 servings.

4 rainbow trout, butterflied, with bones, heads, and tails removed
   (about ½ pound each)
¼ cup milk
½ cup all-purpose flour for dredging
Salt and freshly ground pepper to taste
2 tablespoons olive or vegetable oil
24 orange sections, with membranes removed
2 tablespoons chopped shallots
4 sprigs fresh lemon thyme, leaves only, or 1 teaspoon dried thyme
1 tablespoon lemon juice
3 tablespoons lemon-flavored vodka
2 tablespoons soft butter
4 sprigs fresh basil or parsley for garnishing

1. Place the trout in a large bowl and pour in the milk. Spread the flour over a flat dish and season with salt and pepper. Remove the trout from the milk and dredge them in the flour, shaking to remove excess flour.

2. Over high setting, heat the oil in a large nonstick skillet or black steel pan. Add the trout and cook for about 3 minutes, or until lightly browned. Turn and sauté for another 2 to 3 minutes or until fully cooked. Remove and set aside. Keep warm.

3. Pour off the excess fat from the pan. Add the orange sections, shallots, and lemon thyme, and cook briefly, just to warm through. Do not brown the shallots. Stir in the lemon juice, vodka, and the soft butter. Blend well.

4. To serve, place a trout on a warm plate and spoon some sauce over it. Garnish with the basil.

Pan-Fried Skate Wings with Capers
◇ ◇

This is the first skate recipe I learned as a young cook. It is a classic, still popular today. It calls for dredging the skate wings in milk and flour and then sautéing them in butter or oil. A quick caper-butter sauce is then made and poured over the fish.

Yield: 4 servings.

4 boneless, skinless skate wings (about 1½ pounds total)
½ cup milk
Salt and freshly ground pepper to taste
4 tablespoons all-purpose flour for dredging
3 tablespoons vegetable or corn oil
4 tablespoons butter
½ cup sweet red peppers, cut into ¼-inch cubes
⅓ cup drained capers
2 tablespoons finely chopped shallots
2 tablespoons red wine vinegar
4 tablespoons finely chopped parsley

1. Put the skate fillets in a dish large enough to hold them in one layer. Pour the milk over them and sprinkle with salt and pepper to taste. Turn the fillets in the milk so they are coated on both sides.

2. Scatter the flour over a large dish. Lightly dredge the fillets on both sides in the flour.

(Continued on next page)

◇

It is remarkable how common skate has become on restaurant menus. It is not yet well known to home cooks. Skate is a delectable fish with a mild flavor and—if cooked properly—a delicate texture. Incorrectly prepared, it can be tough and fibrous. A kind of ray, it has a flat body and a short, spineless tail. It is found in oceans worldwide, weighing anywhere from several pounds to 2 tons. The wings are the only edible portion.

Skate improves when left to stand refrigerated for a day or two. As it matures, the flesh becomes firmer and more palatable. When purchased, it has usually been aged slightly.

3. Heat the oil in a large nonstick skillet over medium-high setting. When the oil is hot but not smoking, add the fillets. If it is necessary to do this in two batches, use the same oil. Sauté on one side until golden brown, about 3 minutes. Turn and cook on the other side until golden brown, about 3 minutes more. When the fillets are done, transfer them to a warm platter or serving plate.

4. Wipe out the pan with a paper towel and return it to the heat. Melt the butter and add the red peppers, shaking the pan frequently until the butter turns light brown. Add the capers, cook briefly, and add the shallots, vinegar, and parsley. Cook briefly; then stir and pour the sauce over each fillet evenly. Serve immediately.

Marinated Broiled Tuna Steaks with Sauce Niçoise
◇ ◇

Sometimes in summer I go out to the fishing piers in Montauk, Long Island, and watch fishermen haul in the monstrous tunas. If I'm lucky, I'll buy a few steaks from local retailers. Tuna's fatty flesh goes very well with fresh summer vegetables and a little vinegar.

Yield: 4 servings.

4 center-cut tuna steaks, about 1 inch thick (6 ounces each)
Salt and freshly ground pepper to taste
6 tablespoons olive oil
4 sprigs fresh thyme or 2 teaspoons dried
2 crumbled bay leaves
4 small sprigs fresh rosemary or 2 teaspoons dried
⅛ teaspoon red pepper flakes
4 ripe plum tomatoes
½ cup thinly sliced fennel bulb (white part only)
½ cup sliced red onions
2 teaspoons coarsely chopped garlic
6 pitted black olives
2 teaspoons grated lemon rind
2 tablespoons red wine vinegar
4 tablespoons coarsely chopped fresh basil or parsley

1. Preheat broiler to high or turn on outdoor charcoal grill.

2. Place the tuna in a dish and sprinkle both sides with salt and pepper. Brush both sides with 2 tablespoons olive oil. Add the thyme, bay leaves, rosemary, and pepper flakes. Cover with plastic wrap and let it stand for 20 minutes.

3. Place the tomatoes in boiling water for about 10 seconds. Drain and pull away the skin. Cut and discard the core and chop the tomatoes coarsely.

4. Place the remaining olive oil in a small saucepan over medium-high heat. When it is hot, add the fennel, onions, and garlic. Cook briefly until wilted. Add the tomatoes, olives, lemon rind, vinegar, salt and pepper to taste. Cover and simmer for 5 minutes.

5. Transfer the mixture into a blender or food processor. Add 3 tablespoons of the basil, then blend for 5 to 7 seconds, taking care that it remain coarse. Transfer the sauce to a saucepan, check for seasoning, reheat briefly. Keep warm.

6. If broiling, arrange the tuna steaks on a rack and place under the broiler about 5 inches from the heat source. Broil 5 minutes with the door partly open. Turn the steaks, and, leaving the door open, continue broiling about 5 minutes longer. (Check after 3 minutes.) The steaks should not be overcooked.

7. If grilling, place the steaks on a hot grill and cover. Cook for 5 minutes. Turn the fish, cover the grill, and continue cooking for about 3 minutes. Check for doneness. Serve with the prepared sauce around the fish and sprinkle with the remaining basil.

Tuna Steaks Moroccan Style

◇ ◇

I am particularly fond of the Moroccan style of seasoning seafood and lamb. It is not difficult to replicate at home—you just need a well-stocked spice rack. This dish has a lot of ingredients, mostly dried spices, but once you spread them out on the counter, the rest of the cooking is quite easy.

Yield: 4 servings.

1 teaspoon paprika
½ teaspoon ground cumin
1 teaspoon turmeric
¼ teaspoon ground aniseed
½ teaspoon ground fresh ginger or ¼ teaspoon dried
⅛ teaspoon ground cinnamon
¼ teaspoon red hot pepper flakes
Salt and freshly ground white pepper to taste
4 tuna steaks, about 1½ inches thick (about 1½ pounds total weight)
1 tablespoon fresh lemon juice
2 tablespoons olive oil
2 tablespoons melted butter
4 tablespoons coarsely chopped coriander

1. In a small mixing bowl, combine paprika, cumin, turmeric, aniseed, ginger, cinnamon, red pepper flakes, salt and pepper, and blend well.

2. Place the tuna steaks on a large platter and rub each side with the spice mixture. Sprinkle evenly with the lemon juice and oil. Cover with plastic wrap. Let stand until ready to cook—no more than 2 hours.

3. If broiling, arrange the steaks on a rack and place under a very hot broiler about 4 inches from the heat. Broil 4 minutes with the door partly open. Turn, continue cooking or broiling, leaving the door partly open for about 3 to 4 minutes for pink inside. For rare, cook less. The steaks should be well browned.

4. For panfrying, heat a heavy cast-iron skillet that is large enough to hold the steaks in one layer. Do not add fat. When the skillet is quite hot, add the tuna steaks and cook until well browned on one side, about 3 minutes. Flip and cook 3 minutes more for rare.

5. Place the tuna steaks on warm plates, brush them with the melted butter, and sprinkle with coriander. Serve with couscous.

NOTE: Here is a presentation tip for the cooked couscous: Take a medium-sized coffee cup and fill it with couscous. Pack it down with the back of a spoon. Invert the cup on a serving plate, tapping it lightly to demold. You will have a little tower of couscous.

◇

Couscous is often misidentified as a grain; in fact, it is a tiny semolina pasta that can be flavored in countless ways. It is a nice alternative to rice. This one is sweetened with raisins and sweet peppers. You could add any kind of chopped, cooked vegetables of choice.

Couscous with Raisins and Red Peppers
◇ ◇

Yield: 4 servings.

1 tablespoon olive oil
⅓ cup finely chopped onions
½ cup sweet red pepper, cut into small cubes
1¼ cups boiling water
⅓ cup raisins
⅛ teaspoon ground cinnamon
¼ teaspoon ground cumin
½ teaspoon grated orange rind
Salt and freshly ground pepper to taste
1 cup quick couscous

1. In a saucepan with a tight lid, heat the olive oil. Add the onions and red peppers and cook, stirring, until wilted. Do not brown the onions. Add the water, raisins, cinnamon, cumin, orange rind, salt, and pepper. Bring to a boil.
2. Remove from the heat, add the couscous and stir well. Cover and let stand for 5 minutes. Uncover, and fluff well with a fork. Serve with the Moroccan-style tuna steaks.

Rolled Fillets of Sole à la Nage

◇ ◇

The terms sole *and* flounder
are often confused. Many North
Atlantic flatfish are called sole
even though they may belong to
the flounder family. Sole of all
kinds is the most popular
American eating fish, so it
behooves cooks to know its
variations.

I had second thoughts about putting this classic French recipe in
the book, since it does require a little handiwork. But it is so attractive on the plate, and so flavorful, that I think it is worth the
effort. The term *nage* refers to a method of cooking in which the
ingredients are poached in a seasoned broth.

Yield: 4 servings.

4 large boneless, skinless lemon sole fillets (about 6 ounces each)
2 small zucchini (about ½ pound)
1 pound mussels
4 thin slices gingerroot
2 sprigs fresh thyme or 1 teaspoon dried
1 bay leaf
2 cups dry white wine
12 baby carrots, all about the same size, trimmed and scraped
Salt to taste
8 tablespoons butter
2 tablespoons chopped shallots
Freshly ground pepper to taste
8 sprigs fresh coriander

1. Put fillets of sole on a flat surface. A thin line runs lengthwise
down the center of each fillet. Run a sharp knife in the center to divide
the fillets. Now you have 8 fillets.

2. Cut off zucchini ends. If you have a mandoline-like device that
makes long strips, make long, thin spaghetti-like pieces; if you have no
such device, just slice the zucchini into thin rounds.

3. Clean the mussels (page 17) and drain. Place them in a saucepan.
Add the ginger, thyme, bay leaf, and wine. Cover tightly and bring to a
boil. Cook 30 seconds or until mussels open. Let cool. Remove meat
from shells and set aside. Strain liquid and set aside.

4. Place the carrots in a saucepan with water to cover and salt. Bring
to a boil and simmer for 10 minutes or until tender. Drain. Keep warm.

5. Roll fillets like small jelly rolls. Insert a toothpick to hold them
together. Place 1 tablespoon butter in a skillet large enough to hold the
rolls in one layer. Sprinkle shallots over bottom of the skillet and add salt
and pepper.

6. Arrange the rolls in the pan. Salt and pepper well. Pour the mussel broth over the fish. Cover closely and bring to a boil. Simmer for about 3 minutes. Do not overcook. Remove the fillets and keep them warm. Strain the cooking liquid.

7. Transfer the cooking liquid to a saucepan over medium-high heat. Reduce the liquid to two-thirds. Add the remaining butter bit by bit to the saucepan, beating rapidly with a wire whisk. Add the zucchini and simmer for 10 seconds, stirring with a fork. Keep very hot.

8. To serve, give each diner 2 fish fillets (in a shallow soup bowl). To each plate, add 3 slices carrots and a few mussels around the fillets. Pour the broth over them. Add zucchini. Garnish with coriander sprigs. Serve hot.

◈

What exactly is lemon sole?

Lemon sole, a popular fish in markets, is actually a flounder. This cold-water fish from the Atlantic usually weighs more than 3 pounds when caught. The fillets are off-white and mild in flavor. Gray sole, also a flounder, is slightly smaller and commands a premium price because of its clear white color and delicate texture. It is the fish for people who don't like fish. The biologically correct term for these fish is witch flounder.

What is Dover sole?

Dover sole, technically speaking, is the only authentic member of the sole family sold in this country. The name derives from the English port of Dover, a major market for the thick, meaty fish. Dover sole used to be sold frozen, but jet transportation now makes it available fresh in restaurants and markets, although for a hefty price.

Sautéed Fillet of Sole with Fresh Tomatoes and Ginger Sauce

◈ ◈

Yield: 4 servings.

4 ripe tomatoes (about 1 pound)
1 tablespoon olive oil
2 tablespoons chopped shallots
1 teaspoon finely chopped garlic
2 tablespoons grated fresh ginger
1 teaspoon ground cumin
Salt and ground pepper to taste
4 tablespoons butter
4 skinless fillets of lemon sole (about 1 pound)
4 tablespoons milk
½ cup flour
2 tablespoons vegetable oil
1 tablespoon fresh lemon juice
4 sprigs fresh basil or parsley

1. Place the tomatoes in boiling water for about 10 seconds. Drain, and pull away skins; remove cores. Cut tomatoes crosswise and into ¼-inch cubes.

2. Heat olive oil in saucepan, add shallots and garlic. Cook briefly. Do not brown. Add tomatoes, ginger, cumin, and salt and pepper to taste. Bring to a boil and simmer 5 minutes.

3. Place tomato mixture in a blender. Add 1 tablespoon butter and blend quickly to a fine texture. Check seasoning; transfer to a small saucepan and keep warm.

4. Meanwhile, sprinkle fillets with salt and pepper to taste. Pour milk into a shallow bowl; put the flour on a dish. Dredge each fillet in the milk, then in the flour, patting so a thin coating of flour adheres—shake to remove excess flour.

5. Heat vegetable oil in a large nonstick skillet over medium-high setting. Place as many fillets in the pan as will fit in one layer without crowding.

6. Brown fillets thoroughly on one side; turn, and brown on other side. Cooking will take about 2 to 3 minutes on each side, depending on the thickness of the fillets. Do not overcook.

7. Divide tomato mixture equally among 4 warm serving plates. Place fillets over tomatoes, and keep warm.

8. While the pan is still warm, wipe it out with a paper towel and return it to medium-high heat. Add the remaining butter, and cook until hazelnut brown. Add lemon juice, and pour equally over each serving. Top with basil or parsley.

Snapper Fillets Provençal Style

◇ ◇

I have made this recipe successfully with gray sole, lemon sole, swordfish, grouper, pompano, and other white-fleshed species. Red snapper, a particularly delicate and delicious fish, is the most popular of the hundreds of species of snapper found in the oceans. It is found in the Atlantic from Brazil to as far north as North Carolina.

The broth in this dish is delicious with rice. The quick saffron rice recipe here takes only 17 minutes to cook. It is seasoned with onions, garlic, almond slivers, saffron, thyme, and bay leaf.

Yield: 4 servings.

◇

Braising is an excellent and little-used method for cooking mild white-fleshed fish like snapper. The braising liquid and slow cooking impart flavors from the seasonings. This method for snapper Provençal style is not only simple and relatively risk-free, but also abundant with flavor.

2 tablespoons olive oil
2 teaspoons finely chopped garlic
1 cup finely chopped leeks
2 cups peeled and chopped fresh plum tomatoes
½ cup chopped fennel
1 teaspoon turmeric
Salt and freshly ground pepper to taste
½ cup dry white wine
½ cup fish broth (page 61) or bottled clam juice
1 bay leaf
4 sprigs fresh thyme or 1 teaspoon dried
⅛ teaspoon Tabasco
4 snapper fillets with skin on (about 6 ounces each)
2 tablespoons Ricard or other anise-flavored liquor
2 tablespoons chopped fresh basil or parsley

(Continued on next page)

If you don't have expensive saffron, you can substitute ground turmeric, which is the root of a tropical plant. The yellowish powder has a slightly bitter flavor, so you don't want to use too much. It gives food a lovely golden color. Store dried turmeric in a cool, dry place.

1. Heat 1 tablespoon of the olive oil in a saucepan and add the garlic, leeks, tomatoes, fennel, and turmeric. Season with salt and pepper. Cook, stirring, over medium heat about 3 minutes. Add the wine, broth, bay leaf, thyme, and Tabasco. Bring to a boil and simmer for 5 minutes.

2. In a large pan, add the remaining tablespoon of oil, arrange the fillets of fish in one layer. Season with salt and pepper. Pour the leek-tomato mixture evenly over the fish fillets. Sprinkle the Ricard, cover and simmer for about 5 minutes or until cooked. Sprinkle with basil and discard bay leaf before serving.

Saffron Rice

Yield: 4 servings.

1 tablespoon olive oil
¼ cup finely chopped onions
1 teaspoon finely chopped garlic
1 cup converted rice or parboiled rice
¼ cup almond slivers
½ teaspoon saffron stems or ½ teaspoon turmeric
2 sprigs fresh thyme
1 bay leaf
1½ cups water
Salt and freshly ground white pepper to taste

1. Heat the oil in a saucepan and add the onions and garlic. Cook, stirring, until the onions are wilted. Add the rice, almonds, saffron, thyme, bay leaf, water, salt, and pepper. Bring to a boil, stirring. Cover tightly and simmer for 17 minutes.

2. Discard the thyme and bay leaf. With a fork, toss the rice lightly. Keep the rice covered in a warm place until it is served.

Steamed Halibut Fillets
with Scallion-Ginger Vinaigrette
◇ ◇

This is an extremely healthful and flavorful dish. You could make it with cod as well.

Yield: 4 servings.

½ cup coarsely chopped scallions, including greens

1 tablespoon grated ginger

3 tablespoons coarsely chopped parsley

1 teaspoon minced garlic

6 tablespoons olive oil

1 tablespoon wine vinegar

1 tablespoon fresh lemon juice

2 tablespoons Dijon-style mustard

Salt and freshly ground pepper to taste

1 hard-cooked egg, quartered

4 boneless, skinless halibut or salmon fillets (about 6 ounces each)

4 slices lemon

1. Combine the scallions, ginger, parsley, garlic, oil, vinegar, lemon juice, mustard, salt and pepper to taste in a food processor or blender. Blend until the herbs are finely chopped—the ingredients should retain some texture.

2. Add the quartered egg and process briefly, until coarsely blended.

3. Pour water into the bottom of a steamer. Season the fillets with salt and coarsely ground pepper. Place them on a steamer rack. Lay 1 lemon slice over each fillet. Cover, bring the water to a boil, and steam for 4 to 5 minutes. Do not overcook.

4. Transfer the fish fillets to a serving plate and place some sauce over them. The dish can be served cold or at room temperature. This is nice served over a bed of spinach.

◇

I have a little gadget at home that makes grating ginger easy. It is ceramic, about the size of an endive leaf, and has a grate on one side. It is available in many kitchenware shops. You can also use a regular kitchen grater and run the ginger over the side of the smallest grate.

Poached Halibut Steaks with Lemon Sauce

◇ ◇

To my taste, a simple lemon sauce sweetened with shallots is a sublime combination with just about any type of fish.

Yield: 4 servings.

4 halibut steaks, each about 1 inch thick (about ½ pound each)
¼ cup milk
6 peppercorns
1 bay leaf
2 sprigs fresh thyme or ½ teaspoon dried
⅛ teaspoon cayenne pepper
¼ cup sliced onion
4 sprigs fresh parsley
Salt and freshly ground pepper to taste
2 tablespoons butter
2 tablespoons finely chopped shallots
2 tablespoons olive oil
2 tablespoons fresh lemon juice
2 tablespoons finely chopped parsley

1. Arrange the steaks in a skillet large enough to hold them in one layer (or use 2 pans). Add water to cover. Add the milk, peppercorns, bay leaf, thyme, cayenne, onion, parsley sprigs, salt, and pepper. Bring to a simmer and cook gently 4 to 5 minutes. Cooking time will depend on the thickness of the fish. Cook only until the fish flakes easily when tested with a fork.

2. Heat 1 tablespoon of the butter in a saucepan and add the shallots. Cook briefly, stirring. Remove ¼ cup of the cooking liquid from the fish and add it to the shallots. Bring to a boil and simmer about 3 minutes or until reduced by half. Add the remaining butter, the olive oil, and lemon juice. Bring to a simmer. Add the parsley, salt, and pepper.

3. Drain the fish and serve hot with the sauce.

Flounder with Chervil Butter Sauce

◇ ◇

Chervil is one of the more delicate herbs in my garden. I use it mostly with seafood and soups. In this recipe, it nicely complements the mild-tasting flounder.

Yield: 4 servings.

◇

Chervil is a mild-mannered member of the parsley family. It has lacy, pale green leaves, and a faint anise flavor. It is wonderful in salads and sauces.

4 tablespoons butter
Salt and freshly ground pepper to taste
4 fillets of flounder (about 1¼ pounds)
3 tablespoons dry white wine
4 tablespoons chopped fresh chervil or parsley

1. Preheat the oven to 475 degrees.
2. Select a baking dish large enough to hold the fillets in one layer. Grease the bottom with 1 tablespoon of the butter. Sprinkle with salt and pepper.
3. Arrange the fillets close together in the pan. Sprinkle with salt and pepper and brush the top with 1 tablespoon of the wine.
4. Place the fish in the oven and bake 5 minutes.
5. Meanwhile, place the remaining 3 tablespoons butter in a saucepan. Add the remaining wine. Bring to a boil and cook for 1 minute. Add salt, pepper, and chervil. Blend well with a wire whisk.
6. Transfer the fish to a warm serving plate. Pour the sauce evenly over the fish and serve immediately.

Flounder Fillets with Mushrooms and Tomatoes

◇ ◇

This recipe can be made with flounder or lemon sole. The sesame seeds give the fish a pleasant crunch.

Yield: 4 servings.

1 tablespoon butter
1 tablespoon olive oil
⅓ pound mushrooms, cut into small cubes
2 teaspoons finely chopped garlic
4 ripe plum tomatoes, cored, peeled, and cut into small cubes
1 tablespoon fresh lemon juice
2 sprigs fresh thyme or 1 teaspoon dried
Salt and freshly ground pepper to taste
6 tablespoons sesame seeds
1¼ pounds fillet of flounder
2 tablespoons corn or vegetable oil
3 tablespoons chopped fresh parsley

1. Heat butter and olive oil in a skillet. Add mushrooms, and cook briefly over medium-high heat, shaking the pan until the mushrooms are lightly browned. Add garlic; do not brown. Add tomatoes, lemon juice, thyme, and salt and pepper to taste. Cook, stirring, for 5 minutes. Remove from heat and keep warm.

2. Spread sesame seeds on a large platter. Season fillets with salt and pepper. Lay the fillets over the sesame seeds on one side, then on the other, to coat them lightly.

3. Heat corn oil in a large nonstick skillet and place fillets in it without crowding. Cook over high heat until fillets and seeds are lightly browned on both sides. Time will vary depending on thickness of fillets.

4. Spoon sauce onto warmed serving plates. Place fish fillets over sauce, sprinkle with parsley, and serve.

Monkfish Stew with Red Wine (Matelote)

Yield: 4 servings.

2 tablespoons butter

½ pound small mushrooms (if large, cut into quarters)

½ cup finely chopped onion

¼ cup finely chopped shallots

¼ cup finely chopped carrots

¼ cup finely chopped celery

1 teaspoon finely chopped garlic

2 teaspoons chopped fresh thyme or 1 teaspoon dried

1 bay leaf

2 tablespoons flour

1½ cups dry red wine

1 cup fresh fish broth (see page 61) or bottled clam juice

2 cloves

1½ pounds monkfish fillets, cut into ½-inch cubes

Salt and freshly ground pepper to taste

2 tablespoons cognac

2 tablespoons finely chopped parsley

1. Heat the butter in a saucepan and add the mushrooms, onion, shallots, carrots, celery, garlic, thyme, and bay leaf. Cook, stirring, until the onion is wilted. Add the flour and stir. Add the wine, fish broth, and cloves, stirring with a wire whisk. Bring to a boil. Simmer for 20 minutes and reduce liquid to about 1¾ cups.

2. Add the fish, salt, and pepper, stirring gently so that the fish is coated with the sauce. Simmer for about 5 minutes and add the cognac. Sprinkle with parsley and serve.

One of the classic dishes of my home region of Burgundy, matelote *is made with freshwater fish, vegetables, and red wine. As a young boy, I would fish in the nearby river and bring the catch home for my mother to make* matelote. *There are variations on the dish from region to region. In the northeast region of Touraine, for example,* matelote *contains prunes. In this version, there is boneless fillet of monkfish, whose firm texture holds up well to any kind of wine cooking. You could substitute any firm-fleshed, non-oily fish.*

The base for the stew here, loosely based on matelote, *is made by sautéing some mushrooms, onions, shallots, carrots, celery, thyme, bay leaf, and garlic. Flour is added as a binder. Then comes the wine— obviously Burgundy is best— and the fish broth. This is reduced for 20 minutes; then the fish is added. The monkfish should be finished in about 5 minutes.*

Marinated Monkfish Brochettes

◇ ◇

Monkfish are excellent for grilling since their flesh is so firm. In this quick recipe, the monkfish cubes marinate with rosemary, garlic, hot red pepper flakes, cumin, mustard, lemon juice, and red peppers. They should marinate only about 15 minutes (too long and you risk cooking the fish in the acidic marinade).

I love to grill outside, and I do it all year long—even in the snow! Monkfish is ideal for grilling because of its meaty, firm flesh.

Yield: 4 servings.

1¾ pounds monkfish fillets

2 medium-size sweet red peppers

Salt and freshly ground black pepper to taste

2 tablespoons lemon juice

1 tablespoon coarse Dijon-style mustard

1 teaspoon ground cumin

⅛ teaspoon hot red pepper flakes

2 teaspoons finely chopped garlic

1 tablespoon chopped fresh rosemary

4 tablespoons melted butter

4 tablespoons chopped fresh parsley

1. Cut the monkfish into 1½-inch cubes. There should be about 24 pieces.

2. Cut away and discard the core and veins of the peppers and cut them into about 24 pieces about 1 inch square.

3. Blend remaining ingredients except the butter and parsley in a large bowl. Add the monkfish, cover with the mixture, and cover with plastic wrap. Let marinate up to half an hour at room temperature.

4. Heat the grill or oven broiler to high. Soak 4 large wooden skewers in cold water until ready to use.

5. On each skewer arrange alternately 6 or so pieces of monkfish and peppers. Brush with the marinade. Set aside the leftover marinade.

6. Put the skewers on the grill or under the broiler and cook about 4 minutes. Turn the skewers over and cook 3 to 4 minutes longer. While cooking, brush them with the reserved marinade. Put them on a warm serving platter and brush with melted butter and sprinkle with parsley. Serve immediately, with rice or couscous.

Poached Lobsters with Basil Sauce

◆ ◆

I harvest all of my basil in early September. Half goes into pesto, which I freeze; the other half is simply puréed with some olive oil, salt, and pepper so I have a base sauce to work with throughout the year. This is the kind of dish I would make with it.

Yield: 4 servings.

4 lobsters, preferably female (about 1¼ pounds each)
4 small zucchini (totaling about 1 pound)
2 tablespoons butter
2 tablespoons finely chopped shallots
½ cup dry white wine
8 fresh basil leaves, coarsely chopped
½ cup cream
Salt to taste
⅛ teaspoon cayenne pepper
1 tablespoon melted butter for zucchini

1. Bring enough water to a boil to cover the lobsters when they are added. Put in lobsters and let water return to boil. Cook 10 minutes.

2. Meanwhile, trim off ends of zucchini and cut into ¼-inch rounds. Steam or boil them. To steam, place zucchini in top of a steamer rack and put rack over the steamer bottom containing boiling water. To boil, bring enough water to a boil to cover zucchini when added. Add the zucchini. Steam or boil the zucchini 4 minutes or until tender but still crisp. Drain.

2. In the meantime, heat 1 tablespoon butter in a saucepan and add shallots. Cook until wilted. Add wine and basil. Bring to a boil and cook until the liquid is almost evaporated. Add cream and bring to a boil. Cook about 30 seconds. Swirl in remaining butter, salt, and cayenne.

3. Line a small saucepan with a sieve and pour the sauce into it. Press as much liquid as possible from the solids.

4. Serve hot. Drain lobsters. It is best to remove meat from shells. It is easier, however, to split lobsters in half lengthwise and spoon small amounts of sauce on top. Serve zucchini slices with melted butter brushed on top.

◆

It is best to cook lobsters the day you buy them. If you need to store them in the refrigerator, wrap them in a wet towel and place them in the coldest part, which is the bottom.

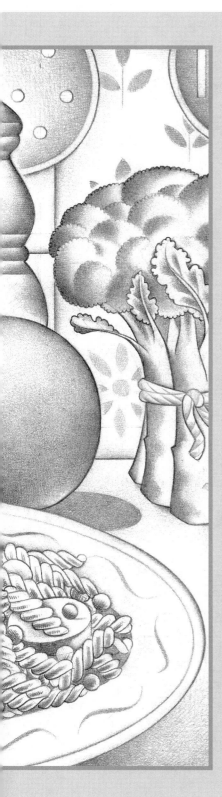

Pasta

◇ ◇ ◇

Ziti with Scallops and Shrimp

Turkey Lasagna with Fresh Tomato Sauce

Fettuccine with Goat Cheese and Asparagus

Shrimp and Fettuccine Medley

Spaghettini with Zucchini

Fusilli with Eggplant and Zucchini

Ziti with Mussels and Broccoli

Fettuccine with Ham and Asparagus

Spaghetti with Shrimp and Eggplant

Spaghetti with Southwestern-Style Meatballs

Penne with Broccoli Rape

Spaghettini with Vegetables and Pepper Vodka Sauce

Linguine with Mussels

Angel Hair with Prosciutto and Wild Mushrooms

Linguine with Clam Sauce

Ziti with Chicken and Broccoli

Penne with Smoked Salmon

Fusilli with Zucchini, Prosciutto, and Tomatoes

Ziti with Scallops and Shrimp

◇ ◇

I like to combine two types of seafood in certain pastas, each with different textures and flavors. Shrimp and scallops are a good example. Just remember not to overcook either one, for they will become rubbery.

Yield: 4 servings.

¼ cup plus 1 tablespoon olive oil
½ cup minced onion
2 cloves garlic, peeled and minced
½ cup dry white wine
½ cup canned crushed tomatoes (imported is best)
1 teaspoon fresh tarragon, chopped, or ½ teaspoon dried
¼ teaspoon dried red pepper flakes, or to taste
Salt to taste
Freshly ground black pepper to taste
1 pound ziti
3½ cups broccoli florets (approximately), cut into bite-sized pieces
1 pound sea scallops (halve the biggest ones)
¾ pound shrimp
¼ cup minced parsley

1. Fill a large pot with salted water and place it over high heat. Meanwhile, heat ¼ cup olive oil in a pan and add the onion and garlic. Cook over medium heat, stirring, for about 3 minutes—do not brown the garlic. Add wine, tomatoes, tarragon, pepper flakes, salt, and pepper. Bring sauce to a boil, stir, and set aside.

2. When the water boils, add the pasta and cook, stirring often, about 10 minutes—the pasta should be short of al dente, still slightly firm. Add broccoli to the water with the pasta. When the water returns to a boil, cook for 4 minutes. Test pasta for doneness, then drain the pasta and broccoli, reserving 1 cup of cooking water. Add them to the sauce and place over medium heat.

3. Meanwhile, pour the remaining tablespoon of oil into another large pan over medium heat. Add the scallops. Cook for about 1 minute, flipping the scallops once. Add the scallops to the sauce. Add the shrimp. Cook about 2 minutes more. Remove from the heat. If the sauce seems too thick, add some of the reserved cooking water. Serve garnished with parsley.

Turkey Lasagna with Fresh Tomato Sauce

◇ ◇

I am a great proponent of lean, healthful turkey parts, which can substitute in many cases for beef and veal. Here is a wonderful recipe using ground turkey. After it is seasoned and sauced, your guests will think it is beef. Get ground turkey from the leg—it is more moist than meat from the breast. This recipe has many steps, but nothing is difficult. You can make a large portion and freeze it.

Yield: 4 to 6 servings.

For the Sauce

2½ pounds ripe plum tomatoes or 4 cups canned crushed tomatoes
1 tablespoon olive oil
2 tablespoons minced garlic
⅛ teaspoon hot red pepper flakes, or to taste
1 teaspoon chopped fresh oregano or ½ teaspoon dried
Salt and freshly ground pepper to taste

For the Lasagna

2 tablespoons olive oil
2 pounds ground turkey meat (or minced leftover cooked turkey)
1 teaspoon minced garlic
½ cup dry red wine
1 teaspoon chopped fresh oregano or ½ teaspoon dried
Salt and freshly ground pepper to taste
12 lasagna strips (available in supermarkets)
2 cups cold water
Oil for greasing the dish
2 cups ricotta cheese
¼ cup hot water
½ cup grated Parmesan cheese

1. To make the sauce, core the tomatoes and cut them into 1-inch cubes. Put the tomatoes in a food processor or blender and blend until coarsely chopped. There should be about 4 cups. *(Continued on next page)*

2. Heat the oil in a skillet and add the garlic. Cook briefly but do not brown it. Add the tomatoes, red pepper flakes, oregano, salt, and pepper. Bring to a boil and simmer for 10 minutes.

3. Preheat the oven to 400 degrees.

4. To prepare the turkey, heat the oil in a nonstick pan and add the meat. Cook, stirring to break up the particles, until lightly browned.

5. Add the garlic, stir, and add the wine. Bring to a boil over high heat and cook until the wine has evaporated. Add the tomato sauce, oregano, salt, and pepper. Simmer for 5 minutes.

6. Meanwhile, cook the lasagna in salted water according to package instructions, adding the lasagna strips one at a time. Cook until tender. Drain and add the cold water to cool. Drain again and spread the strips one at a time on a damp cloth.

7. Lightly grease a 2-quart oblong baking dish. Add a layer of lasagna.

8. In a bowl, beat the ricotta with the hot water to make it spreadable. Spread about one-third of the ricotta over the lasagna strips. Spread a layer of the meat sauce over this and then sprinkle over it about a quarter of the Parmesan cheese.

9. Continue making layers, ending with a layer of lasagna on top. Sprinkle with the remaining Parmesan cheese. Bake for 15 to 20 minutes or until the lasagna is piping hot and bubbling.

Fettuccine with Goat Cheese and Asparagus

◇ ◇

Now that goat cheese is widely available, I like to create recipes using it. Fresh, young goat cheese is just faintly tart. The older it gets, the more sharp it becomes. This recipe calls for a young goat cheese.

Yield: 4 servings.

1¼ pounds fresh asparagus, scraped and trimmed
2 quarts water
Salt to taste
1 pound fettuccine
4 ripe plum tomatoes
2 tablespoons olive oil
2 tablespoons butter
2 teaspoons minced garlic
¼ pound soft goat cheese
4 tablespoons coarsely chopped fresh basil leaves
Freshly ground pepper to taste
Freshly grated Parmesan cheese

1. Slice the asparagus spears on the bias, creating ½-inch lengths.

2. In a large pot, bring the water to a boil and add salt. Add the fettuccine. Boil about 9 to 10 minutes—the pasta should be al dente. Reserve ¼ cup of the cooking liquid. Drain the pasta.

3. Dip the tomatoes into boiling water for 10 seconds to loosen skins. Remove them from the water and skin them with a paring knife. Core, seed (slice them in half and squeeze out the seeds), and dice them.

4. Heat the oil and butter in a pan and add the asparagus, tomatoes, and garlic. Cook over medium heat for 2 minutes, stirring. Add the fettuccine, cheese, basil, reserved cooking liquid, salt, and pepper. Toss well over medium heat. Serve immediately with Parmesan cheese on the side.

Shrimp and Fettuccine Medley
◇ ◇

Yield: 4 servings.

1 pound fettuccine or dry egg noodles
4 tablespoons olive oil
1 cup coarsely chopped red onions
1 pound small zucchini, cut into 1-inch-thick slices (about 3 cups)
2 sweet red peppers, cored and seeded, cut into ½-inch cubes
Salt and freshly ground pepper to taste
1¼ pounds medium shrimp, peeled and deveined
6 ripe plum tomatoes, cut into ½-inch cubes, or 2 cups canned
   crushed tomatoes
1 tablespoon minced garlic
1 tablespoon minced ginger
¼ teaspoon red pepper flakes
¼ cup pitted small green olives
4 tablespoons chopped fresh coriander or basil
1 tablespoon red wine vinegar

1. Bring salted water to a boil. Add the fettuccine, stir, and cook according to package instructions. The pasta should be al dente. Drain and reserve ¼ cup of cooking liquid.

2. Meanwhile, heat 2 tablespoons of the olive oil in a large skillet or wok. Add the onions, zucchini, red peppers, salt, and pepper. Cook, stirring, over high heat until wilted, about 5 minutes.

3. Add the shrimp, tomatoes, garlic, ginger, pepper flakes, and olives. Cook and stir about 5 minutes longer over high heat.

4. Add to the skillet the remaining 2 tablespoons of olive oil, the drained noodles, the coriander, the vinegar, and, if needed, the reserved cooking liquid. Toss and stir well. Bring to a simmer and cook for 2 minutes. Serve immediately.

Spaghettini with Zucchini

◇ ◇

I devised this simple recipe out of desperation—zucchini were taking over my garden. This utterly simple recipe is a good way to fight back. Add any other herbs that you like.

Yield: 4 servings.

1 pound spaghettini
1 tablespoon olive oil
3 medium-size zucchini, trimmed and sliced very thin
Salt and freshly ground pepper to taste
¼ teaspoon red pepper flakes
1 tablespoon butter
4 tablespoons minced fresh basil or Italian parsley

1. Drop the spaghettini into salted boiling water and cook, stirring, until al dente. Drain and reserve ¼ cup of the cooking liquid.

2. Meanwhile, pour the olive oil into a pan over medium-high heat and add the zucchini, salt and pepper to taste, and the pepper flakes. Cook briefly, shaking the pan, until the zucchini are tender.

3. In a deep pan, add the butter, spaghettini, zucchini mixture, half of the reserved cooking liquid, and the basil or parsley. Heat over medium setting and toss gently. (If the sauce seems too thick, add remaining cooking water and stir.) Check for seasonings.

TIPS FOR PERFECT
PASTA

◇

• *Start out with plenty of water, roughly 4 quarts per pound. This prevents the pasta from sticking together without adding oil to the pot.*

• *Stir frequently to keep the pasta moving around in the boiling water.*

• *Keep the water boiling. If it stops when you put the pasta in, place a lid on the pot to bring back to the boil as quickly as possible.*

• *Drain the pasta well before adding sauce to it. Wet pasta dilutes the sauce.*

• *Count on about 4 ounces of pasta per person—about one-quarter of a 1-pound box.*

• *To test pasta for doneness, taste a strand. It should be slightly firm to the bite—just about al dente. It is best to remove it just short of al dente because the pasta will continue to cook from residual heat when you put it in the colander.*

FRESH VERSUS DRIED PASTA

◇

About fifteen years ago, fresh pasta was all the rage, and home cooks were cranking away on their shiny pasta machines. That has gone the way of bell-bottoms, and only the dedicated continue. In truth, fresh pasta is not necessarily better than dried pasta—it's just different.

Fresh pasta is lighter and finer-textured, and it must be watched carefully, as it cooks quickly. Packaged pasta is drier, with a more toothy texture. Dried pasta also is better suited to hearty, full-flavored sauces. Fresh pasta is excellent with vegetable sauces and seafood.

INSTANT PASTA

◇

If you are really rushed, you can make a meal by placing a pound of cooked, drained pasta of choice in a large bowl and drizzling good olive oil over it. Salt and pepper generously, squeeze over the juice of ½ lemon, and add your favorite chopped fresh herbs (basil, thyme, oregano, chervil). Sprinkle over some Parmesan or Romano cheese. Toss well. Serve immediately. Serves 4.

Fusilli with Eggplant and Zucchini

◇ ◇

I have experimented with several pasta recipes, including zucchini. This one is the best. The zucchini add color and a different flavor.

Yield: 4 servings.

4 tablespoons olive oil
1 tablespoon minced garlic
1 28-ounce can crushed tomatoes
4 tablespoons chopped fresh Italian parsley
2 tablespoons dried oregano
⅛ teaspoon red pepper flakes, or to taste
Salt and freshly ground black pepper to taste
1 pound eggplant
½ pound zucchini
1 pound dry pasta, like fusilli, shells, or rigatoni
4 tablespoons coarsely chopped fresh basil
4 tablespoons grated Parmesan cheese

1. Heat 1 tablespoon of the olive oil in a saucepan and add the garlic. Cook and stir without browning. Add the tomatoes, parsley, oregano, pepper flakes, salt, and pepper. Stir to blend, bring to a boil, and simmer for 15 minutes.

2. Meanwhile, cut off the ends of the eggplant and peel it. Cut it into 1-inch cubes. Cut the ends off the zucchini and slice into 1-inch-thick rounds.

3. Heat the remaining olive oil in a large skillet. When the oil is very hot, add the eggplant, zucchini, salt, and pepper. Cook, tossing, until nicely browned and tender. Add to the tomato sauce. Mix well and cook for 15 minutes.

4. Drop the pasta into salted boiling water and cook to al dente. Drain and reserve ½ cup of the cooking liquid.

5. Return the pasta to the pot and add the reserved cooking liquid, the vegetable mixture, basil, and Parmesan cheese. Toss and serve hot.

Ziti with Mussels and Broccoli

◇ ◇

One summer day at my beach house in East Hampton some friends dropped in unexpectedly and we invited them to dinner. I had just been out digging mussels and decided to make a pasta around them. The broccoli was an afterthought, and it goes very well with the soft-textured mussels.

Yield: 4 to 6 servings.

2 pounds mussels, with beards and barnacles removed

1 bay leaf

4 cloves

1 bunch broccoli (about ¾ pound)

Salt to taste

1 pound ziti

4 tablespoons olive oil

1 tablespoon minced garlic

2 cups canned crushed tomatoes

3 tablespoons tomato paste

1 tablespoon chopped fresh oregano or 1 teaspoon dried

1 small jalapeño pepper, chopped

Freshly ground pepper to taste

1. Place the mussels in a saucepan with the bay leaf and cloves. Cover tightly and cook over high heat, shaking the pan occasionally, about 3 minutes or until all the mussels are opened.

2. Remove the mussels with a slotted spoon and set aside to cool. Strain and reserve the broth from the mussels. When the mussels are cool enough to handle, remove the meat and discard the shells.

3. Cut the broccoli into florets. Remove the stems and peel them. Cut into ¼-inch-thick rounds. Drop the broccoli into boiling salted water to cover. When the water returns to a boil, cook for 1 minute. Scoop out the broccoli, set aside, and return water to a boil.

4. Add the ziti to the boiling water, stir, and cook about 9 minutes, or until al dente. Drain.

(Continued on next page)

REHEATING LEFTOVER
PASTA

◇

If you have leftover unsauced pasta, store it in a plastic bag and refrigerate. The best way to reheat pasta is to place it in a glass bowl and put it in the microwave on low power for a minute or two. Another method is to place the pasta in a colander, boil some water, and pour the water over the pasta. Drain well and sauce it immediately.

5. Meanwhile, heat the oil in a large pan. Add the garlic and cook briefly, but do not brown. Add the tomatoes, tomato paste, the reserved mussel cooking liquid, oregano, jalapeño pepper, salt, and pepper. Bring to a boil and simmer 5 minutes.

6. Add the drained ziti and cook, stirring, for 2 minutes. Add the mussels and the broccoli. Toss, check seasonings, and serve.

Fettuccine with Ham and Asparagus
◇ ◇

Yield: 4 servings.

1¼ pounds fresh asparagus
Salt to taste
1 pound fettuccine
2 tablespoons olive oil
1 cup diced boiled ham (about ⅓ pound)
4 ripe plum tomatoes, peeled, seeded, and diced
2 teaspoons minced garlic
¼ pound soft goat cheese, broken apart with your fingers into bite-
    sized pieces
¼ cup cream or half-and-half
4 tablespoons coarsely chopped fresh basil leaves or Italian
    parsley
Freshly ground pepper to taste
Grated Asiago or Parmesan cheese to taste

1. Scrape and trim the asparagus; break off the tough bottoms. Slice the spears on a bias into 1-inch lengths. In a large saucepan, bring 2 quarts of water to a boil. Add salt and the fettuccine. Boil gently for 9 minutes, or until al dente. Reserve ¼ cup of the cooking water and drain the pasta.

2. Heat the olive oil in a large pan and add the asparagus, ham, tomatoes, and garlic. Cook, stirring, over medium heat for 3 minutes. Add the drained fettuccine, goat cheese, cream, basil leaves, half of the reserved water, and salt and pepper to taste. Toss well over medium heat until blended well (it may need the rest of the reserved water). Serve immediately with grated Asiago or Parmesan cheese on the side.

Spaghetti with Shrimp and Eggplant

◇ ◇

The only time-consuming part of this pasta is peeling and deveining the shrimp, but once you get the technique down, it goes quickly (page 9).

Yield: 4 servings.

1¼ pounds medium-size shrimp

1 eggplant (about 1 pound)

4 tablespoons olive oil

1 tablespoon minced garlic

4 cups imported canned crushed tomatoes

1 teaspoon honey

¼ teaspoon hot red pepper flakes, or to taste

¼ cup coarsely chopped fresh basil or Italian flat parsley

Salt and freshly ground pepper to taste

4 quarts water

1 pound spaghetti

¾ cup grated Parmesan cheese (optional)

1. Peel and devein the shrimp and set aside.

2. Trim the ends of the eggplant and peel it. Cut into ½-inch cubes.

3. Heat 1 tablespoon of the oil in a pan and add the garlic. Cook, stirring, without browning. Add the tomatoes, honey, pepper flakes, basil, salt, and pepper. Stir to blend, cover, and simmer, stirring frequently, about 15 minutes.

4. In another pan, heat 2 tablespoons of the oil. When it is very hot, add the eggplant and season well with salt and pepper. Cook the eggplant, tossing, until it is nicely browned. Drain and add the eggplant to the tomato sauce. Stir, then cover and simmer for 15 minutes.

5. Add to the eggplant pan the remaining 1 tablespoon of oil and the shrimp. Salt and pepper generously. Cook over high heat for 1 minute, stirring. Add the shrimp to the sauce, blend well, and cook for 1 minute. Keep warm.

6. Meanwhile, salt the water and bring to a boil. Add the spaghetti and cook to al dente.

7. Drain the spaghetti and return it to the pot. Add the shrimp and eggplant mixture, toss well, and serve immediately—with grated Parmesan cheese if desired.

◆

Almost all shrimp sold in the Northeast and interior United States is frozen. Much of it comes from the Gulf States or the Deep South. Flash-frozen shrimp can be excellent when handled and stored properly. Its shelf life is about six months if well wrapped. When buying shrimp, inspect it carefully for dried-out or white patches, which are signs of freezer burn.

Shrimp is generally best purchased in the shell and not precooked. Stale shrimp are easy to identify—they have an offensive ammonia odor. The recipe here combines medium-sized shrimp with eggplant, garlic, crushed tomatoes, and hot pepper flakes. It should be served immediately so the shrimp do not overcook in the sauce.

Spaghetti with Southwestern-Style Meatballs

◇ ◇

Whenever I create a dish like this, I ask my expert tasters—my young grandchildren—what they think of it. In this case, they got a real kick out of the cross-cultural dish of spaghetti with spicy southwestern-style meatballs. The meatballs, healthful and inexpensive, can be made with lean ground beef, ground turkey, ground veal, ground pork, or any combination of these. The sauce is simple to prepare and also goes well with chicken breasts or pork chops.

While the list of ingredients may look daunting, the recipe is absolutely simple, mainly a matter of mixing the ingredients together and cooking quickly.

Yield: 4 to 6 servings.

The Meatballs

2 tablespoons olive oil
¾ cup minced onions
2 teaspoons minced garlic
1½ pounds ground beef chuck or other ground meat
½ cup fresh bread crumbs
¼ cup chopped fresh coriander
1 egg, lightly beaten
1 teaspoon cumin powder
1 teaspoon chili powder
Salt and freshly ground pepper to taste

The Sauce

2 tablespoons olive oil
1 cup minced onions
1 tablespoon minced garlic
1 cup sweet red pepper, cored, cleaned, and cut in ½-inch pieces
1 cup green pepper, cored, cleaned, and cut in ½-inch pieces
1 teaspoon chopped jalapeño pepper (optional)
1 28-ounce can imported crushed tomatoes
⅛ teaspoon red pepper flakes, or to taste
1 cup water
Salt and freshly ground pepper to taste

The Spaghetti

  1 pound spaghetti
  8 cups water
  Salt to taste
  2 tablespoons olive oil

1. Start your large pot of salted water over high setting. To make the meatballs, heat 1 tablespoon of the oil in a pan and add the onions and garlic. Cook, stirring, until wilted. Let cool.

2. In a bowl, combine all ingredients except the remaining tablespoon of oil, and blend well. Shape the mixture into 20 or more 1½-inch-diameter meatballs.

3. Heat the remaining tablespoon of olive oil in a large nonstick skillet over medium heat. Add the meatballs. Cook, turning so they brown evenly, about 10 minutes. Keep them warm.

4. To make the sauce, heat the oil in a saucepan. Add the remaining ingredients, blend well, and bring to a boil. Simmer for 10 minutes. Add the meatballs and simmer for 10 minutes more.

5. Cook the spaghetti in the pot of boiling salted water until al dente. Drain and return the spaghetti to the pot. Add the remaining olive oil and toss. Serve immediately with the meatballs and sauce.

Penne with Broccoli Rape

◇ ◇

Broccoli rape has a tart, peppery taste that adds an invigorating edge to pasta sauces. It is long and leafy with little green buds. Look for broccoli rape with thin, tender stalks and firm green buds. It is great simply sautéed with olive oil and garlic. Cut off the hard section of the stems.

This quick pasta is not only tasty but also very healthful—broccoli rape is filled with vitamins C and E. It is simply sautéed with garlic. The anchovies in the sauce provide an intriguing counterbalance.

Yield: 4 servings.

1½ pounds broccoli rape
¼ cup olive oil
1 teaspoon minced garlic
⅛ teaspoon dried hot red pepper flakes, or to taste
4 anchovy fillets, finely minced
8 cups water
Salt to taste if desired
1 pound penne or ziti
1 tablespoon butter

1. Trim off the larger, tough stems of the broccoli rape, leaving only the tender, slender stems, leaves, and bulbous shoots.

2. Rinse the edible portions, leaving the water that clings to the leaves.

3. In a saucepan over medium setting, heat the oil and add the garlic, pepper flakes, and anchovy. Stir and add the broccoli rape. It is not necessary to add more liquid, but watch the vegetable carefully as it cooks so that it does not stick to the pan and burn. Cover closely and cook over moderate heat. Turn the broccoli rape pieces over several times so they cook evenly. Cook 4 to 5 minutes, or until the pieces are tender. Do not overcook, or they will become mushy.

4. Meanwhile, bring the salted water to a boil. Add the pasta and cook, stirring often, until tender. Drain. Put the pasta over the broccoli rape and stir in the butter. Toss gently to blend. Taste for seasonings before serving.

Spaghettini with Vegetables and Pepper Vodka Sauce

◇ ◇

Yield: 4 servings.

1 bunch broccoli, about 1¼ pounds
¼ pound snow peas
5 ripe plum tomatoes, about 1 pound
12 cups water, approximately
Salt to taste
1 pound spaghettini
2 tablespoons olive oil
1 tablespoon minced garlic
¼ pound sliced prosciutto, cut into ¼-inch strips
⅛ teaspoon red hot pepper flakes, or to taste
½ cup lemon-flavored vodka
½ cup cream or half-and-half
Freshly ground pepper to taste
½ cup Pecorino Romano cheese
12 basil leaves, coarsely chopped
½ cup chopped fresh chives

1. Cut the hard stems off the broccoli and separate the florets. Cut away the stems' outer skin. Cut the stems into 1¼-inch lengths, then into ½-inch slices. There should be about 5 cups of stems and florets.

2. Trim the snow peas. Core the tomatoes. To peel them, drop the tomatoes into boiling water for about 10 to 12 seconds. Remove with a slotted spoon and peel. The skin should come off easily if you use a paring knife. Cut the tomatoes into ½-inch cubes. There should be about 2 cups.

3. Bring the salted water to a boil and add the broccoli. Bring to a simmer and cook for 5 minutes. Add the snow peas and bring to a boil. Cook for 2 minutes. Do not overcook; the vegetables must remain crisp. Drain and reserve the cooking liquid.

4. Return the reserved cooking liquid to a boil and add the spaghettini. Stir and cook according to package directions. The pasta should be al dente. Drain and reserve ½ cup of the cooking liquid.

(*Continued on next page*)

◇

When I first encountered pasta sauce spiked with vodka, I was dubious. But I found that it does add a certain warmth and flavor—if it is a flavored vodka—to pasta sauce. You do not really taste the alcohol, most of which evaporates in cooking, but lemon vodka adds a kind of smooth, citric sensation. Many herb-flavored vodkas are sold today, and it can be fun to experiment with them. If you don't have lemon vodka, just squeeze half a lemon into regular vodka.

When making this kind of pasta dish, be sure not to overcook the vegetables. The broccoli florets simmer for only about 3 to 5 minutes; the snow peas for 2 minutes. Also, always reserve the poaching liquid from the vegetables and cook the pasta in it, which adds extra flavor. A bit of the vegetable poaching liquid should be set aside to be used at the very end to bind the finished sauce. Once you have this technique down, you can add other vegetables to the recipe.

5. Heat the oil in a large skillet. Add the garlic and prosciutto. Cook, stirring, briefly without browning. Add the tomatoes, snow peas, broccoli, red pepper flakes, and cook, stirring, 1 minute. Add the vodka, cream, and salt and pepper to taste. Bring to a simmer and cook for 1 minute.

6. Transfer the pasta to the pan holding the tomato mixture. Add the cheese, basil, chives, and reserved ½ cup cooking liquid. Bring to a simmer and toss well for 1 minute. Serve immediately.

Linguine with Mussels
◇ ◇

Yield: 4 *servings.*

1 tablespoon plus ¼ cup olive oil
2 teaspoons minced garlic
4 pounds small mussels (about 12 cups)
3 tablespoons plus 10 cups water
2 cups fresh peas or a 10-ounce frozen package
1 cup ricotta cheese
1 pound packaged dried linguine
⅛ teaspoon dried hot red pepper flakes, or to taste
¼ cup minced fresh basil or 2 tablespoons dried
Salt to taste if desired
Freshly ground pepper to taste

1. Heat 1 tablespoon of the oil in a large kettle. Add garlic and cook, stirring, without browning, about 1 minute. Add mussels and 3 tablespoons water. Cover closely and cook about 4 minutes or until all of the shells open. As the mussels cook, shake kettle to redistribute them so they steam evenly.

2. Place a colander over a bowl and drain mussels. There should be about 1½ cups of broth. Reserve broth.

3. If fresh peas are used, drop in a pot of boiling water, cook 3 minutes and drain. If frozen peas are used, put in a sieve and run very hot tap water over them until defrosted. Set aside.

4. When mussels are cool enough to handle, remove meat from the shells. There should be about 1½ cups. Set aside. Discard the shells.

5. Pour the reserved mussel liquid through a strainer into a large skillet and add ricotta cheese. Stir until blended and simmering.

6. Meanwhile, bring the remaining 10 cups of water to a boil and add linguine. Cook until al dente. Drain the linguine and add it to ricotta sauce. Add remaining ¼ cup of oil and stir. Add peas, pepper flakes, basil, salt, pepper, and mussels. Cook until mussels are heated through.

Angel Hair with Prosciutto and Wild Mushrooms
◇ ◇

The major risk with angel hair pasta is overcooking. Be sure to cook it very al dente because it continues to cook when it is added to the sauce at the end.

Yield: 4 servings.

½ pound wild mushrooms, such as shiitake, morels, or oyster
    mushrooms
2 ripe tomatoes or 1 cup canned crushed tomatoes
¼ pound thinly sliced prosciutto
½ pound snow peas
¼ cup olive oil
Salt to taste
Freshly ground black pepper to taste
1 tablespoon finely minced garlic
1 teaspoon minced jalapeño peppers (optional)
1 sprig fresh rosemary or ½ teaspoon dried
1 pound fresh angel hair (capellini) or vermicelli or dried
1½ cups cream or half-and-half
¼ cup freshly grated Parmesan cheese, plus additional cheese to
    be served on the side
½ cup shredded fresh basil

1. Rinse the mushrooms and pat them dry. Cut off and reserve the stems. Cut the caps into thin strips. There should be about 4 cups of caps and stems combined.

(Continued on next page)

2. Core the tomatoes and cut into ½-inch cubes.

3. Cut the prosciutto into very thin strips.

4. Pull off any tough "strings" from the pea pods. There should be about 2 cups of pea pods. Put them in a saucepan and add water to cover. Bring to a boil and simmer 1 minute. Drain.

5. Meanwhile, heat the oil in a large, heavy casserole and add the mushrooms, salt, and pepper. Cook, stirring, about 3 minutes, and add the garlic, jalapeño peppers, and prosciutto. Cook, stirring, about 1 minute. Add the rosemary.

6. Bring 3 quarts of water to a boil and add the angel hair. Stir so that the strands are submerged. Cook about 2 to 4 minutes or until al dente. Reserve ½ cup of the cooking liquid. Drain the pasta.

7. Add the tomatoes to the mushroom mixture and stir. Add the cream and bring to a boil. Add the pasta, pea pods, and half of the reserved pasta cooking liquid to the casserole and stir. Add ¼ cup of Parmesan cheese and shredded basil. Toss to blend. Taste for seasonings. Serve with additional Parmesan cheese on the side (if the sauce seems a bit dry, add remaining ½ cup reserved cooking liquid).

Linguine with Clam Sauce

◇ ◇

When I don't have fresh clams, I make this dish with canned chopped clams, which are actually quite good.

Yield: 4 servings.

18 cherrystone clams or 4 6½-ounce cans clams, in natural juices
½ pound small zucchini
4 ripe red tomatoes, peeled (about ¾ pound)
¼ cup olive oil
2 tablespoons finely minced garlic
⅛ teaspoon hot red pepper flakes, or to taste
Salt to taste
Freshly ground black pepper to taste
18 whole basil leaves, rinsed and patted dry
1 pound fresh or dried linguine

1. Shuck clams or have them shucked. Reserve the juice and clams separately. Chop clams coarsely. There should be about 1 cup clams and 2 cups juice.

2. Trim the ends of the zucchini. Cut zucchini lengthwise into quarters and each quarter into thin slices crosswise.

3. Cut the tomatoes into ½-inch cubes.

4. Bring 2½ quarts of salted water to a boil.

5. Heat the olive oil in a pan and add the garlic and pepper flakes. Cook briefly, stirring, and add zucchini and tomatoes. Sprinkle with salt and pepper and stir. Add reserved clam juice. Bring to a boil and add basil leaves.

6. Drop the linguine into the water. When cooked al dente, drain quickly.

7. Put linguine in the sauce and add the clams. Toss to blend. Taste for seasonings and serve immediately.

Ziti with Chicken and Broccoli

◇ ◇

You can substitute broccoli rape for regular broccoli if you wish.

Yield: 4 servings.

2 skinless, boneless whole chicken breasts (about 1 pound)
1 bunch broccoli (about 1¼ pounds)
Salt to taste
1 pound ziti
2 tablespoons olive oil
Freshly ground pepper to taste
1 tablespoon minced garlic
3 ripe tomatoes, peeled and cut into ½-inch cubes (about 1 pound)
2 teaspoons chopped fresh rosemary or 1 teaspoon dried
2 teaspoons chopped fresh oregano or 1 teaspoon dried
⅛ teaspoon red hot pepper flakes (optional)
½ cup cream or half-and-half
4 tablespoons coarsely chopped Italian parsley
4 tablespoons grated Parmesan or pecorino cheese

1. Place the chicken breasts one at a time on a flat surface. Using a sharp knife, cut the breasts in half lengthwise, then crosswise, into ½-inch-thick strips.

2. Cut off the broccoli florets; peel the stems and cut them into thin slices.

3. Bring 4 quarts of salted water to a boil and add the broccoli. Cook for 5 minutes. Do not overcook—the broccoli must remain crisp. Drain and reserve the cooking liquid.

4. Bring the reserved cooking liquid to a boil and add the ziti. Stir and cook according to package directions. The pasta should be al dente. Drain and reserve ½ cup of the cooking liquid.

5. Heat the oil in a large pan. Add the chicken breasts, salt, and pepper. Cook and stir over medium-high heat for 1 minute. Add the garlic, stir and cook briefly; do not brown. Add the tomatoes, rosemary, oregano, pepper flakes, and cook, stirring, for 1 minute. Add the cream, bring to a boil, then simmer for 2 minutes.

6. Add the broccoli and the pasta to the tomato mixture. Add the reserved ½ cup of cooking liquid, salt, and pepper. Bring to a simmer, add the parsley and cheese and toss well for 1 minute. Taste for seasonings. Serve immediately.

Penne with Smoked Salmon

◇ ◇

Yield: 4 servings.

5 ripe plum tomatoes (about 1 pound)
¾ pound penne or any tubular pasta of your choice
Salt to taste
2 tablespoons olive oil
1 tablespoon minced garlic
2 tablespoons minced shallots
Freshly ground pepper to taste
¼ cup cream
¼ cup pepper vodka
½ pound sliced smoked salmon, cut into 1½-inch strips
½ cup coarsely chopped fresh basil or coriander
Freshly grated Parmesan or pecorino cheese (optional)

1. Core the tomatoes and drop them into boiling water for 10 to 12 seconds. Drain immediately and peel. The skin should come off easily if you use a paring knife. Cut the tomatoes into ½-inch cubes. There should be about 2¼ cups.

2. Cook the penne in salted boiling water according to package directions. The pasta should be al dente. Drain and reserve ¼ cup of the cooking liquid.

3. Meanwhile, heat the oil in a large pan and add the garlic and shallots. Cook briefly, stirring, without browning. Add the tomatoes, salt, and pepper. Cook, stirring, for 1 minute. Add the cream and vodka. Bring to a simmer and cook 1 minute.

4. Add the pasta and reserved cooking liquid to the tomato sauce. Blend well and simmer 1 minute.

5. Add the salmon and basil. Toss well and cook 1 minute. Serve with cheese if desired.

Fusilli with Zucchini, Prosciutto, and Tomatoes

◇ ◇

I added the prosciutto to this dish to add a touch of salt and a textural contrast to the vegetables.

Yield: 4 servings.

1 pound ripe plum tomatoes, cored
4 small zucchini (about 1 pound)
4 quarts water
Salt to taste
1 pound fusilli
¼ cup olive oil
1 tablespoon chopped garlic
¼ pound thinly sliced prosciutto, cut into 1½-inch strips
Freshly ground black pepper to taste
⅛ teaspoon hot red pepper flakes
½ cup chopped fresh basil
1 cup freshly grated Parmesan cheese

1. Cut the tomatoes into ½-inch cubes.

2. Trim the ends of the zucchini and cut them crosswise into thin slices.

3. In a large pot, bring the water to a boil. Add salt and the pasta. When the water returns to a boil, cook the pasta, stirring, until al dente. Do not overcook. Drain the ziti, reserving ½ cup of the cooking liquid.

4. Meanwhile, heat the oil in a large pan. Add the garlic and cook briefly, stirring, but do not brown. Add the zucchini, prosciutto, salt, pepper, and pepper flakes. Cook, stirring, for 3 minutes. Add the tomatoes and reserved cooking liquid. Cook briefly.

5. Add the pasta, stir, and cook for 1 minute. Add the basil and cheese. Toss well and serve immediately.

Vegetables

◇ ◇ ◇

Fresh Spinach with Cumin

Kale Southern Style

Lyonnaise Potatoes

Garlic Potatoes

Potato and Parsnip Purée

Eggplant with Tomatoes

Carrot Pudding

Ratatouille à la Minute

Brussels Sprouts with Sesame Seeds

Braised Red Cabbage with Orange

Yam Purée

Broiled Fennel and Zucchini with Parmesan

Carrots with Egg Noodles and Lemon

Eggplant Caviar with Tomato

Asparagus with Shallot Butter

Grilled Asparagus

Oven-Broiled Tomatoes

Asparagus Soufflé

Zucchini-Garlic Soufflé

Carrot Soufflé

Green Beans with Cumin

Snap Peas with Mint

Snow Peas with Sesame Seeds

Potato Salad with Sugar Snap Peas

Sautéed Turnips

Fresh Spinach with Cumin

◇ ◇

I often discuss experimenting with herbs and spices to come up with your own flavor combinations. This is one example. I wasn't sure that fresh spinach and cumin would go together—although I had used it in creamed spinach—so I gave it a try. In small doses, it adds a nice flavor and aroma.

Yield: 4 servings.

1½ pounds fresh spinach leaves
2 tablespoons butter
Salt and freshly ground pepper to taste
¼ teaspoon freshly ground cumin

1. Cut away and discard any tough spinach stems and blemished leaves. Rinse the spinach and drain well.

2. Heat the butter in a large pan and add the spinach, salt and pepper, and the cumin. Stir as the spinach wilts. Cook and stir over high heat until the spinach is totally wilted and the moisture has evaporated. Do not overcook. Remove from heat and serve.

Kale Southern Style

◇ ◇

Kale, a crinkly, dark green powerhouse of vitamins and minerals, is terrific when steamed or sautéed. It is a cold weather plant that flourishes even in the snow. When buying kale, look for heads that have no yellow leaves. Refrigerate in a plastic bag.

Yield: 4 servings.

2 pounds kale
2 slices bacon, diced
½ cup finely chopped onion
½ cup water
1 bay leaf
¼ teaspoon ground cumin
Salt and freshly ground pepper to taste
4 lemon wedges

1. Wash kale thoroughly and strip leaves from the tough center ribs. Cut out any blemished areas.

2. In a heavy pan, lightly brown the bacon over medium heat. Add the onion, kale, water, bay leaf, cumin, salt, and pepper. Cover and simmer for 15 minutes or until tender, stirring occasionally. Discard bay leaf and serve with lemon wedges.

Lyonnaise Potatoes

◇ ◇

This recipe comes from Lyons, the capital of French gastronomy. It is quite easy to make. If you like, add fresh herbs of choice.

Yield: 4 servings.

1 pound small red potatoes (about 12 to the pound)
Salt and pepper to taste
2 tablespoons vegetable oil
1 cup sliced onions
1 tablespoon unsalted butter
4 tablespoons fresh chopped parsley

1. Wash potatoes and dry well. Put into a saucepan and cover with lightly salted water. Bring to boil, return to simmer, and cook for 20 minutes. Drain and let cool.

2. Slice potatoes, with skins, ¼ inch thick.

3. Put oil into the pan and heat over medium-high setting. Add potatoes. Season with salt and pepper. Sauté, flipping occasionally, until golden brown on both sides, about 5 minutes.

4. Add onions and butter and cook until onions are brown. Taste for seasonings. Serve with sprinkled parsley.

Garlic Potatoes
◇ ◇

Yield: 4 servings.

4 russet potatoes (about 1½ pounds)
6 cloves garlic, peeled
Salt to taste
3 tablespoons butter
1½ cups milk
Freshly ground white pepper to taste

1. Peel potatoes and cut them crosswise into ¾-inch-thick slices. Put slices in a saucepan with water to cover. Add garlic and salt.

2. Bring to a boil and cook 15 minutes or until potatoes are tender. Drain and put potatoes and garlic through a food mill and back into the saucepan.

3. Add butter, milk, salt, and pepper to potatoes and beat with a potato masher to blend.

The recipe for garlic potatoes calls for russet potatoes (also known as Idahos), which are round, light brown, and have a low moisture content (preferred for baking and French fries). Here are a few others you will encounter in the market.

YUKON GOLD. *This has a golden skin and a moderate moisture content. They are best boiled—and they make great mashed potatoes.*

NEW POTATOES. *These are young potatoes that have not fully converted their sugar into starch. That leaves them smooth and waxy and well suited to boiling.*

FINGERLINGS. *Narrow, finger-thin, these are delicate and mild-flavored. Good for sautéing.*

IDAHO. *A good all-around baking potato, also goes by the name russet.*

I enliven mashed potatoes in many ways to achieve different flavors and colors. You can blend in cooked carrots, spinach, turnip, garlic (first baked until pulp softens), cheese, fresh herbs, and much more. It is best to mash potatoes by hand or with a ricer. Food processors make them gummy.

Potato and Parsnip Purée

◇ ◇

In the winter, I cook a lot with root vegetables. Parsnips are an underappreciated vegetable, for it has a sweet flavor and is great in purées of all types.

Yield: 4 servings.

4 russet potatoes (about 1½ pounds)
2 parsnips (about ½ pound)
1 large onion
2 cloves garlic, peeled
Salt to taste
½ cup milk or cream
2 tablespoons unsalted butter
1 pinch freshly grated nutmeg
Salt and freshly ground pepper to taste
½ cup chopped chives or any herb of your choice

1. Peel and quarter the potatoes. There should be about 3½ cups.
2. Trim and scrape the parsnips and slice them crosswise. There should be about 2 cups.
3. Peel and slice the onion. There should be about 2 cups.
4. Combine the potatoes, parsnips, onion, and garlic in a large saucepan. Add water to cover and salt to taste. Bring to a boil and cook about 15 minutes, or until tender. Drain.
5. Return the vegetables to the saucepan. Add the milk or cream and the butter. Using a potato masher, mash the ingredients until they are coarse. Add the nutmeg, salt, pepper, and chives. Blend thoroughly, taste for seasonings, and serve.

Eggplant with Tomatoes

◇ ◇

Eggplant got its name from the small white variety that flourished several hundred years ago. Most eggplant on the market today has a glossy black-purple skin and weighs about 1½ to 2 pounds. Avoid those with soft or brown spots. The flesh is spongy, so many cooks dredge it in flour to prevent the eggplant from getting soggy. Refrigerate eggplants in plastic bags.

Yield: 4 servings.

1 medium-size eggplant (about 1 to 1½ pounds)
4 medium-size tomatoes (about 1 pound)
2 teaspoons finely minced garlic
½ teaspoon dried rosemary
½ teaspoon dried oregano
Salt to taste
Freshly ground black pepper
6 tablespoons olive oil
1 tablespoon finely chopped parsley

1. Preheat oven to 450 degrees.
2. Trim each end of the eggplant. Cut eggplant lengthwise in half. Place each half, cut side down, on a flat surface and cut crosswise into half-moon shapes, each about ⅓ inch thick. There should be a total of about 34 slices.
3. Trim off the ends of the tomatoes and cut away the cores. Cut tomatoes crosswise into slices, each about 2 inch thick. There should be about 32 pieces. In a baking dish, compactly alternate tomato slices with eggplant slices.
4. Combine garlic, rosemary, and oregano and sprinkle over layered eggplant. Sprinkle with salt and pepper and drizzle oil over all.
5. Place dish in the oven and bake 30 minutes. Baste the layered eggplant with any juices that have accumulated around it. Sprinkle with parsley and serve.

Carrot Pudding

◇ ◇

I like to make puddings with all sorts of vegetables. Carrot pudding is particularly good—sweet, faintly peppery, and with a touch of nutmeg.

Yield: 4 servings.

6 large carrots (about 1¼ pounds)
¾ cup chopped, trimmed scallions, green part included
2 large eggs, beaten
1 cup milk
Salt to taste
Freshly ground pepper to taste
⅛ teaspoon freshly grated nutmeg
2 teaspoons butter plus additional butter for greasing the baking dish

1. Preheat oven to 400 degrees.

2. Trim carrots and scrape them. Cut carrots crosswise into ¼-inch rounds. There should be about 4 cups.

3. Put carrots in a saucepan and add water to cover. Bring to a boil and cook 5 minutes. Drain.

4. Put carrot rounds into the container of a food processor or electric blender and blend thoroughly. Add scallions and blend a second time. There should be about 3 cups. Put the mixture in a bowl.

5. Beat the eggs with the milk, salt, pepper, and nutmeg. Add this to the carrot mixture and beat to blend. Generously butter the inside of a 4-cup baking dish (a soufflé dish is recommended). Pour the mixture into the baking dish. Dot the top with 2 teaspoons butter. Bake 25 minutes.

Ratatouille à la Minute

◇ ◇

I have streamlined the classic ratatouille recipe for home cooks. The flavors are essentially the same, although it has fewer ingredients.

Yield: 4 to 6 servings.

3 tomatoes (about 1¼ pounds)

2 cups zucchini, cut into ¾-inch cubes (about ¾ pound)

1½ cups coarsely chopped onions

1½ cups cored, seeded, deveined green peppers, cut into ½-inch cubes

2 cups eggplant, unpeeled and cut into ¾-inch cubes

2 to 4 tablespoons olive oil

1 tablespoon finely minced garlic

1 teaspoon finely chopped fresh thyme or ½ teaspoon dried

1 bay leaf

Salt if desired and freshly ground pepper to taste

2 tablespoons finely chopped parsley

1. Core the tomatoes, cut in half crosswise and squeeze to remove seeds. Cut into 1-inch cubes. There should be about 3 cups.

2. Prepare other vegetables and set aside.

3. Line mixing bowl with sieve.

4. Heat oil in a pan and add zucchini. Cook, shaking pan and stirring, for 4 minutes. Drain and reserve oil. Set zucchini aside.

5. Pour reserved oil back into pan and add onions and green pepper. Cook, shaking pan and stirring, for 4 minutes. Drain and reserve oil. Set green pepper and onions aside.

6. Pour reserved oil back into pan, adding more if necessary. Add eggplant and cook, shaking pan and stirring, for 3 minutes. Drain and again reserve oil. Set eggplant aside.

7. Return reserved oil to pan and add more if necessary. Add garlic, thyme, and bay leaf and cook, stirring. Add tomatoes and salt and pepper and stir. Add cooked vegetables and any oil accumulated around them. Cook, stirring to blend, for 5 minutes. Sprinkle with chopped parsley. Remove the bay leaf and serve.

◇

Probably the reason many people shun cabbage is because it is often overcooked and watery. When steamed or boiled properly, it has a toothsome texture and mild flavor. There are basically four types of cabbage.

GREEN CABBAGE. *This is the most common type, mild-flavored and suitable for steaming and boiling with an array of seasonings.*

RED CABBAGE. *Deep reddish purple, this is about the same size as green cabbage and slightly more tart. It is good in salads and soups.*

NAPA CABBAGE. *A form of Chinese cabbage, this has a celery shape and a peppery flavor. Good for stir-frying.*

BOK CHOY. *Also used in stir-frying, this resembles Swiss chard and tastes much like green cabbage.*

Brussels Sprouts with Sesame Seeds

◇ ◇

Brussels sprouts were among the few foods that were periodically sent back to the kitchen when I was a chef. They certainly are a love/hate vegetable. Maybe that is because people just boil them and serve them without a little seasoning. Here is a combination I like.

Yield: 4 servings.

1 pound fresh Brussels sprouts
Salt to taste if desired
2 tablespoons butter
2 tablespoons sesame seeds
¼ teaspoon ground cumin

1. Trim off the end of each Brussels sprout. Using a sharp, small knife, cut a cross about ½ inch deep in the base of each sprout.
2. Put the sprouts in a saucepan, add cold water to cover, and salt. Bring to a boil and cook 10 minutes until tender. Drain.
3. Add the butter and stir until melted.
4. Put the sesame seeds in a separate pan and cook, shaking the pan and stirring, until the seeds are lightly toasted. Add the Brussels sprouts and sprinkle with cumin. Toss to blend and serve.

Braised Red Cabbage with Orange

◇ ◇

I cook a lot with orange, especially when the main ingredient has some sweetness, as in red cabbage. Season generously with black pepper to counteract the sweetness.

Yield: 4 servings.

1 medium-size red cabbage (about 2 pounds)
3 tablespoons butter
½ cup finely chopped onion
2 whole cloves
Salt to taste if desired

Freshly ground pepper to taste
1 cup freshly squeezed orange juice

1. Quarter and core cabbage and shred the quarters. There should be about 10 cups.

2. Heat 2 tablespoons of the butter in a large pan and add the onion. Cook, stirring, until wilted. Add cabbage, cloves, salt, and pepper and cook, stirring, 5 minutes. Add orange juice and cover. Cook, stirring occasionally, about 45 minutes. Stir in remaining butter and serve.

Yam Purée
◇ ◇

Yield: About 3½ cups.

4 yams or sweet potatoes (about 2 pounds)
Salt to taste if desired
2 tablespoons butter
¼ cup heavy cream
½ cup milk

1. Place yams in a saucepan and add cold water to cover. Bring to a boil and cook 30 minutes or until tender. Drain.

2. When yams are cool enough to handle, peel them. Cut yams into 1-inch cubes and put them through a food mill or potato ricer.

3. Put the potatoes in a pan and add the salt, butter, cream, and milk. Heat thoroughly, stirring.

Broiled Fennel and Zucchini with Parmesan

◇ ◇

Fennel is one of my favorite vegetables, refreshing and distinctive. It is a nice addition to salads, sliced, or cooked. It has a large white bulb and a pale green stalk. The bulb has a lovely hint of sweet anise. Cut off the stalk and slice the bulb. The lacy greens of fennel can be used as a garnish. The recipe here for broiled fennel goes particularly well with seafood.

Yield: 4 servings.

1 large unblemished fennel bulb (about 1 pound)
2 zucchini (about ½ pound)
Salt and freshly ground pepper to taste
2 tablespoons olive oil
¼ cup freshly grated Parmesan cheese
2 tablespoons chopped parsley

1. Preheat the broiler to high.
2. Cut the fennel bulb lengthwise into ½-inch slices.
3. Trim the zucchini but do not peel them. Split in half lengthwise.
4. Put the zucchini and fennel in one layer in a baking dish. Sprinkle them with salt and pepper and brush the tops with oil. Put them under the broiler about 6 inches from the heat source, leaving the door partly open. Broil for 5 minutes. Turn and broil 3 minutes more.
5. Sprinkle the vegetables with Parmesan. Return to the broiler and cook until nicely browned. Sprinkle with parsley and serve.

Carrots with Egg Noodles and Lemon

◇ ◇

I serve this dish with roasts of all kinds, as well as with barbecued meats. You could substitute orzo, the rice-shaped pasta, for noodles if you like.

Yield: 4 servings.

4 carrots, trimmed and scraped (about ¼ pound)
1 tablespoon butter
1 teaspoon grated lemon rind (yellow skin only)
¼ cup dry white wine
2 tablespoons lemon juice
1 cup cream
4 quarts water
Salt to taste if desired
¾ pound very thin egg noodles
¼ cup freshly grated Parmesan cheese

1. Cut the carrots crosswise into 1-inch lengths. Cut the pieces lengthwise into very thin slices. Stack the slices and cut them into very thin strips. There should be about 2 cups or slightly more, loosely packed.

2. Heat the butter in a saucepan and add the carrot strips and lemon rind. Cook, stirring, about 2 minutes. Add the wine and cook about 1 minute.

3. Add the lemon juice and cook about 3 minutes, stirring occasionally. Add the cream and bring to a boil.

4. Meanwhile, bring the water to a boil in a pot and add salt to taste. Add the noodles, and cook 3 minutes or until noodles are tender.

5. Drain the noodles and return them to the hot pot. Add the sauce and the cheese. Stir to blend and serve immediately.

Eggplant Caviar with Tomato

Many recipes call for seeded tomatoes. Take a tomato and slice it in half widthwise. Pick up the half, hold it cut side down over a sieve with a bowl underneath, and squeeze gently. The seeds will fall out. Cook with tomato juices.

This has little to do with caviar, but it is a pleasing blend of eggplant pulp, fresh vegetables, and herbs.

Yield: 6 or more servings.

1 eggplant (about 1 pound)
1 ripe tomato, cored, peeled, seeded, and finely chopped
  (about ¼ cup)
¼ cup finely chopped onions
1 teaspoon finely minced garlic
4 tablespoons finely chopped coriander or parsley
2 tablespoons olive oil
2 tablespoons sesame oil (or use more olive oil)
Salt to taste
Freshly ground black pepper to taste
¼ teaspoon sugar
2 tablespoons lemon juice

1. There are two ways to prepare the eggplant for this dish. It may be charred over charcoal or a gas burner, or it may be baked in the oven. To cook over charcoal or a gas burner, place the untrimmed, unpeeled eggplant over the coals or gas flame (the latter method can be very messy). Cook, turning on all sides, until the eggplant is thoroughly charred and soft from the skin to the center, 30 to 45 minutes. If you wish to cook the eggplant in the oven, preheat the oven to about 375 degrees and place the eggplant on a sheet of aluminum foil. Place in the oven and bake until soft throughout, about 30 minutes.

2. Peel the eggplant and chop the flesh. There should be about 2¼ cups. Put the eggplant in a mixing bowl.

3. Drain the tomato well and add it to the eggplant. Add the onions, garlic, coriander, olive oil, sesame oil, salt, pepper, sugar, and lemon juice. Blend well. Refrigerate for several hours. Serve at room temperature with slices of dark bread.

Asparagus with Shallot Butter

◇ ◇

When the first thin stalks of spring asparagus poke through my garden, I usually steam or boil them and serve them with a little shallot butter. Contrary to belief, the first spring asparagus are not the most flavorful. Later in the season, they are more mature and tasty.

Yield: 4 servings.

1 pound medium-size asparagus
Salt to taste
3 tablespoons finely chopped shallots
3 tablespoons water
4 tablespoons butter, cut into small pieces
Freshly ground black pepper to taste

1. Peel the asparagus, starting about 2 inches from the top. Snap off tough ends.

2. Boil enough water to cover the asparagus. Add salt. Add asparagus and cook until crisp-tender, 2 to 3 minutes. Drain well. Arrange on warm platter and set aside.

3. Place shallots and 3 tablespoons water in a pan. Bring to a boil and cook over high heat until half of the liquid evaporates. Add butter gradually, stirring rapidly with a whisk. Season with salt and pepper. Cook, stirring rapidly, for 1 minute.

4. Spoon mixture onto asparagus and serve hot.

◇

The next time you grill out-doors, try grilling asparagus. First cook them in boiling salted water for about 3 minutes. Drain well and pat dry with a towel. Brush with olive oil, season with salt and pepper, and place on the grill. Cook for about 3 to 5 minutes, turning frequently. They will have a nice toasty flavor. Serve with lemon butter.

Oven-Broiled Tomatoes

◇ ◇

Sometimes I vary this recipe by inserting slivers of garlic into the cut side of the tomatoes.

Yield: 4 servings.

4 ripe tomatoes (about 1¾ pounds)
Salt to taste if desired
Freshly ground pepper to taste
2 tablespoons olive oil
½ teaspoon fresh chopped rosemary or ¼ teaspoon dried

1. Preheat broiler to high.
2. Core each tomato. Bring a pot of water to a boil. Add tomatoes and let stand about 15 seconds. Remove tomatoes and, when they are cool enough to handle, peel them.
3. Cut each tomato in half. Place each tomato, round side down, on a clean cloth. Pull up edges of the cloth, in order to make a bag to enclose each tomato half, one at a time, evenly. Squeeze bag gently to extract most of the liquid and shape the tomato halves into balls.
4. Arrange each tomato ball in one layer on a baking dish. Sprinkle with salt and pepper. Blend oil and rosemary and brush the tomatoes with the mixture. Place under the broiler for 3 to 5 minutes.

Asparagus Soufflé

◇ ◇

Yield: 8 servings.

2½ pounds asparagus, trimmed and peeled

2 small white potatoes, peeled and cubed (about ½ pound)

1¼ tablespoons sesame seeds

½ cup ricotta cheese

Salt and freshly ground pepper to taste

2 teaspoons fresh grated ginger

¼ teaspoon hot pepper flakes, or to taste

2 tablespoons finely minced scallions

8 eggs, separated

1. Preheat oven to 425 degrees. Butter well and chill eight 1¼-cup soufflé dishes or 1 large dish (all must have vertical sides).

2. In separate pots, boil the asparagus and potatoes in lightly salted water until soft. Drain well. Meanwhile, lightly toast the sesame seeds by placing them in a hot nonstick fry pan. Set aside.

3. Place asparagus and potatoes in a food processor or blender with ricotta. Purée slightly. Add salt, pepper, ginger, pepper flakes, and scallions and purée well. You should have about 3 cups. Transfer mixture to a bowl.

4. Add egg yolks to mixture and blend well with a wire whisk. In another bowl, whisk whites until they form soft peaks. Fold a quarter of the whites into the asparagus mixture, then the rest. Do not overwork mixture. Taste for seasoning. Fill the soufflé dishes.

5. Place soufflé dishes in a roasting pan with sides and fill with water about 3 inches up the sides of the dishes. Sprinkle sesame seeds evenly onto the soufflés. Before placing in the oven, run your thumb around the rim of each dish to remove any overflow, which could cling and prevent the mixture from rising fully. Bake for approximately 10 minutes.

◇

Making soufflés is a little bit like dancing a waltz: from the sidelines, it appears more difficult than it actually is, so a good many people hesitate to try for fear of falling flat in front of an audience.

Traditional soufflés are made by mixing a roux (a combination of butter and flour), and then adding milk and egg yolks. To that cooked combination is added a primary ingredient (vegetables, meat, fish, fruit, etc.), as well as beaten egg whites. That takes some time and elbow grease. However, there is a shortcut that eliminates the roux and yields a quicker, lighter soufflé.

Elimination of the roux and milk, which help bind a soufflé and make it puff, cuts out a significant amount of fat. For example, a traditional vegetable soufflé that would serve 6 calls for about ½ stick (¼ cup) of butter and 4 tablespoons of flour to make the roux. To this are added 1 cup of milk and 4 to 5 egg yolks to bind the other ingredients further.

To compensate for the absent roux, the new-style soufflés can be bound with ricotta cheese, which is much lower in fat than butter (cream cheese would work

(continued on next page)

as well, but the fat level would be higher). The egg content is about the same for both, 1 yolk per serving. The technique here works with almost any fresh produce.

These soufflés can be made in individual serving dishes or in one large one. It is easier to work with individual dishes because the soufflés cook more quickly—in about 10 minutes—and more evenly. Making a large soufflé risks having it browned and crisp on the outside while still uncooked in the center. Small soufflés can be served directly from the oven in their baking dishes or demolded and served upside down. You might add a light herb sauce for the savory mixtures or a fruit sauce for the dessert soufflé.

FOLDING EGG WHITES

◆

The term folding refers to taking a quantity of whipped whites (best using a rubber spatula) and, using a turning motion from bottom to top, incorporating the whites into other ingredients. You do not want to beat the mixture. Use a slow, even movement. Do not fold any more than necessary.

Zucchini-Garlic Soufflé

◇ ◇

As you can see, the basic technique for all of these soufflés is the same. Only the flavoring ingredients change.

Yield: 8 servings.

4 cloves garlic, minced (about 1¼ tablespoons)
2 tablespoons olive oil
2 pounds zucchini, thinly sliced
¼ teaspoon hot pepper flakes
½ teaspoon oregano
Salt and freshly ground pepper to taste
½ cup ricotta cheese
¼ cup grated Parmesan cheese
8 eggs, separated

1. Preheat oven to 425 degrees. Butter well and chill eight 1¼-cup soufflé dishes or 1 large dish.

2. Sauté garlic in olive oil over medium heat for several minutes. Do not let brown. Add zucchini slices, hot pepper flakes, oregano, salt, and pepper. Cover and cook over medium heat 10 minutes, shaking the pan and stirring often. Uncover and cook until all moisture evaporates.

3. Place the zucchini in the bowl of a food processor along with the ricotta and Parmesan cheese. Purée well. Taste for seasoning. You should have about 3 cups.

4. Transfer mixture to a bowl and add the egg yolks. Blend well with a wire whisk. In another bowl, whisk whites until they form soft peaks. Fold a quarter of the whites into mixture, then the remainder. Do not overwork. Taste for seasoning. Pour into the soufflé dishes.

5. Place soufflé dishes in a baking pan and fill with enough water to reach about 3 inches up the soufflé dishes. Before placing in the oven, run your thumb around rim of each dish to remove any overflow, which could cling and prevent the soufflé from rising fully. Bake for approximately 10 minutes.

Carrot Soufflé

◇ ◇

I like to serve carrot soufflés at dinner parties because they are so attractive coming out of the oven. Cumin and dill add a pleasing flavor and aroma.

Yield: 8 servings.

2 pounds carrots, chopped (about 4½ cups)
½ cup ricotta cheese
¼ teaspoon powdered cumin
3 tablespoons minced fresh dill
Salt and freshly ground pepper to taste
8 eggs, separated

1. Preheat oven to 425 degrees. Butter well and chill eight 1¼-cup soufflé dishes or 1 large dish.

2. Boil carrots in salted water until soft. Drain well.

3. Place carrots in a food processor or blender with ricotta, cumin, dill, salt, and pepper. Purée well. You should have about 3 cups. Transfer to a bowl.

4. Add egg yolks to the mixture and blend well with a wire whisk. In another bowl, whisk egg whites until they form soft peaks. Fold a quarter of the whites into the carrot mixture, then the rest. Taste for seasoning. Pour the mixture into the soufflé dishes.

5. Place soufflé dishes in a baking pan and fill with water about 3 inches up the outside of the dishes. Before placing in the oven, run your thumb around rim of each to remove any overflow, which could cling and prevent the soufflés from rising fully. Bake for approximately 10 minutes.

Green Beans with Cumin
◇ ◇

Yield: 4 servings.

¾ pound fresh green beans
Salt to taste
1 tablespoon butter
Juice of ½ lemon
¼ teaspoon ground cumin
2 tablespoons finely chopped parsley
Freshly ground pepper to taste

1. Pull or cut off the ends of the green beans. Rinse the beans and set aside.
2. Place the beans in a pan and add cold water to cover. Add salt. Bring to a boil and let simmer 5 to 6 minutes or until tender. Drain.
3. Place the pot over medium heat. Toss the green beans with the butter, lemon juice, cumin, parsley, and pepper. Taste for seasonings. Serve.

Snap Peas with Mint
◇ ◇

My garden overflows with mint, but I find that you have to be cautious cooking with it. Mint has a very strong flavor that can be wonderful with desserts and other sweets, and with some vegetables like snap peas. Always put a little in and taste.

Yield: 4 servings.

1 pound sugar snaps or snow peas
Salt to taste
4 plum tomatoes, cored (about ¾ pound)
2 tablespoons butter
1 tablespoon shredded fresh mint
Freshly ground pepper to taste
2 teaspoons lemon juice

1. Pluck off and discard the end of each pea pod.

2. Bring a pot of salted water to a boil. Add the peas. When the water returns to a boil, cook the peas for about 3 to 4 minutes. Do not overcook. Drain.

3. Meanwhile, drop the tomatoes into boiling water and blanch them for 10 seconds. Drain, let cool. Remove the skins and cut the tomatoes into ¼-inch cubes.

4. Heat the butter in a saucepan. Add the tomatoes and stir for 1 minute. Add the peas, mint, and salt and pepper to taste. Stir to blend. Cook for 1 minute. Add the lemon juice and serve.

Snow Peas with Sesame Seeds
◇ ◇

Yield: 4 servings.

Salt to taste
1 pound snow peas
1 tablespoon olive oil
2 tablespoons sesame seeds
2 tablespoons chopped scallions
Freshly ground pepper to taste

1. Fill a large pot with salted water. Bring to a boil and add the snow peas. Blanch them for 1 minute and drain.

2. Heat the oil in a nonstick skillet over medium-high setting. Add the sesame seeds and brown them lightly. Add the snow peas, scallions, salt, and pepper. Sauté for 1 minute and serve.

Potato Salad with Sugar Snap Peas

◇ ◇

In France, we often served this salad warm—with a crisp white wine, of course.

Yield: 4 servings.

½ pound sugar snap peas (if not available, snow peas can be used)
Salt to taste
¾ pound small red new potatoes
2 tablespoons white wine vinegar
4 tablespoons peanut or vegetable oil
3 tablespoons finely chopped shallots or scallions
½ teaspoon finely chopped garlic
4 tablespoons finely chopped chervil or parsley (or both combined)
Freshly ground pepper to taste

1. Trim off ends of snap peas and remove strings.

2. Place the snap peas in a pot of boiling salted water. Cover, return to a boil, and cook for 3 to 4 minutes, or until crisp and tender. Drain.

3. Place potatoes in a pot of boiling water. Return to a boil, then lower heat to simmer and cook for about 20 minutes or until potatoes are tender. Do not overcook. Drain. The salad should be made while potatoes are still warm, with the skins on.

4. When the potatoes are cool enough to handle, peel them and cut them into ¼-inch slices. Place the potato slices in a bowl and add snap peas. In a bowl, whisk together the vinegar, oil, shallots, garlic, chervil, salt, and pepper. Pour over the salad and toss well. Serve immediately.

Sautéed Turnips

◇ ◇

I like to serve these sweet and crispy turnips with roasted pork or roasted ham.

Yield: 4 *servings.*

½ cup vegetable oil

3 tablespoons butter

3 pounds turnips, peeled and sliced as thin as possible (a mandoline works best for this)

Salt and freshly ground black pepper to taste

¼ teaspoon ground cumin

¼ cup chopped parsley

1. In a large pan (preferably nonstick), heat a third of the oil and a third of the butter. Add a third of the turnips and shake pan well. Season with salt, pepper, and about a third of the cumin. Continue cooking until slices are evenly golden brown on both sides, about 7 minutes. Repeat twice with similar portions of oil, butter, turnips, and cumin.

2. Drain turnips on paper towels as you make each batch and set aside. Transfer turnips to a warm serving bowl and garnish with parsley.

A mandoline is a French-made metal slicing device with an adjustable blade that can save you lots of time. It is used for slicing all kinds of vegetables to varying thicknesses. A less expensive Japanese-made mandoline does much the same thing. You may use either one in this turnip recipe.

Desserts

❖ ❖ ❖

Lemon and Yogurt Trifle

Frozen Yogurt Soufflé with Raspberry Sauce

Raspberry Sauce

Banana Cream Pie

Short Dough Pie Shell

Pastry Cream

Lemon-and-Chocolate Tart

Lemon Cream

Walnut and Ginger Cake

Fig Spice Cake

Crêpes with Strawberries and Cream

Strawberry Shortcake with Grand Marnier Sauce

Cream Cheese Pastry Rounds

Grand Marnier Sauce

Chocolate Brownie Cheesecake

Chocolate Brownies

Poached Pears in Red Wine and Cassis

Apples with Calvados and Ice Cream

Persimmon and Buttermilk Pudding

Chocolate Amaretto Cake

Prunes in Beaujolais

Summer Fruit Salad

Chilled Rhubarb Soup with Strawberries

Grapefruit and Campari Sherbet

Honeydew and Melon Liqueur Ice

Rosemary and Mint Ice

Chocolate Mousse

Harvest Bread Pudding

Lemon and Yogurt Trifle

◇ ◇

My grandchildren love this festive, layered dessert—and most adults dig in with gusto, too. The classic English trifle is made by layering sponge cake and cooked fruits with a vanilla custard—it looks so good that you want to dive into it. In Scotland, when Drambuie is poured in, it is called a Tipsy Laird. Here is a lower-fat version of the trifle, made with yogurt and lemon cream. Using yogurt cuts down on the calories. Add some rum if you like.

Yield: 4 to 6 servings, depending on the size of the wine goblet in which it is served. The shortbread recipe makes more cookies than needed for the dessert.

The Lemon Cream

4 whole eggs
3 egg yolks
1 cup sugar
1 cup fresh lemon juice
6 tablespoons unsalted butter, softened

The Yogurt Cream

2 cups cream
1 teaspoon vanilla extract
1 tablespoon sugar
8 ounces unflavored yogurt

The Shortbread Cookies

¾ cup unsalted butter, softened
½ cup sugar
1½ cups all-purpose flour
⅓ cup cornstarch

The Garnishes

Fresh mint
8 strips candied lemon zest
1 pint raspberries

(Continued on next page)

The term to cream *means simply to whisk (or stir with a wooden spoon) a combination of soft ingredients, often butter, until they achieve a creamy texture. Most often you are asked to cream butter and sugar. An electric mixer makes for an effortless task.*

1. Make the lemon cream. In a large, stainless-steel mixing bowl, place the whole eggs, egg yolks, sugar, and half the lemon juice. Set the bowl over a pot of boiling water and whisk vigorously until frothy, about 5 minutes. Add the remaining lemon juice and continue whisking until the mixture is thick and creamy.

2. Remove the bowl from the heat and whisk in the butter until well incorporated. Cover and refrigerate until cool.

3. Make the yogurt cream. In a bowl, combine the cream, vanilla, and sugar. Whisk with an electric mixer or by hand until soft peaks begin to form. Add the yogurt and continue whipping until well blended. Refrigerate.

4. Make the cookies. In a bowl, cream the butter and sugar (you may want to cut the butter into tablespoon-size pieces and add a few at a time). Sift the flour and cornstarch together and add to the butter mixture. Mix until smooth. Wrap well and refrigerate for 1 hour.

5. Preheat the oven to 300 degrees.

6. Roll the dough into a ⅛-inch-thick circle. Cut out the cookies with a wide-mouth wineglass (red wine glass). You will have more cookies than you need for this recipe. Place the cookies on a baking sheet and bake until they turn golden brown, about 15 minutes.

7. To assemble, place a few raspberries in the bottom of each wineglass. Spoon (or pipe with a pastry bag) 1 inch of the yogurt cream over the berries. Cover with a cookie, pressing gently to flatten the cream. Arrange 5 more berries around the perimeter of the cookie, making sure they touch the side of the glass. Pour or spoon enough lemon cream to cover the berries. Top the dessert with another inch of yogurt mixture. Garnish with fresh mint, candied lemon zest, and more berries. (This dessert is best when served within 8 hours of being assembled. Both the lemon cream and the cookies can be made ahead.)

Frozen Yogurt Soufflé with Raspberry Sauce

◇ ◇

I like to make frozen soufflés for dinner parties because they can be made in advance and taken out of the freezer a few minutes before serving.

Yield: 6 servings.

4 large eggs, separated
1½ cups sugar
½ cup coarsely chopped, glazed fruitcake mix (available in supermarkets)
2 tablespoons chopped candied ginger
4 tablespoons Grand Marnier
½ cup sour cream
2 cups plain yogurt, drained for about 15 minutes in a fine sieve or cheesecloth
Raspberry sauce (see page 282)
Candied flowers for garnishing (optional)

1. Select a 2-quart mixing bowl that will fit snugly inside a large saucepan. Add about 2 inches of water to the saucepan and bring to a simmer.

2. Place the egg yolks and 1 cup of the sugar in the mixing bowl. Before placing the bowl over the heat, whisk vigorously until the mixture forms a ribbon (see sidebar).

3. Place the mixing bowl over the saucepan, whisk constantly and vigorously for 10 minutes or until the egg mixture is a very thick, smooth, and creamy custard. The temperature of the egg mixture at this point should be 130 to 140 degrees on a cooking thermometer.

4. Remove the bowl from the saucepan and stir in the fruitcake mix, candied ginger, and the Grand Marnier. Place the mixture in a cool bowl and refrigerate. When cool, fold in the sour cream and the yogurt. Blend well until smooth.

5. Place the egg whites in a mixing bowl (copper is best). With a balloon whisk, beat them to a soft peak. Beat in the remaining ½ cup of sugar until the mixture is stiff and peaks are formed. With a large rubber spatula, fold the whites into the egg mixture. *(Continued on next page)*

◈

Step 2 of the frozen soufflé recipe calls for whisking egg yolks and sugar until they "form a ribbon." That simply means the mixture becomes so thick that when you drizzle some on top of itself, it does not sink in right away. The "ribbon" is the strip of the beaten egg yolks that lies on top of the mixture.

6. Pour the mixture into six 1-cup soufflé dishes, smooth the top and place in the freezer. Let stand for several hours or overnight until frozen.

7. When ready to serve, dip the molds into hot water and remove immediately. Wipe off and unmold upside down onto serving plates. Place raspberry sauce around and decorate with candied flowers for garnish if desired.

Raspberry Sauce
◇ ◇

Yield: About 1¼ cups.

1 pint fresh raspberries or 1 10-ounce package frozen
Juice of ½ lemon
½ or ¼ cup sugar, depending on type of raspberries used (fresh or frozen)
2 tablespoons Grand Marnier

1. If fresh raspberries are used, rinse and drain them. Place the fresh or frozen raspberries into the container of a food processor or blender. Add the lemon juice. If fresh raspberries are used, add ½ cup sugar. If frozen are used, add ¼ cup sugar. Blend thoroughly. If you wish to remove the seeds, drain and push through a fine sieve.

2. Add the Grand Marnier. Blend well.

Banana Cream Pie

◇ ◇

When I first started cooking in this country, banana cream pie was a great discovery. Creamy, custardy, and frothy, banana cream pie is an American classic. Note that the crust here is precooked so the custard doesn't sink in and make it soggy. Once you cook the crust, you can cover it with plastic wrap and refrigerate for a day.

Yield: 8 to 10 servings.

1 8-inch baked pie shell (see page 284)
4 pounds unpeeled, unblemished ripe bananas
1 tablespoon lemon juice
1 tablespoon cold water
Pastry cream (see page 285)
2 cups heavy cream
2 teaspoons sugar

1. Prepare the pie shell and let it cool.

2. Peel the bananas and cut them into ½-inch rounds. There should be about 7½ cups. Put the banana rounds into a bowl. Blend the lemon juice with the water and pour this over the banana pieces. This will prevent discoloration. Blend to coat the pieces well. Pat the bananas dry with a clean white kitchen towel or a napkin.

3. Put the banana pieces in a mixing bowl and spoon the pastry cream over all. Stir to blend. Pour the filling into the baked pie shell. Chill thoroughly.

4. Whip the cream, with the sugar, until stiff. Take a pastry bag with a star tube (No. 14) and spoon the whipped cream into the bag. Pipe the cream out onto the banana filling in a decorative pattern.

Short Dough Pie Shell

◇ ◇

Yield: *1 pie shell.*

1¾ cups plus 2 tablespoons (approximately) all-purpose flour for
    making and rolling out the dough
8 tablespoons cold, unsalted butter, cut into small cubes
1 egg yolk
1 teaspoon sugar
Salt to taste
3 tablespoons cold water, approximately

1. Put 1¾ cups flour into the bowl of an electric mixer. Add the butter and beat until the mixture has the granular texture of cornmeal.

2. Combine the egg yolk, sugar, and salt in a small glass measuring cup. Beat well. Add the cold water.

3. Pour the egg yolk mixture down the sides of the mixing bowl holding the flour and continue beating until the liquid is thoroughly incorporated. Gather the resulting dough into a ball. Press a forefinger into the dough to test it for firmness. If the dough keeps an imprint, there is no need to refrigerate. If the dough tends to close in on itself, chill for half an hour or so.

4. Preheat the oven to 400 degrees.

5. Sprinkle the top of a flat surface, preferably cold marble, with 2 tablespoons of all-purpose flour. Turn the dough out onto it and roll the dough into a circle about 14 inches in diameter. Use this to line an 8- to 9-inch tart tin, preferably with a removable bottom. Press the dough against the inside.

6. Chill the dough for 15 minutes. Line the bottom and sides of the dough gently with aluminum foil and place in the oven. Bake 20 minutes, or until golden brown. As the dough bakes, the pastry may rise slightly. If it does, press it gently in the center to make it lie flat once more. Remove the shell from the oven and let cool. Remove aluminum foil.

Pastry Cream

◇ ◇

Yield: About 1⅓ cups.

1 cup milk
6 tablespoons sugar
1 tablespoon all-purpose flour
2 teaspoons cornstarch
1 egg
3 tablespoons butter
¼ teaspoon vanilla extract

1. Put the milk in a saucepan and bring to a simmer.

2. Meanwhile, in a bowl, combine the sugar, flour, and cornstarch and blend with your fingers to break up any lumps.

3. Put the egg in a second mixing bowl and beat, gradually adding the cornstarch mixture, until smooth.

4. Add about ¼ cup of the hot milk to the egg mixture, stirring rapidly with a wire whisk. Pour the warmed egg mixture back into the remaining milk that is still simmering, stirring constantly and rapidly with the whisk. Stir until it reaches the bubbling stage. Immediately turn off the heat. Stir in the butter and vanilla. There should be about 1⅓ cups.

5. Pour the pastry cream into a bowl to chill.

Lemon-and-Chocolate Tart

◇ ◇

Yield: 6 to 10 servings.

1 8-inch baked pie shell (see page 284)
¼ pound unsweetened chocolate
1 recipe for lemon cream (see page 287)
Sweetened whipped cream for decorating (optional)

1. Preheat the oven to 350 degrees.
2. Prepare the pie shell and let cool.
3. Chop the chocolate as finely as possible by hand, or use a food processor.
4. Scatter the chopped chocolate over the bottom of the pie shell. Pour the lemon cream over the chocolate, smoothing it over. Place the pie shell in the oven and bake 15 minutes.
5. If desired, decorate the top with sweetened whipped cream before serving.

Lemon Cream

◇ ◇

Yield: About 3 cups.

3 large eggs
¾ cup sugar
½ teaspoon finely grated lemon rind
½ cup freshly squeezed lemon juice
6 tablespoons cold, unsalted butter cut into cubes

1. Break the eggs into a metal mixing bowl. There should be about ¾ cup.

2. Add the sugar and beat by hand or with an electric mixer until light and fluffy. Beat in the lemon rind and juice.

3. Select a saucepan in which the bottom of the mixing bowl will at least partly fit. Bring about 1 quart of water to a boil in the saucepan. Place the metal mixing bowl on top of the water (but not touching the water). Cook, stirring constantly, until the sauce thickens, about 2 minutes longer.

4. Remove the mixing bowl from the heat and beat in the butter. Let stand at room temperature.

Walnut and Ginger Cake

Madeira wine comes from the Portuguese island of the same name. Ranging from pale golden to tawny, it is a fortified wine, which means alcohol is added to it. Generally very sweet, Madeira is used often in desserts.

Yield: 10 or more servings.

1 pound butter, cut into 1-inch cubes, plus butter for greasing pan

3 cups sifted all-purpose flour, plus flour for dusting pan

½ pound candied ginger, cut into ¼-inch cubes (about 1 cup)

½ pound golden raisins (about 1½ cups)

1 pound walnuts, preferably black walnuts, broken into pieces (about 3¾ cups)

1 teaspoon baking powder

Salt to taste if desired

2 cups sugar

6 egg yolks (about ⅓ cup)

⅓ cup Madeira or dry sherry

6 egg whites (about 1 cup)

1. Preheat oven to 275 degrees.

2. Lightly butter the inside of a 10-inch, 12-cup cake pan. Sprinkle with flour and shake pan to coat inside. Shake out excess.

3. In a mixing bowl, combine the ginger, raisins, and walnuts.

4. In another bowl, sift together 3 cups flour, baking powder, and salt. Sift this mixture over the ginger and nut mixture.

5. Put the pound of butter into the bowl of an electric mixer. Start beating while gradually adding sugar. Cream the mixture well and gradually beat in the yolks. Beat in the Madeira.

6. Pour this mixture over the nuts and flour mixture. Blend the ingredients thoroughly. This is best done by hand.

7. Beat the egg whites until stiff and fold in thoroughly until they do not show.

8. Pour batter into prepared pan and smooth over top with spatula. Set the pan on a baking sheet and place in the oven. Bake about 2¼ hours or until cake is puffed above the pan and nicely browned on top—or until the internal temperature is 200 degrees on a thermometer.

9. Remove the cake from the pan shortly after baking. To unmold, tap the bottom of the pan with heavy knife. Store cake for at least 10 days. Keep closely covered, wrapped in cheesecloth and foil, and refrigerated until ready to use.

Fig Spice Cake

◇ ◇

Whenever I am in the South of France, I make a point of buying fresh figs, which are sweet, moist, and terrific. We don't generally find fresh figs here, but dried ones work well in this tasty cake.

Yield: 12 or more servings.

1 pound dried figs
½ cup plain yogurt
2 cups sifted cake flour
1 teaspoon baking powder
1 teaspoon salt
1 teaspoon cinnamon
¼ teaspoon ground cloves or allspice
¼ teaspoon baking soda
½ cup shortening (like Crisco)
1 cup sugar
2 eggs
1 teaspoon vanilla
1 cup chopped walnuts or pecans
Confectioners' sugar

1. Preheat oven to 350 degrees.

2. Cover figs with boiling water. Let stand 10 minutes; drain and reserve water. Chop off the fig stems and, using scissors, cut the figs fine. Mix ½ cup of reserved fig water with yogurt. Set aside.

3. Sift flour, baking powder, salt, cinnamon, cloves, and baking soda together twice.

4. In a bowl, cream the shortening and sugar together until fluffy. Add eggs, one at a time, beating well after each addition. Add vanilla.

5. Add sifted ingredients alternately with yogurt mixture, beating until smooth after each addition. Add nuts and figs.

6. Turn mixture into greased 9-inch tube pan (see sidebar) and bake 50 minutes to 1 hour. Remove and let stand for 5 minutes.

7. While still warm, unmold cake onto a round dish. Sprinkle with confectioners' sugar.

◇

A tube pan, also known as an angel food pan, is about 4½ inches high with a funnel-like tube rising in the center. The cake batter goes around the funnel and leaves a hole in the middle.

Crêpes with Strawberries and Cream

To save time, I often make crêpes ahead of time and stack them between sheets of waxed paper, then freeze them. Reheat them in a warm oven before serving. There is an old French saying, "The first crêpe is for the dog," indicating the first crêpe never comes out right. Don't give up.

Yield: Approximately 20 crêpes.

Crêpes (to be made in advance)

> 2 eggs
> 1 cup flour
> 1 cup plus 4 tablespoons milk
> 2 teaspoons sugar
> ½ teaspoon vanilla extract
> 4 tablespoons unsalted butter

1. Put the eggs and flour into a mixing bowl and start beating and blending with a wire whisk. Add the milk, stirring. Add the sugar and vanilla extract and stir well.

2. Melt 2 tablespoons butter in a 7- or 8-inch nonstick pan. When the butter is melted, pour it into the crêpe batter.

3. Place a strainer over a mixing bowl and pour the batter into the strainer, pushing solids through with a rubber spatula.

4. Melt remaining butter and use this to grease the pan. Brush the pan lightly with butter and place it on the stove. When the pan is hot but not smoking, add 2 tablespoons of batter and swirl it around to completely cover the bottom of the pan. Cook over moderately high heat for about 30 seconds or until the crêpe is slightly brown on the bottom. Flip it and cook for another 15 seconds. Remove the crêpe and place on waxed paper. Repeat until all the batter is used. When the crêpes are cool, wrap in aluminum foil and refrigerate until used (they also can be frozen).

Crêpe Filling

Yield: 6 servings.

> ¾ cup cream
> 4 tablespoons sugar
> 4 tablespoons Grand Marnier (or liqueur of your choice)
> 2 pints strawberries, stems removed, sliced into thirds

1. In a large pan, combine the cream, sugar, and Grand Marnier. Place the pan over medium-high heat and reduce volume by half. Add the strawberries and mix to coat them. When they are warm, lay 3 overlapping crêpes on a plate, pour some sauce over them, and serve.

Strawberry Shortcake with Grand Marnier Sauce

◇ ◇

I use orange-scented Grand Marnier in many dessert sauces. It is wonderful in this strawberry shortcake, giving this traditional dish a lively twist.

Yield: 6 to 8 servings.

12 to 16 baked cream cheese pastry rounds (see page 292)
Grand Marnier sauce (see page 293)
2 pints fresh strawberries
½ cup sugar

1. Prepare the pastry rounds and set aside. Prepare the Grand Marnier sauce and chill.
2. Trim off the stem ends of the strawberries and put the berries in a bowl. Sprinkle with sugar and refrigerate, stirring occasionally so that they are equally sweetened.
3. When ready to serve, arrange 1 pastry round on each of 6 to 8 dessert plates. Arrange half the strawberries, stemmed side down, on the pastry rounds. Cover with another pastry round. Arrange the remaining berries on the top rounds. Spoon a portion of the Grand Marnier sauce over each and serve.

These pastry rounds are not very sweet, so I sometimes eat them at breakfast or pair them with a dinner soup or stew. If you like, add a little fresh minced dill, tarragon, thyme, or black pepper. Grated orange and lemon rind also give the biscuits a lively edge.

Cream Cheese Pastry Rounds

◇ ◇

These pretty little cookielike rounds make a nice light nibbler after a substantial meal.

Yield: 12 to 16 rounds or biscuits.

¼ pound cream cheese
¼ pound butter, plus 1 teaspoon for greasing cookie sheet
1 cup flour, plus 2 tablespoons for dusting the kneading board
2 tablespoons sugar

1. The pastry for this should be made at least 2 hours in advance or, preferably, the night before.

2. Put the cream cheese, butter, flour, and sugar in the container of a food processor. Blend thoroughly, scraping the bowl with a plastic spatula as necessary. (If a food processor is not used, put the cream cheese, butter, flour, and sugar in a mixing bowl. Blend thoroughly, using 2 knives or a pastry blender.)

3. Scrape the mixture onto a lightly floured board and pat gently all over with flour, using as little as possible. Shape the pastry into a ball and flatten it slightly. Wrap in plastic wrap and chill 2 hours or, preferably, overnight.

4. When ready to bake, preheat the oven to 400 degrees.

5. Roll out the dough to ⅛-inch thickness. Using a wide biscuit cutter (about 3¾ inches in diameter) or a drinking glass roughly that size, cut out rounds of pastry. There should be about 12 to 16 rounds. Scraps of dough may be gathered together and rolled out a second or third time.

6. As the "biscuits" are cut, arrange them on a greased baking sheet. Place on the middle rack of the oven and bake 10 minutes, watching carefully so that they do not burn.

7. Remove from the baking sheet and let cool.

Grand Marnier Sauce

◇ ◇

Yield: enough for 6 to 8 portions of strawberry shortcake.

2 egg yolks
¼ cup sugar
2 tablespoons Grand Marnier
1 cup heavy cream, chilled

1. Combine the egg yolks and the sugar in a mixing bowl and whisk until it forms ribbons.

2. Bring water to a boil in a saucepan. Reduce to simmer and place the bowl snugly over it. Whisk vigorously for up to 10 minutes or until the mixture is thick and pale yellow (you can use an electric hand mixer for this).

3. Remove the bowl from the saucepan and stir in the Grand Marnier. Scrape the mixture into a cool bowl and refrigerate for 2 hours minimum.

4. When the Grand Marnier mixture is cool, whip the cream until stiff and fold it into mixture. Serve.

Chocolate Brownie Cheesecake

◇ ◇

This is an unrepentantly rich dessert, but watch how fast it disappears.

Yield: 10 servings.

Butter for greasing a cake pan
2 pounds cream cheese, at room temperature
1 teaspoon vanilla extract
⅛ teaspoon salt (optional)
1½ cups sugar
4 large eggs
3 large brownies (see page 295), frozen or partly frozen
½ cup graham cracker crumbs (optional)

1. Preheat the oven to 350 degrees. Arrange a rack one-third of the way up from the bottom of the oven.

2. Generously butter a round cake pan that is 8 inches in diameter and 3 inches deep, including the rim.

3. Place the cream cheese in the bowl of an electric mixer and beat until it is uniformly smooth. Scrape the bottom and sides as you mix. Add the vanilla, salt, and sugar and beat until it is thoroughly and evenly blended without lumps.

4. Start beating on moderate speed and add the eggs one at a time, beating briefly after each addition. Do not beat more than necessary. Remove the bowl from the mixer.

5. Pour enough of this batter into the prepared pan to make a layer about ½ inch thick.

6. Cut the brownies into ½-inch cubes and fold these into the remaining batter, taking care not to break up or crumble the cold cubes. Pour the batter into the pan and smooth the top.

7. Place the pan in a larger pan and pour hot water into the larger pan. The water should be about 1½ inches deep.

8. Place the pans in the oven and bake about 1½ hours. The cake will rise about ¼ inch above the rim of the pan while baking. Remove the cake pan from the water and place it on a rack to cool. When it cools, it will sink to the original level. Let stand 2 to 3 hours. Refrigerate until cold. Unmold. If desired, you may sprinkle the cake with graham cracker crumbs.

Chocolate Brownies
◇ ◇

Yield: 4 *large brownies.*

Butter for greasing the liner of a pan
1 cup sifted flour
3 tablespoons unsweetened cocoa powder
8 tablespoons unsalted butter
2 squares (2 ounces) unsweetened chocolate
1 teaspoon powdered espresso coffee
½ teaspoon pure vanilla extract
¼ teaspoon almond extract
⅛ teaspoon salt if desired
1 cup sugar
2 large eggs
1 cup walnuts, broken into quarters

1. Preheat the oven to 350 degrees. Arrange a rack one-third of the way up from the bottom of the oven.

2. Prepare a liner for an 8-inch square pan. To do this, invert the pan onto the center of a 12-inch square of aluminum foil (shiny side down). Shape the foil to the diameter of the pan. Carefully remove the foil. Turn over the pan and place the foil in it. Press all around to make the foil fit the inside of the pan bottom. Butter the inside of the foil. Set aside.

3. Sift together the flour and cocoa. Set aside.

4. Put the butter and the chocolate in a 2½- to 3-quart saucepan. Heat, while stirring, until the two ingredients are melted and blended. Add the coffee, vanilla, almond extract, and salt. Stir. Add the sugar and stir. Add the eggs, one at a time, beating well after each addition. Add the flour mixture and stir. Add the nuts and blend well.

5. Pour the mixture into the foil-lined pan and smooth the top. Place in the oven and bake 23 to 25 minutes, until a cake tester or toothpick inserted in the center of the cake comes out clean.

6. Remove the cake to a rack and let cool. When the cake is cool, place the pan in the freezer and let stand until the cake is quite firm. To unmold, cover with a rack and invert the pan onto the rack. Remove the pan and peel off the foil. Cover with a second rack or a cookie sheet and invert the cake, leaving it right side up.

(Continued on next page)

7. Cut the cake into quarters while it is still totally or partly frozen. Cut into 4 brownies. Use three-quarters of the brownies in preparing a cheesecake (see page 294). Put the remainder to another use. Store in the freezer the brownies to be used in making the cake.

Poached Pears in Red Wine and Cassis
◇ ◇

Cassis, or crème de cassis, is a rich, dark purple, syrupy liqueur made from black currants. It is wonderful over ice cream or in other desserts. It also can be poured into a flute of Champagne to make a kir royale.

I find that cassis goes exceptionally well with pears and apples. Adjust the quantity to suit your taste.

Yield: 6 servings.

6 Bartlett pears, peeled, with stems left on (about 1½ pounds)
1¼ cups dry red wine
¾ cup sugar
2 tablespoons lemon juice
½ stick cinnamon
¼ cup cassis
½ teaspoon vanilla extract

1. Trim the bottom of the pears so they stand upright.
2. In a pot large enough to hold the upright pears, combine the wine, sugar, lemon juice, cinnamon, cassis, and vanilla extract. Bring to a boil, then lower to a simmer. Arrange the pears in the liquid, cover, and poach for about 20 to 30 minutes or until the pears are soft.
3. Place a pear on each serving plate. Turn the heat to high and reduce the cooking liquid by a quarter. Pour around the pears.

NOTE: This dish is great with a scoop of vanilla ice cream.

Apples with Calvados and Ice Cream

◇ ◇

Calvados is an apple brandy made in Normandy and is often used in cooking there. In this recipe, it enhances the flavor of the apples.

Yield: 4 servings.

4 firm, slightly tart apples such as McIntosh or Granny Smith
3 tablespoons butter
½ teaspoon grated lemon peel
4 tablespoons sugar
¼ teaspoon ground cinnamon
¼ cup Calvados or applejack
4 scoops vanilla ice cream

1. Peel and core the apples and cut each into 12 equal slices. There should be about 4 cups.

2. Melt the butter in a skillet and add the apple slices and the lemon peel. Sprinkle with sugar and cinnamon, and cook over medium-high heat, gently stirring the apples and shaking the skillet so that they cook evenly. When the apples start to brown, add the Calvados. Turn up the heat and tilt the pan. Ignite the sauce with a long match (the alcohol will burn off quickly). Blend well.

3. Put a scoop of ice cream into each of 4 individual serving dishes. Pour the apples on top and serve.

Persimmon and Buttermilk Pudding

◇ ◇

This all-American pudding comes from my friend Larry Forgione, chef-owner of An American Place in Manhattan and The Beekman 1776 Tavern in Rhinebeck, New York. Persimmons are autumn fruits known for their extreme sourness when young and intense sweetness when ripe. For this pudding, you want ripe ones. The persimmon tree grows wild in the southeastern United States. In the fall, the fruit turns from green to bright orange, signaling ripeness.

Yield: 8 or more servings.

1½ cups fresh or canned persimmon purée, or use canned pumpkin
2½ cups buttermilk
1½ cups sugar
1½ cups flour
1½ teaspoons baking powder
1½ teaspoons baking soda
Salt to taste if desired
½ teaspoon powdered cinnamon
½ teaspoon freshly grated nutmeg
4 eggs
¼ cup melted butter, plus butter for greasing the baking dish

1. Preheat the oven to 400 degrees.

2. Make a persimmon purée by putting enough ripe, pitted persimmons through a sieve to produce 1½ cups. Stir well. Put the persimmon purée into a mixing bowl and add the buttermilk. Beat well with a mixer.

3. Sift together the sugar, flour, baking powder, baking soda, salt, cinnamon, and nutmeg.

4. In a bowl, beat the eggs and add them to the persimmon mixture. Add the sifted dry ingredients and beat with the mixer. Beat in the butter. There should be about 6 cups.

5. Butter a 6-cup baking dish and pour the batter into it. Set the baking dish in a larger utensil and pour boiling water into the larger dish—it should reach 3 to 4 inches up the sides of the baking dish.

6. Place in the oven and bake 35 to 40 minutes or until the pudding is set and a cake tester inserted in the center comes out clean. If desired, top with whipped cream.

Chocolate Amaretto Cake

◇ ◇

This recipe for a chocolate amaretto cake calls for cake flour. I often use cake flour, which is widely available, because it is finer than all-purpose flour and has less gluten. It yields a lighter cake. If you don't have cake flour, use all-purpose flour.

Yield: 10 or more servings.

The Cake

2 teaspoons corn, peanut, or vegetable oil

2 tablespoons all-purpose flour

2 tablespoons cocoa powder

½ cup cake flour

½ cup plus 3 tablespoons sugar

4 eggs, beaten

4 egg yolks, beaten

½ cup liqueur such as amaretto, Kahlúa, or Grand Marnier

¼ cup unsalted butter, melted

The Topping and Filling

1 cup milk

½ pound semisweet or bittersweet chocolate, finely chopped

2½ cups heavy cream

6 tablespoons liqueur such as amaretto, Kahlúa, or Grand Marnier

½ pint raspberries, rinsed and well drained

Sweetened whipped cream for decorating (optional)

1. Preheat the oven to 325 degrees.

2. Lightly oil the sides of a 9½-inch springform cake pan. Trace out a circle of parchment paper or aluminum foil to fit over the bottom of the pan. Spoon 2 tablespoons of all-purpose flour inside the pan and shake it around to coat the bottom and sides of the pan. Shake out excess.

3. Combine the cocoa powder, cake flour, and 3 tablespoons of sugar and shake it through a sieve. Set aside.

(Continued on next page)

4. In a mixing bowl, combine the beaten eggs, beaten yolks, and remaining ½ cup of sugar. Select a saucepan that can hold the metal bowl securely. Bring 1 quart of water to a simmer in the saucepan. Set the metal bowl containing the egg mixture on top, but not in, the simmering water. Start beating with a wire whisk for 2 minutes or until the egg mixture is hot to the touch. Do not overcook or the eggs will scramble. Use a cooking thermometer to ensure that the temperature is 130 degrees.

5. Pour the mixture into the bowl of an electric mixer and beat on high speed about 5 minutes, or until the mixture has tripled or quadrupled in volume. To tell if it is ready, run your finger through the batter. It should leave a furrow that does not close right away.

6. Sprinkle the top with the cocoa mixture, pour in ½ cup of amaretto, and carefully fold it into the batter. Fold until the cocoa is totally incorporated.

7. Pour a fourth of the batter into a mixing bowl and pour in the melted butter. Fold the butter into this portion of the batter. When the butter is folded in, pour this portion of the batter into the mixing bowl with the amaretto.

8. Pour and scrape the batter into the prepared cake pan. Tap the pan solidly onto a flat surface to smooth the top.

9. Place the pan in the oven and bake for about 60 to 80 minutes. The cake is done when the center springs back when touched lightly with the fingers. Let the cake rest a full 10 minutes.

The Filling

1. To make the filling and topping for the cake, bring milk to a boil in a saucepan. Add the finely chopped chocolate (it may be chopped by hand or in a food processor) and turn off the heat. Shake the pan gently in a circular motion, while stirring, until the chocolate is melted and well blended. Use a wire whisk for stirring. When ready, pour and scrape the liquid into a mixing bowl and let cool to room temperature.

2. Whip the cream until it is stiff and beat in the melted chocolate mixture until well blended.

3. With a long serrated knife, split the cake widthwise into two thin round layers of equal size. Turn the top layer over so you have two cut sides exposed. Brush the top of each layer with 3 tablespoons of amaretto or another liqueur. Spread 1½ cups of the filling onto one layer and smooth it over the top. Scatter the raspberries over all and press them

into the filling. Center the second layer on top. Pour and scrape the remaining filling onto the cake and smooth it gently over the top and sides. If desired, decorate the top of the cake with sweetened whipped cream, putting it through a pastry tube. Let the cake stand 15 minutes before cutting and serving.

Prunes in Beaujolais

◇ ◇

Around the holidays, I often make batches of prunes in Beaujolais, put them in Mason jars, wrap a ribbon around them, and give them away as presents.

Yield: 6 to 8 servings.

2 pounds large dried prunes (with pits)
3 cups Beaujolais wine
1 teaspoon pure vanilla extract
2 cups sugar
Rind from 2 lemons (only yellow part, not bitter white pith)

1. Place the prunes in a mixing bowl and add the wine. Let stand 24 hours at room temperature until the prunes have softened well.

2. Place the prunes and wine in a saucepan. Add the vanilla, sugar, and lemon rinds. Bring to a boil; simmer for 30 minutes. The mixture should be syrupy. Chill. Remove rinds. Serve alone or with vanilla ice cream.

Summer Fruit Salad

◇ ◇

Yield: 4 or more servings.

2 cups water
1 vanilla bean or ½ teaspoon vanilla extract
1 2-inch piece of lemon peel or zest
4 4-inch pieces of orange peel or zest
3 sprigs fresh mint
½ cup sugar
1 ripe mango (about ¾ pound)
1 large orange, peeled (about ½ pound)
1½-inch-thick slice of fresh, ripe pineapple
6 large ripe strawberries, stems removed (about ½ pound)
1 peach (about 6 ounces), peeled
⅔ cup fresh blueberries
⅔ cup fresh raspberries
1 teaspoon finely minced fresh mint leaves

1. Put the water in a pot and bring to a boil. Split the vanilla bean in half lengthwise. Add this to the pot. Add the lemon and orange peels, mint sprigs, and sugar. Bring to a boil and remove from the heat. Cover closely and let the syrup stand until cool. If vanilla bean is not used, add vanilla extract. Chill thoroughly.

2. Peel the mango and cut the flesh from the pit. Cut the flesh into thin strips. Cut the flesh from each orange section and discard any seeds. Keep the fruit on separate plates.

3. Peel the pineapple and cut away any black spots that may remain. Cut the flesh into small pieces. Cut the strawberries into thin slices. Cut the peach in half and discard the pit. Cut the peach flesh into ½-inch cubes. Combine the pineapple, peach, blueberries, and raspberries in a bowl and strain the syrup over all. Garnish the top with the strawberry, orange, and mango pieces arranged symmetrically and slightly overlapping in concentric circles. Sprinkle minced mint over all. Serve chilled.

Chilled Rhubarb Soup with Strawberries

◇ ◇

Few home cooks use rhubarb for desserts, but whenever I serve it to guests or at a cooking demonstration, people love its slightly sour flavor.

Yield: 8 servings.

12 cups chopped fresh rhubarb, trimmed of leaves (for the soup)
⅓ cup fresh lemon juice
1 vanilla bean, split lengthwise
2 cups sugar plus 3 tablespoons, or to taste
3 cups thinly sliced fresh rhubarb, from the tender narrow end, sliced on a bias (for garnish)
4 strawberries, stems removed, diced into ⅛-inch cubes (about ½ cup)
¾ pint vanilla ice cream, slightly softened

1. To make the soup, place the 12 cups of the chopped rhubarb, lemon juice, and the vanilla bean in a pot and cover with 8 cups water. Add 2 cups of the sugar.

2. Bring to a boil, reduce heat, and simmer for 90 minutes. When the liquid has cooked for about 15 minutes, remove the vanilla bean and squeeze out the tiny black seeds inside into the pot. (To do this, pinch the bean with your thumb and forefinger and run your fingers down the length of the bean. Toss the skin back into the pot.)

3. Meanwhile, place the 3 cups of rhubarb garnish in a pot and add ¾ cup water and 3 tablespoons of sugar. Bring to a boil and simmer until soft, about 5 minutes. When the rhubarb is cooked, remove the pot from the heat and place it in a bowl filled with ice to stop the cooking.

4. When the first rhubarb soup mixture has finished cooking, strain it through a fine sieve or chinois (do not press the solids). You should have about 7 cups of liquid. Chill thoroughly. Before serving, taste for sweetness (you may need more sugar).

5. To serve, place equal amounts of the rhubarb garnish in serving bowls. Add equal portions of the diced strawberries. Ladle in the soup mixture. Place a scoop of vanilla ice cream in the center.

Grapefruit and Campari Sherbet

Campari is an Italian apéritif with a bitter, astringent flavor. It is usually drunk with soda water or alone. It adds a sharp, cleansing edge to sherbets and sorbets.

Campari is another liquor that I like to use in desserts. Its tart flavor complements sweet sherbets and fruit salads.

Yield: 10 to 12 servings.

3 large pink grapefruit, the redder the flesh the better (about 1
    pound each)
2 cups water
1½ cups sugar
¼ cup Campari

1. Peel the grapefruit, cutting away and discarding all the outer white membrane. Carefully section it, running the knife between each segment. There should be about 3 cups of flesh (save any juice that drips out).

2. Combine the grapefruit sections and juice in the container of a food processor or electric blender and blend as thoroughly as possible. There should be about 3⅓ cups. Put the mixture in a mixing bowl.

3. Combine the water and sugar in a saucepan and bring to a boil. Cook about 5 minutes and let cool. Add to the grapefruit mixture and blend. There should be about 5½ cups. Add the Campari and chill thoroughly.

4. Pour the mixture into the container of an electric or hand-cranked ice cream machine and freeze according to the manufacturer's instructions. Freeze to the desired consistency.

Honeydew and Melon Liqueur Ice

◇ ◇

A dinner guest once gave me a bottle of melon liqueur as a gift, so I used it in this dessert. If you don't have it, use a splash of Grand Marnier.

Yield: 10 to 12 servings.

1 honeydew melon (about 3 pounds)
2 tablespoons freshly squeezed lemon juice
2 cups water
1 cup sugar
5 tablespoons bottled green melon liqueur

1. Cut the honeydew into eighths. Scrape away and discard the inner seeds, fibers, and outer peel. The prepared melon should weigh about 1½ pounds.

2. Cut the melon into small pieces, place in a bowl and add the lemon juice. Toss to coat the pieces.

3. Meanwhile, bring the water and the sugar to a boil in a saucepan and let simmer about 3 minutes. Add the melon pieces and cook 2 minutes. Drain but reserve both the melon pieces and cooking liquid. Let cool.

4. Put the melon pieces into the container of a food processor or electric blender and blend thoroughly. There should be about 3⅓ cups. Put the mixture in a bowl. Add the reserved cooking liquid and blend. There should be about 5 cups. Chill well. Add the green melon liqueur.

5. Pour the mixture into the container of an electric or hand-cranked ice-cream freezer and freeze according to the manufacturer's instructions.

Rosemary and Mint Ice

◇ ◇

You might not think of rosemary as a dessert ingredient, but I use it occasionally in desserts, as well as mint and coriander (in baked goods). Fresh rosemary is much better than dried in this ice.

Yield: 6 to 8 servings.

3 cups water
1 cup sugar
2 tablespoons chopped fresh rosemary or 1 tablespoon dried
2 tablespoons lemon juice
1 tablespoon crème de menthe

1. Combine the water and sugar in a saucepan and let simmer 3 minutes. Add the rosemary and stir. Cover closely and let stand 15 minutes.

2. Line a bowl with a sieve and line the sieve with cheesecloth. Strain the liquid and discard the solids. Let the liquid stand until cool. Add the lemon juice and crème de menthe and chill thoroughly.

3. Pour the mixture into the container of an electric or hand-cranked ice cream freezer. Freeze according to the manufacturer's instructions.

Chocolate Mousse

◇ ◇

I get many letters from people asking for a foolproof recipe for chocolate mousse. As this recipe demonstrates, it is quite easy. To alter it, you may use bitter or semisweet chocolate instead of sweet chocolate. You also may use any number of garnishes as decoration. Add sweetened whipped cream with candied violets, or toasted almonds, hazelnuts, walnuts, and so on.

Yield: 4 servings.

4 ounces sweet chocolate, broken into pieces
¼ pound butter, cut into small pieces
3 eggs, separated
¼ cup sugar

1. Place a metal mixing bowl (about 2 quarts) atop a saucepan so that the two fit snugly. Remove the mixing bowl and add boiling water to the saucepan. Set the bowl over it. Bring water to a simmer. Add the chocolate to the mixing bowl and stir.

2. When the chocolate starts to melt, add the butter. Continue stirring until well blended and remove the bowl from the heat. Add the egg yolks and stir until thoroughly blended.

3. Place the bowl briefly in the refrigerator until the mixture is slightly cooler than lukewarm. If it becomes too chilled, it will harden.

4. Meanwhile, beat the egg whites until they form soft peaks. Gradually add sugar, beating briskly. Continue beating until whites are stiff. Fold the whites into the chocolate mixture. Spoon the mousse into 4 serving dishes. Chill until ready to serve. If desired, top with minimally sweetened whipped cream.

Harvest Bread Pudding

◇ ◇

Bread pudding is another all-American dish that I have come to love. This one has apples and berries in it; if you want, you could eliminate one or more.

Yield: 8 to 10 servings.

1 tablespoon vegetable oil
About 12 small apples, peeled and cut into ¼-inch slices (8 cups)
1⅓ cups sugar
6 cups cubed challah, Portuguese sweet bread, or firm white
     bread (about 1½ pounds)
2 cups nonfat milk
2 cups heavy cream
5 eggs
4 teaspoons grated orange zest (about 1 medium orange)
½ cup dried blueberries
½ cup dried cranberries
Powdered sugar for garnish

1. Preheat the oven to 350 degrees. Lightly oil an 8-cup casserole. Set aside.

2. Place the sliced apples and ⅓ cup of the sugar in a heavy saucepan set over medium heat. Stir the apples to evenly coat them with the sugar. Cover the pan and cook the apples for 20 minutes or until they soften.

3. While the apples are cooking, combine the bread with the milk and cream. Let the bread absorb the liquid for about 15 minutes.

4. When the apples are soft, stir them into the bread mixture. In a separate bowl, beat the eggs with the remaining sugar and the orange zest. Add the egg mixture to the bread and apples. Stir in the dried fruit.

5. Pour the pudding into the prepared pan and place it in the oven. Bake for 45 minutes or until it is set and lightly browned on top.

6. Dust the pudding with powdered sugar before serving. Serve at room temperature.

Index

whisking egg yolks, 281
white beans and lamb with vegetables, 184–85
white button mushrooms, 135
wild rice, 50
   and almond salad, 51
   and lobster salad, 50
wine:
   classic *boeuf à la bourguignonne*, 143–44
   deglazing with, 131
   ham steaks with Madeira sauce, 150–51
   prunes in Beaujolais, 301
   red, monkfish stew with (*matelote*), 225
   red, poached pears in cassis and, 296
   red, sauce, fillet of beef in, 125

red, sauce, sautéed chicken in, with spaetzle, 101–2
roast fillet of beef with Madeira-mushroom sauce, 136–37
winter vegetables, poached fillet of beef with, 126

yam purée, 263
yellow squash, couscous with, 173
yogurt:
   buying, 201
   cooking with, 204
   and cucumber soup, cold, with fresh mint, 69
   frozen soufflé with raspberry sauce, 281–82
   and lemon trifle, 279–80
   -paprika sauce, shrimp in, 201

in sauces, 201
-scallion vinaigrette, 54
Yukon Gold potatoes, 257

ziti:
   with chicken and broccoli, 248
   with mussels and broccoli, 237–38
   with scallops and shrimp, 230
zucchini:
   curried soup with apple garnish, 76
   and fennel, broiled, with Parmesan, 264
   fusilli with eggplant and, 236
   fusilli with prosciutto, tomatoes and, 250
   -garlic soufflé, 270
   skewered shrimp and, 27
   spaghettini with, 235